Advance Praise

"*The Gent's Prayer* is a treasure. It reads like a modern-day Horatio Alger story but with a twist. How refreshing and how genuinely honest to read a story of a tremendously successful man who understands why he is successful and who made him that way. Knowing him as I do, he is a man at tremendous peace with himself because he is at peace with God and God's purposes for his life. A deeply moving and heartwarming story, sure to bring hope and inspiration to all its readers."

Rev. Roger McPhail
Senior pastor, New Hope Fellowship

"Lou is a man of integrity at home as well as in the marketplace and in government. I believe Lou to be a marketplace minister doing the work of the Lord where he is: in government. Like Daniel or Nehemiah who influenced government, Louis Gelormino is being used by God today. *The Gent's Prayer* will delight you and give you hope as well as challenge you to 'let your light shine.'"

Rev. Vincent Fusco
Apostle, (Paul and Silas Serving Internationally Fivefold
Office Ministries and Networking Churches) PASSION Network

"Lou continues to amaze me with his steadfast faith, his optimistic approach to life and love for his family. He inspires me to be a better person."

Alex Martins
President of the Indian-American Association
Vice president for the Association for the Deaf and Blind

"This is a true success story: A man who has—through the healing power of love, first given to him by grace from without, and later cultivated within—conquered himself. Not by conquering in the manner of breaking the spirit of a fine horse. Conquering in the way of love: Integration of all aspects of himself into a whole, and from that center Lou has become a beacon of hope and understanding for others."

Joseph Cardieri
Deputy commissioner and counsel to the NYC Department
of Children Services

"New York City is crying out for some more Lou Gelorminos as pillars of light to shine through the darkness."

Bishop Gerald Williams
Bishop and Pastor of the Above Ministry

"This book is a testimony of blessings received and blessings recognized. It is a story and a half for anyone searching for Jesus Christ or struggling to be as fully human as possible."

Father Donald Kenna
Pastor, All Saints Roman Catholic Church

"*The Gent's Prayer* is more than just another book. It's a heartwarming and powerful testimony of how God changed the destiny of a man headed for disaster and transformed him into a mighty instrument for good. Once you start reading this book, you'll find it almost impossible to put down."

Curt Blattman
Author of *The Challenge*
Officer of the Full Gospel Businessman's Association

"Louis was hurtling headlong towards his own destruction when grace turned him from a Brooklyn gangster to the Deputy Commissioner and Counsel. This is the poignant life story of deliverance and hope when Jesus came in. A must-read testimony of my friend and brother."

Bishop Moses Yang
Chinese Evangelical Mission

"Lou's inspiring story is one of perseverance, being strong in one's faith, and a desire to become what God destined and created all of us to become."

Terri M. Williams
Author and founder of The Stay Strong Foundation

"Having spent more than forty years as a member of the New York City Board of Corrections, I believe that Probation, properly administered, may offer one of the few ways of stopping the 'revolving door' system of the Criminal Justice System. Read this book to find out why."

Daniel Shulte
Member of the Board of Corrections of NYC

"When you read *The Gent's Prayer*, you will realize that through the events of Lou's life—which are colorful, sad, funny, and unbelievable at times—you will not only be entertained, but you will find a message of faith, hope, and enlightenment. Read it and pray!"

Mathew W. Daus
President of Council for Understanding and Racial Equality (CURE)
Commissioner of the Tour and Limousine Commission for NYC

"What impressed me was the transformation that took place in Lou's life. I would never have believed that he was a gang member and was able to make it to the top by becoming a lawyer. God still works miracles, and Lou is a miracle."

Rev. Michael Bacchus
Senior pastor, Full Gospel Assembly

"Louis Gelormino's life is an amazing adventure, a triumph of grace, an inspiration for today's inner city youth, and a legacy for his son. I've been on part of the journey with him and it has enriched my life. Hollywood, are you listening? You need stories like this!"

Ed Morgan
President, The Bowery Mission, New York

"Louis Gelormino takes us into his life, which is nothing short of inspirational. Through his weaknesses, faults, and battles, he comes out a winner and over-achiever by way of faith. He is truly a messenger of God."

John Abi-Habib
Chairman, Middle Eastern Christian Coalition
Chairman, Mahrajan of Middle Eastern Churches
CEO, MSI Net Inc.

"This is a story of how one man found his true potential . . . and then some. Lou shows what is possible in life and provides a shining example of what lies within each and every one of us."

John McCole
NYC Fire Department lieutenant and author of
The Second Tower's Down

"This compelling story will show all who read it the secret of his success. It will inspire everyone irrespective of their background or religious beliefs."

Pastor Joseph Mattera
Author of *Ruling in the Gates*
Pastor of Resurrection Church and director of City Covenant Coalition

"It is with great honor that I write to acknowledge *The Gent's Prayer*. Knowing something of the life Lou has led really gives meaningful insight to man's ability, with the help of God, to turn one's life to a positive testimony for others."

Dr. Kerry A. Gulston
Faith Mission Christian Fellowship, Harlem, NYC

"Louis's example as a godly attorney and his 'ministry of law' have inspired attorneys throughout New York to reach out to the widow, orphan, and all those in need. This book will move you to make a loving difference in your family, job, and community!"

Joseph A. Ruta
Chapter president, New York City Christian Legal Society

"George Bernard Shaw wrote that 'Most men live their lives in quiet desperation.' In *The Gent's Prayer*, Louis tells us how Jesus led him from a life of poverty and desperation to wealth in spirit and victory in life. His story will be an inspiration to all who travel the journey of *The Gent's Prayer*."

Frank Arthur Banks
Board of Directors member
Italy for Christ Ministry

"*The Gent's Prayer* will inspire you to accept life's difficult circumstances and to revel in how God will turn them into good not only for yourself, but for thousands of others. God has done this in Louis Gelormino."

Mary Szto
Professor

Professor and former president of the Christian Legal Society "Louis Gelormino sets an example of how you can make a difference if you believe in yourself and in the strength of your convictions. Our world is better because of Lou, and I'm proud of our association and friendship."

Rick Del Mastro
President, City Outdoor, Inc.
President, Working Organization for Retarded Children and Adults, Inc.
President, New Era Democrats

"Louis M. Gelormino's life is like poetry in motion or a beautiful painting that you hang on a wall for all to see. Our Lord has certainly molded 'Crazy Louie' into a golden vessel."

Fred J. Gioffre
Deputy commissioner, NYS Liquor Authority

"Lou Gelormino's journey through the years of poverty, oppression, violence, and loss, to his successful turnaround and ultimate spiritual revelation, gives all of us the hope, desire, and fortitude to persevere in our journey to reach our own success and happiness. This book is fascinating and uplifting reading. I recommend it to everyone."

Salvatore Aspromonte
President, Congress of Italian American Organizations (CIAO)

"This book will reveal the real work of rehabilitating former lawbreakers and changing them into useful members of society by the life-changing power of a relationship with Jesus Christ."

Daniel J. Staatz
President, Greater New York Chapter,
Full Gospel Business Men's Fellowship International

"I'm proud to endorse a book written by a man whose life and history are a true testament to successfully overcoming adversity and achieving his lifelong dream of serving the interest of the public."

Raul Russi
Former commissioner, NYC Department of Probation
Executive director of Bronx Addiction Integral Concepts System
(BASICS)

"Lou has been a constant source of inspiration to me. His life has come full circle, from the streets of South Brooklyn to a very successful career, together with his wife and son. Through this book he will be able to reach out and touch even more people than he did till now."

Laurian Jacoby, MD
Fellow American Academy of Physical Medicine and Rehabilitation
(FAAPMR)

"Lou has been a resource person for our church on many occasions. His advice has helped us to steer many in our congregation in the right direction."

Rev. Michael Bacchus
Senior pastor, Full Gospel Assembly

"There are so many positive messages that can be found in this book, in the way that my father lived and continues to live his life. I do not know the words to describe how much of a blessing he is as both a father and a friend. *The Gent's Prayer* is a testimony to courage, determination, strength, faith, joy, happiness, and maximizing our effectiveness as human beings."

Louis Gelormino III

"God gave me a great treasure of immense and untold worth and brought a touch of heaven into my lifetime here on Earth, for he sent me someone wonderful, an angel from above. He blessed me with a wonderful husband and blessed me again with a wonderful son. Lou, you are my best friend; you are my true love."

Elaine Gelormino

The Gent's Prayer

A tale of transformation through faith in Jesus Christ

Louis M. Gelormino

Authors of Unity Publishing

New York, NY

Authors of Unity Publishing
575 Madison Ave., 10th Floor
New York, NY 10022
www.authorsofunity.com

Cover design © 2004 TLC Graphics

Printed in the United States

ATTENTION ORGANIZATIONS and CORPORATIONS
Bulk quantity discounts for reselling, gifts,
or fundraising are available.
For more information, please contact:
Authors of Unity Publishing
Tel: (800) 935 5430

ISBN: 0-9725250-9-2
Library of Congress Control Number: 2004112000

Contents

Foreword

I have known Lou Gelormino for over twenty years—though it seems like much longer than that. His life continues to serve as an inspiration to me and to so many others. *The Gent's Prayer* captures and portrays his life and provides an uplifting message of hope that will touch many people.

Lou has experienced adversity and the most difficult of times, but he managed, through his faith, to turn these obstacles into empowerment. His life involves a series of events that provided him with spiritual signs that he intercepted and followed on his path. Many of us are presented with these signals or messages throughout our lives—especially at times of tragedy. Whether we understand fully the significance of the message at the time it is happening is not the key. The key is recognizing the power of faith and the difference between good and evil, and knowing when and how to change the course of our lives for the better.

Lou's book, *The Gent's Prayer*, is just that—a prayer that helped him turn his life around full circle—from the neighborhoods of South Brooklyn, to a successful career and fulfilling family life, and back to his beginnings. Lou realized the sign that a very special lady, Mary Sansone, presented him when she visited him and his fellow gang members one evening—and, not knowing exactly where he would end up, he knew he had to follow her path and his prayer. Later, he realized this was the turning point of his life. After weaving his way around one obstacle after another, he realized that the Lord was extending His hand that night, and Lou reached out with nothing other than faith in his heart. From that point on, Lou's life changed. Not only did he become a successful lawyer, high-level government official, and spiritual leader, he also became a husband, a father, and a friend to many. Now he has decided to give back what he learned and share his faith with others. Through his commitment to Nova Ancora and his daily ministry and leadership to those who are needy and astray, Lou extends his hand to all who need his help and guidance. He has helped so many others to follow his lead and turn their lives around before it's too late. Lou Gelormino's life has come full circle, and this book will enable him to reach a greater audience and touch even more lives.

Lou is a trusted friend, and I consider him part of my immediate family. He has helped me, encouraged me, and inspired me at the most difficult times in my life. For this, I am eternally grateful. If you read this book, you will entirely understand how I feel. Nobody tells a story better than Louie. When you read

The Gent's Prayer, you will realize that the events of his life—which are colorful, sad, funny, and unbelievable at times—are not only entertaining, but contain a message of faith, hope, and enlightenment. Read it and pray!

Matthew W. Daus
President of Council for Understanding and Racial Equality (CURE)
Commissioner of the Tour and Limousine Commission for NYC

✝ ✝ ✝ ✝ ✝ ✝ ✝ ✝ ✝ ✝ ✝ ✝ ✝ ✝ ✝ ✝ ✝

Acknowledgments

This is the first book that I have written and completed. I have to admit and confess that it was extremely therapeutic and holistic, a labor of love, and a wonderful spiritual experience and overall joy. Although it has taken me sixteen years to complete this book from the time the Lord had put it in my heart to write it, I find the most difficult part is writing this acknowledgment. When I look back on my fifty-five years of life, there are so many and too many individuals to whom I should thank and express my deep and sincere gratitude.

However, I will thank the obvious people and pray that the many others will know and remember who they are and what they have done for me. And I pray that they will take joy and satisfaction as well as spiritual and emotional comfort in realizing the positive impact they have had on my life. There is no doubt that the good Lord certainly keeps an account, and I am sure that they have been blessed for their acts of kindness, compassion, mercy, grace, and generosity.

I would like to start, appropriately, with God, who created me in my mother's womb and had His hand on me from the moment I was conceived by my mother and father. I would express great appreciation and love for my mother's great faith in God and her persistent prayers and perseverance. I had a wonderful natural father who loved and cared for me unconditionally. I would certainly express a deep love and gratitude to my family, particularly my Aunt Rose, Aunt Anna, and Aunt Doris as well as my three brothers, my sister, and the Gelormino family as a whole.

The Hand of God and His love and light were glaringly obvious and evident over the last forty-one years in my true friends and adopted family, Mary and Zack Sansone. Without them I would never have had the support, love, mentoring, and role modeling that I so greatly needed over these many years. I am eternally grateful to God for giving me these two tremendous blessings, Mary and Zack Sansone, and their family for the rest of my natural life. I truly appreciate and acknowledge my dear friend and brother in the Lord, Dr. Alfred Pecora, who through his obedience to the word of God brought me to the Lord.

I am extremely grateful for and blessed by Elaine, my beautiful wife of twenty-five years as well as a faithful, true, and genuine friend. I pray and hope and expect that I have been the same for her. My son, Louis III, has always been a beautiful dream, a great joy, and at many times a source of comfort, inspiration, and strength. I must express my deep and sincere gratitude to Genie O'Malley, Christian Gurgone, Susan Kendrick, Dina Kuhar, Sara Patton, Cheryl Adam and Authors of Unity for publishing this overdue book. I want to truly thank former Mayor Honorable Rudolph W. Giuliani for appointing me in 1994 as deputy commissioner to the New York City Department of Probation and permitting

✝ ✝ ✝ ✝ ✝ ✝ ✝ ✝ ✝ ✝ ✝ ✝ ✝ ✝ ✝ ✝ ✝

me to put my faith into practice while serving the New York City probationers and all the people of the City of New York. I express a similar gratitude to Mayor Honorable Michael R. Bloomberg for permitting and enabling me to do the same. I wish to also thank the former commissioner of New York City Department of Probation and my friend, Honorable Raul Russi, for supporting and encouraging the Nova Ancora Program.

I would also like to thank my dear friends George McGauglin and Hank Boerner for their inspiration and the great work we undertook in the 1960s to help thousands of underprivileged young people gain vocational training and employment.

I would like to thank my pastor, Roger McPhail of New Hope Fellowship in Bay Ridge, Brooklyn, for his spiritual teaching, enlightenment, and spiritual "meat." I wish to also thank my friend Kurt Blattman for his assistance, cooperation, and support of this project of faith. I wish also to thank my dear friend Father Donald Kenna for being a true brother in Christ as well as being Christlike ever since I met him over thirty-five years ago. I wish also to thank my brother Anthony for his inspiration, insight, and support.

I would like to finish this endorsement the way I began it by saying, "Praise the Lord and thank you Jesus for enabling me and for starting this good work and prayer in me and seeing it to completion." Read this book to be inspired, encouraged, entertained, and above all "blessed."

Louis M. Gelormino, Esq., II
f/k/a Louie from the Little Gents

1 Growing Pains

Welcome! You are about to embark on a journey into the world of Louis Michael Gelormino II. As we travel together, may our voyage help to unlock the wonderful potential that exists within all of us to lead lives of meaning, faith, hope, and joy. There are over 6 billion stories to be written in our world, and this one is mine. Come with me as we stroll down Gelormino memory lane.

South Brooklyn, New York, is where I grew up. We lived in a very tough Italian neighborhood where the Mafia was king, and we were often the pawns in a power struggle that left many lives shattered and destroyed. It's a sad commentary that a little bad often seems to overshadow a lot of good.

Most of the families in my community were closely knit Italian Americans who were basically working-class people. They were warm and loving, had talents and abilities, and were a credit to society. However, the small organized crime element is what everyone seems to remember about South Brooklyn in the 1950s and 1960s. This small but powerful group of men created a stigma for Italian Americans that is not easily shaken. The Mafia helped create the social, economic, and emotional background that I was born into back in the fall of 1948.

Born in poverty and raised in a corrupt neighborhood, my early recollections are of constant violence while growing up on Carroll Street in good old Brooklyn, USA. This is the backdrop to my story and the starting place for our journey. I hope you enjoy the trip!

There is an age-old question that I feel I must throw out to you at this time because it will play heavily on the story about to unfold. Are we the product of our environment, or do we determine our own destiny in life? I believe the answer lies somewhere in between. While certain barometers of success may point to the influence of environment, others point more to our own determination. I will come back to this issue often as I relate my story to you, for while I am a product of my environment, I also, now as I look back, see that I chose the life I have lived.

In my neighborhood, you had two choices: either you conveyed the image of strength or you got beat up by people who viewed you as weak. While all the people I hung out with lived by this code of behavior, there was always a lighter side to the constant pressures of keeping up a tough image.

One such incident I will never forget involved Vinny Mophead. Vinny had just moved into our neighborhood. He was about fifteen years old, and he was always trying to show everyone how tough he was by picking on kids younger than himself. While Vinny was quite successful at this, there was one person who always seemed to destroy the tough image he wanted so much to convey: his mother.

Vinny's mother would come down from her apartment at 12 o'clock every day and force Vinny to go upstairs and eat his lunch. This was very bad for Vinny's image since it showed that his mother dominated him, and that he was basically a sissy because he did what his mother wanted him to do. Vinny had a plan that he thought would help restore his tough-guy image; however, it only made matters worse. He began to tell his mother, "If you keep coming down and forcing me to go upstairs for lunch, one of these days I am going to kill myself."

However, Vinny's mom proved tougher than her son. She would grab him by the ear, slap him on the head, and tell him to go upstairs and eat lunch like a good boy or else she would break his head.

In a desperate attempt to regain some dignity, Vinny did something that will forever immortalize him to those of us who grew up on Carroll Street. One day when his mother came down and demanded that he go upstairs for lunch, he became so disgusted that he went to the top of a four-story brownstone and hung from the face of the brownstone, clutching the top of the roof. He told his mom that if she didn't leave, he would jump.

Vinny's mother proved to be one tough customer herself. She said she was going upstairs and that when Vinny came upstairs, she would give him a nice beating—and if he didn't jump, she would kill him. This went on for several months and proved a real test of wills. Every day, Vinny's mother would come down and bring him upstairs to eat his lunch. And every day, Vinny would go to the top of the roof and hang down, clutching the roof and telling his mother to leave him alone or he would jump.

For this reason, it was never necessary to wear a watch to determine lunchtime. Whenever you saw Vinny Mophead hanging from the four-story brownstone on Carroll Street, you knew it was time to go home for lunch. Fortunately for Vinny, he had a strong pair of hands and never missed a lunchtime meal.

As I look back and reflect on my friend Vinny Mophead, his life seemed to revolve around the image he felt he had to project to others—even if it wasn't who he really was. It was more important to Vinny to project an image of who he thought he should be rather than who he really was. And when I look back at Vinny, I am really looking back at myself. As I was growing up, it wasn't me who was growing up but a composite set of behaviors and images of what I thought I should be.

I guess that was the way many of my friends grew up. We didn't have a real identity, and we looked to the role models around us to establish one. Unfortunately, most of us fixed our eyes and hopes on the wrong models. While in search of an identity, many of us wound up on the wrong side of the tracks.

✝ ✝ ✝ ✝ ✝ ✝ ✝ ✝ ✝ ✝ ✝ ✝ ✝ ✝ ✝ ✝ ✝

Being accepted by our peers was very important and, since we grew up in a very physical neighborhood, we developed our own set of standards for what we felt was important. Being strong and tough, belonging to a gang, and having a nickname became the parameters we felt would bring us identity and respect.

Take, for example, nicknames. First of all, if you wanted to hang out with the guys you had to have a nickname. A person's nickname meant a lot back then—it conveyed self-image and self-worth. To give you a flavor of the types of people I hung out with, let me introduce you to some of my friends: Johnny Dog, Richie Chigot, Ralphie Bopper, Stroll Bracioli, Richie Wax (also known as Gabaybork), Joey Gutless, Nicky Egghead, Anthony Dumbo, and Tommy Lightning. And my nickname was Crazy Louie, which was quite appropriate since I was constantly fighting with other people as I grew up.

As far back as I can remember, hostilities, hatred, and bitterness were the emotions surrounding my childhood. Without having positive, constructive programs to channel my energies toward and to make up for the severe problems I faced at home, it became almost natural for me to place my energies into fighting.

On the home front, my family life was far from normal. I was born to a mother who at age fifteen had a nervous breakdown and developed paranoid schizophrenia, which remained with her till she died at the age of eighty-four. While I loved my mom, it broke my heart to see her in and out of mental hospitals my entire childhood.

Today, I have a wonderful son who has his own room and the love of a mother and father. But back in the 1950s, the Gelorminos lived in a four-room apartment where I not only shared a bedroom with three brothers, but three of us shared the same bed! During winter, it was a sight to behold—the three of us huddled together under the blankets.

My dad was a very dear man. He was a dock worker who worked very hard to not only feed a growing family of four boys and one girl, but also to help pay the enormous medical bills that my mom's condition entailed. Perhaps it was a broken heart or maybe it was the tremendous pressures and stresses my dad had to face year after year that led to his premature death of a heart attack when I was just fifteen.

My older brother, Gene, decided to get married and move out first. My next eldest brother, Anthony, turned to drugs as his way to escape and handle the pressures of our dysfunctional family. My younger brother, James, also turned to drugs in an attempt to make sense of a world that seemed to offer nothing but pain and suffering.

Sadness, unhappiness, and hardship were for the most part what helped to mold my early childhood. I always dreamed of someday breaking out of the

✝ ✝ ✝ ✝ ✝ ✝ ✝ ✝ **✝** ✝ ✝ ✝ ✝ ✝ ✝ ✝ ✝

misery that surrounded me and being a respectable member of society, even though the odds were very much against me.

My dad had dreams too. He had hoped to save up enough money to one day move the whole family to Long Island. But when my mom got sick, his life savings evaporated quickly and so did his dream. It broke my heart and made me angry to watch my father constantly struggling to make ends meet. As we grew older, I saw how our involvement in gangs and Anthony and James's drug problems added to the sorrow my dad had to bear. Seeing my dad's dreams fade away and my entire family life crumbling before my eyes created intense hatred and bitterness in my soul.

Yes, my environment was shaping me, and by the time I reached ten years old I had become a tough but lost young man, desperately searching for love and a sense of belonging. In order to cope with life, I somehow knew that dreams were very important, especially since the harsh realities of life were ever-present. Though I saw my dad finally resign himself to the fact that his dreams and hopes were never going to materialize, I never let go of mine.

Even little dreams, when they come true, can mean all the difference in the world—especially to a little boy who has little to look forward to in life. Nicky Egghead and I had always wanted to see a Dodger game in Ebbets Field. However, being poor, we were never afforded that opportunity. Nicky was an avid Dodger fan whose love for them was enormous. At this point in time, the Dodgers were moving to California and Ebbets Field was about to be knocked down. So Egghead decided that we should go to Ebbets Field and play a game of stickball before they knocked down the home of our beloved Dodgers. So, along with Richie Wax, Ralphie Bopper, Stroll Bracioli, my brother James, and a few others, we decided to travel to Ebbets Field for a friendly game of stickball.

As we set out for Ebbets Field, the excitement seemed to be mounting as we approached the stadium. It was a beautiful Sunday morning, but none of us was prepared for the game we were about to participate in. We all managed to get into the ballpark by squeezing through a small window that couldn't have been more than a six-inch square. As we crawled under a fence, we found ourselves standing on the playing field. Nicky and I were awestruck to actually be on the same field where Duke Snider and Carl Furillo played.

I immediately assumed a position in right field because it was always my dream to be like Carl Furillo. James wanted to be Duke Snider, so he moved to center field. The rest of my friends began to move into the positions of the baseball players they wanted to be.

Nicky always wanted to be a baseball announcer, announcing Dodger games. So he made his way up to the announcer's booth and, as luck would have it, the microphone system throughout the stadium was operable. Nicky began to announce our game, calling out the positions we played on the field.

Pretty soon, the groundskeeper for Ebbets Field appeared. He was so infuriated seeing us playing ball that he began screaming at us at the top of his lungs. He shouted that if we didn't immediately leave the field, he would call the police and run us over. We paid no attention and continued our game. True to his word, the groundskeeper got on his tractor and started chasing us around the field, trying to run us over.

Nicky, still on the microphone system, began to address his comments to the groundskeeper. He told our tractor friend that he was interfering with the baseball game and that if he didn't remove himself from the field at once, he would call the police. Nicky was calling for Don Larsen to come to the pitcher's mound and claimed that the groundskeeper was preventing Larsen from coming to the mound.

This was truly a sight to behold. We did indeed have our dream come true that day—having our stickball game in Ebbets Field, pretending to be the Dodgers whom we idolized. We risked our lives that day—we almost got run over by a tractor or arrested, but it was worth the memory of playing stickball in Ebbets Field.

God bless you, Nicky Egghead, for your vision, daring, and helping dreams come true.

2 Anatomy of a Gang

Just the mention of the South Brooklyn Boys was enough to send shivers throughout the entire community. For many years, they were one of the strongest gangs in Brooklyn. However, with the passing of time their influence slowly began to dwindle, leaving a void in the community. Looking back, it's hard to imagine how the decline of a gang could leave a void in a neighborhood, but back then gangs played a different role than they seem to have in our society today. The gangs back then were a source of community, strength, structure, purpose, and meaning for its members, who usually lacked these things in their family or environment elsewhere. The gang was an organization with a hierarchy, a chain of command, and titles for its officers. The purpose of being in a gang was to obtain a sense of identity and self-image. A member was given a nickname and a title, giving you a sense of belonging. Through the gang, life took on a meaning and purpose.

When we look at some of the gangs today, we see brutality of such an intense nature that it almost makes the gangs of the '50s seem gentle. Many gangs today exist for the sole purpose of inflicting hatred, terror, and acts of senseless violence whenever and wherever they can. With such massive decay in the moral fabric of our country in general, is it any wonder that gangs, which often seem to epitomize the lowest level of a society's moral character, have become so violent and sick?

Now don't get me wrong—the gangs I was involved with in the '50s and '60s were not material to start a church choir with. We participated in a lot of fights, and we had hatred and prejudice toward a lot of people. But the senseless and perverted acts of violence that characterize what we see on the streets of America today were the exception rather than the rule in the gangs of my childhood.

One of the talents God blessed me with was leadership. I was never a follower but a person who had the ability to make things happen, both good and bad. In 1963 I decided to start a new gang in South Brooklyn.

Perhaps if there had been some positive role models in our community, I might have started out in life using my natural leadership qualities for the betterment of our community instead of its decline. The gangsters, politicians, and other people of authority in our community didn't concern themselves with the health, welfare, or well-being of the young people of our community. Their main aim was to enhance their own self-interests, which they did a very good job of.

The really sad thing about not having positive role models was that there were in fact many good, hard-working people we could have admired. But they were, unfortunately, just "regular" people. Instead, we wanted to look up to people of prestige, status, and power, and in so doing totally bypassed the positive images that were there all along. Fortunately, a decade later, these positive role models would enter my life and transform me into a part of the solution to society's problems and evils instead of their cause. But for now, in the year 1963 immediately after my father's death, we began to form the Little Gents. My father was a good, kind, loving man whom I love dearly. He was the only stable figure in my home. In order to fill a void in my life and to cope with the great emotional pain, I, along with Gerard and Robert Serra and Jingles, formed the Little Gents on the roof of the railway located on Sackett Street between 3rd Avenue and Nevins Street.

A great deal of my time began to center around a new gang that we formed called the Little Gents. While "Little Gents" mean little gentlemen, little gentlemen we were not. Fourth Avenue and Sackett Street in Brooklyn became our headquarters, and we immediately held elections. There were only three candidates for office since we only had myself, Gerard, and Robert as members. We decided that Robert would be president, I would be vice president, and Gerard would be Warlord.

Our brand-new gang was now ready to go about the job of recruiting members. But before we started out on our membership drive, we held a strategy meeting to decide on how extensive our turf was going to be. Every gang has to have its own turf, a piece of property that is owned by them. Turf is territory, and is kind of like an exclusive island that can only be entered by nonmembers with the permission of the gang that owns it.

We carefully surveyed the area and decided that the Little Gents' turf would consist of a six- to seven-block area from Fourth Avenue and Union Street down to Fourth Avenue and DeGraw Street and down to Third Avenue. Our headquarters consisted of an old abandoned railway right off Sackett Street and Fourth.

We felt a great sense of power as the leaders of a brand-new gang, and we had high hopes of enlisting a tough band of followers. It was incredible to see how our gang grew as we traveled all over the neighborhood explaining to would-be members the advantages of joining the Little Gents. Within a relatively short time, membership—thanks to the diligent efforts of our senior officers (myself included)—swelled to about 300.

Just how could so many people come to join the Little Gents? I would have liked to think it was my magnetic personality, but there was a very powerful group dynamic that took place. Our organization seemed to provide the youth in our community with something that our community leadership failed to provide. It provided a sense of identity, a sense of position, and a sense of home for these young adolescents, who were seeking to find their place in society.

✝ ✝ ✝ ✝ ✝ ✝ ✝ ✝ **✝** ✝ ✝ ✝ ✝ ✝ ✝ ✝

There was a strong sense of paternity, brotherhood, love, and family in the gang. The Little Gents, as well as other gangs of the time, seemed to be able to provide these individuals with something that families, the community, and churches could not provide.

The need for acceptance and love is so important to the development of the human spirit that our youth naturally gravitated to the place where these basic needs could be met. The Little Gents helped provide this type of atmosphere. It is true that most of the people we recruited had troubles in the home and low self-images. Thus, a gang became a natural place for those who felt out of place everywhere else.

Unfortunately, as I would later come to realize, a gang, although it might temporarily meet some of our social needs, can never meet our need for love and acceptance except in a very superficial way. With so many people in gangs having low self-images, family problems, and a faulty perception of what is right and wrong, it is only a matter of time until the gang begins to turn on itself and create an atmosphere of bondage instead of freedom. As I describe some of my early gang experiences, I think it will become clear why I feel so strongly that gangs seem to offer the promise of a future but only deliver a life of further discouragement and despair.

In my early days as a gang member, before the formation of the Little Gents, I devised an ingenious way to raise money to help support myself. I would charge people fifty cents to join the gang and have protection. However, whenever I needed money—which seemed like always—I would throw them out of the gang and leave them without protection. At this point, I would either beat them up myself or have someone else beat them up. This would then generate the desired outcome: they would always be more than happy to pay me the fifty cents to rejoin the gang and obtain protection.

As time progressed, I logged more and more fights, learned more and more ways to beat the system, and developed more and more into a leader in our neighborhood. By the time I was ready to form the Little Gents, I had developed into a natural gang leader. My book knowledge was learned in school, but my street smarts were carefully cultivated through my associations with the gangs I grew up with.

In order for me to stay in the leadership of the Little Gents, I had to constantly project the image of toughness. Thus, the group dynamic made it necessary for me to get into a continuous series of fights and wars with other gangs to constantly justify my position. I had begun to enjoy the recognition that my position in the gang brought, and started to expand my horizons toward the presidency. My platform as vice president was "a war with every gang." For instance, the Little Gents were constantly fighting with the black and Puerto

Rican gangs in our neighborhood. In order to enhance my platform, I decided to go down to St. Marks and Fourth Avenue and fight a black gang called the Soviet Lords.

The record for going down to St. Marks and Fourth Avenue, fighting and coming back without any injuries, was two times in one night. I decided that it was just the right time to break the record. I felt that if I could break the record, I would be in a great position to become president and be a true gang leader in the community. The status of being president drove me on to attempt the seemingly impossible. If I could only become a well-respected gang leader, it would mean I was now a "somebody." Having a low self-image made it hard for me to feel important unless I was a leader in something, and in my life at that time, I thought the gang was that something.

I decided to go for it. It must have been about midnight, and I had already made two successful battle trips to St. Marks and Fourth and back. By now my body was feeling pretty good, having consumed a substantial amount of alcohol. As I approached this all-too-familiar location for the third time that night, I met a guy named Donald Duck.

Donald was a friend of mine who came from Third Street and Fifth Avenue and had just recently joined the gang. He had on a thin jacket while I was wearing my old, faithful, very thick leather jacket. In an act of spontaneous generosity and concern for my friend, I suggested that if Don was going to come with me on my mission we should switch jackets. With my thick leather jacket on Donald could never get hurt by a knife, aerial antenna, stick, or bat.

It was now my third time at St. Marks and Fourth Avenue. Donald had my thick jacket on while I felt almost naked wearing his thin one. When we arrived, we found three Puerto Ricans standing in a laundromat. It was raining outside as we entered the laundromat to lay down the law to our three Spanish adversaries. I introduced myself as Louis G. and told them to leave this territory. I said that I was expanding my territory and if they didn't leave, I would have to break their heads. Two of them instantly ran away, figuring, "This guy must be crazy."

The third guy, however, remained and came out of the laundromat into the rain. He dropped to his knees and started to search around for something on the floor. He kept smiling at me and made me think that he was either crazy or having a seizure. For the life of me I couldn't understand what he was doing, and I began to feel sorry for him. As he continued on his knees, he kept moving his hands on the ground until I suddenly noticed him coming up with a barber's straight-edge razor blade. As I turned to run, he cut my back with the razor. Because I was so high on alcohol, I never felt the razor cut my back.

Since Donald's thin jacket was on my back, I was without the protective luxury of my own thick jacket; as a result I had gotten sliced. It's kind of ironic

✝ ✝ ✝ ✝ ✝ ✝ ✝ ✝ ✝ ✝ ✝ ✝ ✝ ✝ ✝ ✝ ✝

that on this third journey to St. Marks, I had felt sorry for two different people. In order to protect my friend Donald, I gave him my own protection. And because I felt sorry for the Puerto Rican, I let down my guard and blew my chance to set the record. Even though I was one tough customer, I had a soft spot inside of me that I thank God would one day be used in many wonderful and helping ways. But for now, I had been cut from the top of my back across the spinal cord to the bottom of my back. A quarter inch deeper and I would have been paralyzed.

As I was running away, I ran into a police officer. He put a gun to my head and arrested me for disorderly conduct. With my world now spinning all around me, it struck me as quite absurd that I was running away with my back opened up and here I was getting arrested for disturbing the peace. So much for the caliber of the police enforcement back then.

After I was rushed to the hospital, I passed out on the operating table. They had put forty-eight stitches in my back by the time I came to. The doctor told me that it would cost me fifty cents a stitch. I told him I came from a very poor family and didn't have a dime. I gave him two choices: he could either take my IOU or remove the stitches. He decided to take my IOU.

It was difficult enough to endure the pain I was experiencing in my back, but now I was being marched off to the police precinct. As I arrived, my brother Jamsie and my friend Hornsey were there to greet me. It didn't take long for Jamsie and Hornsey to spread the word that I had gotten myself arrested. Immediately the Little Gents en masse decided to march down to St. Marks and Fourth Avenue and have a few words with the Soviet Lords. One thing led to another, and before the dust had settled a full-blown riot broke out, several guys got beaten up really badly, and Hornsey and Jamsie got arrested.

It's amazing what a few hours can do to the human spirit. Just a short while before, I felt like I owned the world. I was in a great position to become president of my gang and receive all the power, prestige, and respect that came along with the title. And I was on the verge of becoming a legend by placing my name in the record books for accomplishing the three-trip quest.

As the effects of all the alcohol I had consumed finally wore off, I started to reflect back on this recent series of events. Here I was, sitting at the police station under arrest for the third time in my life. My younger brother Jamsie was also keeping me company because he had participated in a riot. I was in quite a lot of physical pain with forty-eight stitches to prove it. My bid for the presidency was going down the drain fast and so was my spirits as deep depression began to grip my heart.

To top all of this off, I was about to participate in something I am not very proud to discuss. In our neighborhood, there was a street cop everybody called

✝ ✝ ✝ ✝ ✝ ✝ ✝ ✝ **✝** ✝ ✝ ✝ ✝ ✝ ✝ ✝ ✝

Prune Face. Prune Face looked a lot like a prune, a face from Dick Tracy days. He knew us and liked me because I was Italian. As he looked at my sorry condition, he asked me if I knew who stabbed me. As I began to say I didn't know, Hornsey, in a loud voice, screamed, "I know who sliced Louis."

Obviously Hornsey could not have known who stabbed me because he was not present at the time I got stabbed. Prune Face took Hornsey down to St. Marks and Fourth Avenue to find out who did it. Hornsey pointed to the first Puerto Rican they encountered and said, "This is the guy that sliced Louis in the back." The police car pulled up to the station and Prune Face, Hornsey, and some Puerto Rican guy surrounded me. Prune Face pointed to this guy and asked me if I could identify him.

I will never forget what I said. As I looked this stranger over carefully, I turned to Prune Face and told him, "Yes, this looks like the person who sliced me." It was just a short time earlier that I had felt sorry for a Puerto Rican who repaid my momentary kindness by slicing me in the back with a razor blade. Now here I was telling a policeman that a totally innocent Puerto Rican was guilty of that stabbing. My motivation for this shameful act on my part was twofold. First, I was really not too happy about being sliced and unjustly arrested; second, I felt that somebody had to pay for what happened to me.

As deplorable as my behavior was, it was equally matched by what Prune Face was about to do. He turned around and smashed this poor kid in the face. This guy spoke no English, and he had no idea what was going on. As he fell to the floor, one of his front teeth came out and his head cracked open. As I turned to Prune Face I said, "You know Prune Face, now that I look at that guy, I don't think he is the one who did it." With my new confession Prune Face picked him up, told him never to hit Italians, and threw him out of the station.

This incident only added to the depression I was experiencing. I really felt sorry for this guy because of the unjust beating he had just received as well as the fact that he had been beaten up without having any idea why. However, he was thrown out of the precinct and went on his merry way. For my reward I spent the night in jail and when I awoke, I again faced the reality that I had forty-eight stitches in my back and had been arrested for the third time. Fear gripped my mind as I began to realize I might not get out of jail this time.

As I contemplated my future, which at the time seemed to be going nowhere fast, little could I imagine that God had a purpose for this incident in my life. As I was growing up, I always knew that there was a God, but He was a very nebulous concept in my life. As I have grown over the years, my knowledge of God has grown greatly and my relationship and faith in Him have been a key to all the positive changes that have taken place in my life.

Just when I thought my future was about to be destroyed, a turning point took place in my life that to me demonstrates how God can turn even the worst of situations into a future blessing. The time was now at hand to go before the judge and await my sentence. I found myself sitting in the "bullpen" at 120 Schermerhorn Street, which is the criminal courts building. While awaiting my court appearance, my fellow bullpen mates consisted of a wide array of characters ranging from con artists to rappers, robbers, and everything in between. While in the bullpen, a silent inner voice said to me, "Louie, look around. This is where you belong. You are a criminal." This I already knew, but oddly enough I then heard this prayer within me, "Dear Lord Jesus, teach me to use my God-given talents and abilities in a constructive way and to maximize my effectiveness as a human being." I later called this "the Gent's Prayer."

I was appointed a Legal Aid lawyer who had long hair and talked like a sissy, possessing a very feminine voice. As he began to speak to me with that high-pitched voice, my hopes for ever getting out of this mess rapidly fled. With each question he asked, I fell into a deeper and deeper depression. I can still remember him asking me, "Where do you live?" and "Where do you come from?"

However, when I went in front of the judge, the lawyer advocated strongly on my behalf. He told the judge that I was just starting college and was active in the community. (At around the time I started college, I was involved with a gentleman named Hank Boerner, attempting to get legitimate jobs for gang members who wanted a job. My life was extremely confusing and conflicted at this time, since I was still a leader in the gang.) The lawyer really painted a very positive picture of me. The judge, based on my lawyer's application, decided to parole me. Eventually the case was dismissed.

This incident represented a significant day in my life. I was so impressed with what this lawyer did for me that, for the first time, I really started to think seriously about leaving the gang and starting to channel my strategies and efforts in a positive direction. How I thank God for this Legal Aid lawyer, whom I firmly believe God placed in my path to open my eyes to the possibility that perhaps I could be a real "somebody" in this world by also becoming a Legal Aid lawyer.

✝ ✝ ✝ ✝ ✝ ✝ ✝ ✝ ✝ ✝ ✝ ✝ ✝ ✝ ✝ ✝ ✝

3 A Legend in the Making

From about age ten to eighteen, my life was wrapped up in various gangs. From my early days of earning fifty cents by throwing guys out of gangs and then allowing them back in, to my closing days of earning forty-eight stitches for my kindhearted jacket switch, I learned a great deal about street life. This roughly ten-year period would prove a valuable asset in my future endeavors, although it would also leave a trail of many emotional scars.

In between my entrance to and departure from gang life, a host of experiences have become permanently etched into my mind. Many of these stories were quite comical, while others reveal tragedy. Nevertheless, they all were an integral part of the life and times of Louis M. Gelormino.

I guess that the idea of one day becoming the president of the Little Gents became a reality after I fought Blackie. If one travels to Sackett Street and Fourth Avenue and talk with the people who have resided in that neighborhood these past twenty-five years or so, few people would be able to say they don't remember a street fight between a skinny Italian and a powerful convicted murderer named Blackie.

When the dust had finally settled in the railway that served as the Little Gents' headquarters, my reputation as a gang leader had reached a level that almost defies description. For on a cool October afternoon back in the mid-1960s, I had fought and won what was then and still is called the greatest street fight in South Brooklyn.

A reflex reaction was soon to lead me into instant stardom and popularity beyond my wildest dreams. From the time that I punched Blackie in the face, twenty-four hours, almost to the minute, would pass before I would emerge as a renowned gang leader in the community. In addition those twenty-four hours were destined to send me on one of the wildest emotional roller coasters of my life.

It all started when Blackie's brother came onto our turf. Several of the Little Gents beat him up and gently kicked him out of our territory. When Blackie found out that we beat up his brother, he became furious. Blackie, whose middle name was Defiant, was not afraid of anybody or anything. He quickly made his way down Fourth Avenue, and when he hit Sackett Street he turned into the old railway.

He immediately slapped the president of the Little Gents on his face. He proceeded to push our Warlord and slap him in the face. Both gave no response. If this was not enough, he then turned to me and slapped me in the face. Now, nobody had ever hit Blackie back because he was a convicted killer and had done some hard time in jail. However, when Blackie slapped me, I just by instinct punched him in the face.

This so enraged Blackie that he looked me straight in the face and barked, "We had better take a walk down the block because I am going to kill you, white punk." Fear instantly gripped my whole body at the thought of having to fight this giant. Blackie was twenty-nine years old and there was little doubt, by viewing the size of his muscles, that he had spent the better part of his eight years in jail pumping iron. He stood 6'1" tall and was 190 pounds of solid mass. Blackie had been in so many fights, yet he still had a baby face because he gave very few people a chance to hit him.

My fears only grew as I thought about my own physique in comparison. I weighed only 130 pounds, and although I was quite fast on my feet, I was also quite skinny—the only thing I ever pumped was air into bicycle tires.

As we walked down the block, it seemed like this was the longest block I had ever traveled. Even though I was deathly afraid to fight Blackie, I did not want to show him I was afraid. As we walked, we began to exchange a series of words: each of us was telling the other that he was going to be killed.

By this stage of my life, I had become somewhat of an expert at hiding my true feelings. Fear was something in which I had lived my entire life. I was afraid of the future and often chose not to reflect back on the past because of all the scars my family situation had inflicted upon me. While I was often afraid to fight, it never seemed to stop me. I had constructed a belief system that showing fear meant weakness and not acting tough meant not being cool and accepted. My fear of not being accepted and respected was greater than my fear of fighting, and thus the stronger of these fears often motivated my behavior. My fighting brought acceptance, and thus I lived much of my early life being afraid but liked.

Well, at least this time nobody could fault me for being scared to fight Blackie. Just as we were about to start fighting, though, a most fortuitous event took place. The sound of a female voice began to call Blackie, and it basically saved my life. Blackie's mom came out of the house and told her son, "You better come in—don't you know it is almost 6:30?" Blackie was on parole and had to be home by a certain hour.

It is really amazing how a change in events can so radically change one's emotions and behavior. As Blackie's mother grabbed her son by the ear and carted him home, my heart felt like its great burden of fear had been lifted. As fear left, or more accurately was put on hold, I began to taunt Blackie by calling him a "mama's boy." I must have been crazy but I yelled out, "Sissy, little sissy. You better not come back onto our territory or I will have to finish the job and beat your behind."

This whole incident was a great source of embarrassment for Blackie. After

✟ ✟ ✟ ✟ ✟ ✟ ✟ ✟ ✟ ✟ ✟ ✟ ✟ ✟ ✟ ✟ ✟ ✟

all, he was a convicted killer and here comes his mother grabbing him by the ear to bring him home. But my moment of courage was to be just that—a moment. The embarrassment and the mocking that Blackie was receiving only made him more enraged. In order to intimidate me, he came right up to my left ear and said softly, "If you are man enough, I'll meet you tomorrow at 4 o'clock and not only will I kill you but after I finish the job no one is going to ever recognize your ugly white face again."

As Blackie went home with his mom, I started to reflect on the upcoming fight I had gotten myself into. As I began to visualize the sixty-pound weight differential and the differences in our hearts—his, vicious, cold, and murderous; mine, basically soft and crafty—my fears became elevated to new heights. My big mouth had done it once again. This time I could see no schemes I could invent to get me out of the first fight I genuinely thought I might get seriously hurt in. Twenty-four hours to think about one's impending doom is not a very pleasant way to spend a day, but I tried to make the best of it. As I began to rehearse the fight in my mind, I tried to focus on my great quickness and speed. I knew that the only way I could survive was really to avoid fighting by staying out of Blackie's fists in the slim hopes that he might tire out, and just maybe I might even land one good punch. There is an old saying, "Sticks and stones will break my bones, but words will never hurt me." Now, old sayings usually have a lot of wisdom, but in this case I would have to make an exception. When I called Blackie a sissy and mocked him, my words were going to lead to my destruction. If I had only backed down, I wouldn't have been faced with this most unwanted fight.

There is another saying that I feel is far more truthful and wise and comes from the greatest book of wisdom ever written—the Bible. While I must admit that the Bible is not a book I often consulted in my young adult life, I somehow knew that it was a good book and that the God who wrote it was always there in my life, watching over me. I didn't really know who He was back then, but I often spoke to God and believed He was there. As I grew older, I would spend a great deal of time reading the Bible and use it to help me solve many of the problems in my life. It would serve as a guide, a blueprint for success, and a great source of inspiration in my life.

Proverbs (18:21) says, "Death and life are in the power of the tongue." My tongue was about to sentence me to a quick death in twenty-four short hours. Yes, it might be the stone fist of Blackie that would break my bones, but it was the words my tongue spoke that were the fuel and the real power behind my upcoming demise.

Well, word of Crazy Louie versus Blackie spread like wildfire in our community. Everybody was talking about the fight. From barbershops to bars, from supermarkets to schools, the word was out that the fighting event of the decade was going to take place shortly. It was amazing to see all the prefight activities that were going on around the neighborhood.

I had always wanted to be the object of discussion and in the limelight, but never in my wildest imagination could I envision all the attention and excitement that the name Louis Gelormino was about to generate. The talk around the community first of all wasn't just limited to the Little Gents and the Soviet Lords. Middle-aged and old folks alike, and even the gangsters, were interested in finding out how this whole fight came about. Every gang that I knew of took an instant interest in this fight, and many of them were making plans to be at ringside for the bout. Even the other young people who were not in the gangs wanted to know all the particulars.

Ringside was to be the old railway at Sackett Street and Fourth Avenue. Instead of a canvas floor and ropes to fence the fight, our arena was filled with broken glass, and the ropes would be the crowd that would surround Blackie and me.

Naturally, the bookies started taking bets on the fight. I went in as a four-to-one underdog, and everyone began to place wagers on the fight. With all of these prefight activities going on, my stomach really began to bother me. This immense attention I was receiving only added to my nervousness and fear, causing my entire body to shake.

Finally the hour of the fight arrived. At about 3:30 in the afternoon Robert Serra, the Little Gents' president, came to my home to let me know it was time to go to the railway to fight Blackie. He said, "Louie, there are already hundreds of people waiting for you to come down and fight Blackie." I told him that I had a very bad stomachache and felt terrible. Fighting Blackie, I told Robert, was something I really didn't want to do.

Robert was not pleased to hear this just before the fight. He raised his voice and said, "You have to go. Everyone is betting on the fight and there is a lot at stake here. You are representing the Italians, and you just have to fight." Robert always had a way of getting people to see things from his viewpoint. I, with great reluctance, agreed to go. The two of us proceeded to walk slowly down to our railway headquarters, but this time it wasn't to hold any Little Gents meetings.

As we walked to the railway, Robert did his best to try to encourage me and build up my confidence. He saw how desperate I looked, and felt if I let Blackie see me in such a scared state, it would only quicken my defeat. We went over strategy and tried to see if Blackie had any weaknesses I could capitalize on. We both agreed that the only chance I had was to use my tremendous quickness and pray for a miracle. Robert's pep talk helped a little, but as we turned into the railway my fears heightened once again at the sight I was now viewing.

✟ ✟ ✟ ✟ ✟ ✟ ✟ ✟ ✟ **✟** ✟ ✟ ✟ ✟ ✟ ✟ ✟ ✟

There were at least 700 or 800 people, all eagerly awaiting my appearance. As I surveyed this huge crowd, I saw many of the faces I grew up with my entire life. The Little Gents were out in force to cheer me on. Many of my classmates were there. Even a healthy number of men in their late fifties and sixties decided to watch the fight. Of course the Soviet Lords were there. Several of the Puerto Rican gangs were on hand, and even some of the ladies decided to make a day of it. It was like a gala event, and all the neighborhood celebrities were there.

The blacks were on one side and the Italians on the other side of the railway. As I scanned the crowd, Robert touched me on the shoulder, and when I turned to him he pulled out a wad from his wallet and said, "Look at all the money I have collected so far. I bet there is at least $1,000 riding on this fight. Louie, if we win we will make a fortune." Of course he was right. Being a four-to-one underdog would bring in a great return on this investment. However, I was still praying that somehow I wouldn't have to fight Blackie.

As my mind kept moving in a million directions, I stopped for a moment and focused on trying to spot the police. It was rare for me to look forward to seeing the cops, but my last hope was that they would arrive on the scene and break up the fight. Back then, cities had various loitering laws on the books to prevent just such occurrences as these from taking place. These laws were enforced back then, too.

At any moment, I was expecting the police to arrive on the scene to break up this huge crowd. After all, the whole neighborhood knew about it, and that certainly meant the cops did. In addition, the crowd was generating was so much noise that it was bound to bring the men in blue to my rescue. As Blackie and I were about to square off, though, there was no sound or sight of police anywhere. I learned after the fight that the police were paid off not to intervene. With this last ray of hope gone, it was time to face Blackie.

While last-minute preparations were taking place before the fight, I took a few moments to warm up with my friend, Waxy. By now, the crowd was ready for action, the whites on one side and the blacks on the other, both sides eagerly placing bets on a winner. With broken glass all around us and my life hanging in the balance, Robert gave the call for the fight to begin.

I immediately began to move and stick, move and stick. Being so thin allowed me to move back and forth with great speed. I had very quick feet and hands. Blackie's big frame, while quite ominous looking, was slow moving. For the first twenty minutes, I gave the crowd an exhibition in dancing and style as I skillfully managed to avoid all of Blackie's punches. While I was dead scared, I knew that I had to avoid his punches or I would be in big trouble.

While a good majority of the crowd was rooting for me, they also wanted to see a little more action than just the few jabs I was landing and the missed punches that Blackie kept throwing. I can't remember exactly what, but I heard Waxy screaming something at me. As I turned to look at him, I lost my concentration and suddenly got hit with a thunderous right hook to the face. I was knocked flat on my back and began to see stars.

Blackie came toward me as if to stomp me and finish me off. But before he had the chance, Robert jumped up and said, "This is supposed to be a fair fight. By the 'rules of the railway,' if any party is knocked down the other party has to let the other one get off the ground." Robert was always a quick thinker, and I thank God he had invented this rule just for this fight. While Blackie was big in the body, he wasn't too big in the head, and he foolishly fell for Robert's trumped-up fair-fight rule.

He backed off and gave me the precious few moments I needed to get off the ground and resume the fight. My nose was bleeding and I was still a little groggy, but something was happening to my mental state that was quite unexpected. Up until this point, the only thing that kept pulsating through my mind was fear and thoughts of survival. However, when I got off the ground my adrenaline was pumping so fast that my body chemistry was no longer signaling impulses of fear but thoughts of power and victory. I was now as mad as hell and ready to attack and kill.

I was no longer moving and sticking but boxing and fighting. I was so enraged by being knocked down that I was looking for just the right opening to return the favor. As Blackie moved toward me, I hit him with the greatest left hook of my career and flattened him. As I began to stomp him, the blacks got up and said that I should let him get up since this was a fair fight.

Robert and several other Little Gents pulled out knives and told the Soviet Lords that the fair-fight rules were out the window and that it was now every man for himself. The blacks backed off, and I continued to stomp Blackie for another minute or two. As quickly as Robert had established the rules of the railway, just as quickly he suspended them. There were never any rules; it was a fight to the death or until one fighter gave up.

Blackie finally got up, and we continued to fight for another two hours. It was a real battle royale—a fight to the finish. Our bare fists were pulsating with pain as we continued to land punches. It was amazing that both of us were still standing. My body was a wreck. I was bleeding from my head, eye, nose, and ear. Every muscle was in a state of pain, and my mind was now numb; I was fighting on instinct. Blackie didn't look much better as blood poured from his nose and mouth. It was a vicious, brutal fight. If nothing else, that day the crowd got to view a brawl they could tell their children and grandchildren they were a part of.

By this time, the whole neighborhood was around the railway watching the fight. Toward the end of the fight, who should appear at the railway but my brother Anthony? At this time, Anthony was at the height of his gang-fighting career. He was the leader of the South Brooklyn Boys, and everybody was afraid of him—even the gangsters.

The South Brooklyn Boys were our mother gang. They were older in age than the Little Gents but were also our allies. They would assist us when we needed them to fight big battles against opposing gangs. The hierarchy of the gangs in South Brooklyn was as follows: the South Brooklyn Boys, then the Golden Guineas, then the Butler Gents, then the Little Gents. We were all allies and friends.

Anthony was six years older than me and as crazy as I was, maybe even more so. He was even more daring. He had built his reputation of being a great gang leader by being able to instill fear in others wherever he went. Anthony was a great fighter, but once he built up his reputation, that reputation was often enough to win his battles for him without him having to throw even one punch.

When Anthony saw me bleeding, he screamed at the top of his lungs, "What the (f….) is going on?" He was very upset to see how badly beaten up I was. I told him I was fighting Blackie and defending the honor of Italians and the Little Gents. He asked me, "Do you want to continue this fight?" My pride once again came into play, and I told him I did—even though I really didn't. I was now totally exhausted and secretly hoping that Anthony would break up the fight; however, he didn't.

I had been fighting for two and a half hours, and now I had to continue this fight. It lasted another ten minutes. Blackie started to get the best of me again, so my brother Anthony intervened. He picked Blackie up and threw him against a wall. With the fair fight rules that Robert had introduced (only for my advantage) out the window, I felt quite comfortable with putting in a temporary replacement. After Blackie was stomped a couple of times, that proved to be the end of him and the fight. He quit.

From that day forward, the word spread like wildfire that I had taken Blackie on and won. Needless to say, I became an instant celebrity. The crowd that day left with a new respect for Louis Gelormino, a.k.a. Crazy Louie. My reputation as a gang leader was really enhanced, and I felt like an important member of our community because I had defended the honor of my fellow Italians.

Respect was something that I always wanted, and after the Blackie fight I found that a lot of people would come up to me and tell me how much they admired me for having the courage to take on Blackie.

Even the bookies were impressed by what I had accomplished. They were so impressed that they paid off on the four-to-one odds, making a lot of my friends quite rich. I was the king of the moment. Prestige followed me wherever

✝ ✝ ✝ ✝ ✝ ✝ ✝ ✝ **✝** ✝ ✝ ✝ ✝ ✝ ✝ ✝ ✝

I went, and I can't say that I didn't like every moment of it. The Blackie fight made me a legend on Sackett Street, and I bet that my name and Blackie's still come up now and then when some of the old-timers of South Brooklyn gather together to reminisce about the past.

✝ ✝ ✝ ✝ ✝ ✝ ✝ ✝ ✝ **✝** ✝ ✝ ✝ ✝ ✝ ✝ ✝ ✝ ✝

4 The Snake Pit

As a teenager in 1964, one of my favorite activities was hanging out on a Friday night at a bar on Fifth Avenue and President Street called the Snake Pit. To me, the Snake Pit was far more than just another bar. It was a place where I could come after a long week of school and the pressures at home and unwind with my best friends. It was a place where the beers would flow freely, and wine, women, and song were just what the doctor ordered to satisfy my weary soul.

The Snake Pit was also a bar with a reputation for attracting many interesting and different types of individuals, many of them criminals and mobsters. People would come from all parts of Brooklyn, Manhattan, and even New Jersey to hang out at the Snake Pit.

On a typical Friday or Saturday night, the Snake Pit would be alive with action. Pool sharks would play until the wee hours of the morning in the back of this establishment while some very attractive women would grace the front of the bar. After having a few drinks with the ladies, some of my friends would get lucky and escort one of these seductive creatures to a more intimate location. It also would prove to be a rare weekend night when a fight or two didn't break out in the bar. When alcohol and hot-tempered Italians were combined, it never took much in the way of a few inappropriate words to start the exchange of fists.

While the Snake Pit was mob-controlled, as far as a lot of the activities that took place within it went, it was not mob-owned. This was not a situation that sat well with the organized crime element that frequented the Snake Pit. They wanted to buy the bar from the owner, but he wasn't interested in selling, even after some gentle but firm threats were made. Now, when the mob wanted something they usually got their way. The threat of having your legs broken for not complying with their wishes was usually enough to convince people that their demands were not so unreasonable after all.

One Friday night, the mob was temporarily suspending its broken-leg tactic in favor of a slightly different persuasive approach to the bar owner. The plan was to recruit one of the neighborhood locals to stick up the bar and hopefully provide enough harassment to scare the owner into selling. That local was Bobby BeBop.

Bebop was a drug addict who shot heroin for many years. In his case, drugs and crime were a family tradition. His older brother, Vinny Bop, was also a drug addict and a convicted bank robber who had spent many years in jail.

That night, as I was hanging out in front of the Snake Pit, Bobby Bebop suggested that I take the guys away from the bar and down to the corner. So around 2 a.m., I asked the guys to come over to the corner with me. I must admit that while I had no idea what BeBop was up to, I was curious.

As we were hanging out discussing the affairs of the day, I saw two people with masks run into the bar. I turned to my friend Allie and said, "I think the bar is being robbed."

It's amazing how the consumption of a large amount of alcohol can numb the senses. By now I had already downed quite a few beers, and having no fear at all, I went back into the bar to see what was going on. As I walked in, one of the robbers came up and put his gun to my head and told me, "Get to the back." With the mask covering his head and face, I had no idea who he was, but I knew that I wasn't crazy enough to argue with his steel friend pointed at my head.

As I got to the back, I saw the other robber put his gun to the bartender's kneecap. The bartender was known as Preacher the Creature and was a friend of mine. Now, before I continue to relate this scene, I want to let you get a little better acquainted with my old friend Preacher.

Preacher was one of those rare individuals who really enjoyed his work. Talking with the patrons and drinking brews with them allowed Preacher to obtain a great deal of personal knowledge of the entire neighborhood. He was a man who could outtalk any other man I have ever known. He called me "Counselor," and we always enjoyed each other's company.

Preacher stood 6'3" tall, and with his hunched back he looked like a giant "S." His potbelly and 220 pounds of flab were not the most masculine form to behold, but he nevertheless was quite a lovable fellow to many of us. He spoke with a slur that kind of grew on you once you got to know him. His real name was Bobby, but no one ever called him that. He was named Preacher after the great Brooklyn Dodger southpaw Preacher Roe. While he was the same height as Preacher Roe, he carried fifty pounds more in cargo space on his body.

Perhaps one of the reasons why we really hit it off was because we both had low self-images. I tried to cover mine by always acting tough, while Preacher tried to talk up a storm and camouflage his. Preacher had a soft heart and desperately wanted to be loved and surrounded by friends. Even if this meant spending a lot of money to secure them, he felt it was worth the expense to be with people and share good conversation.

Whenever you sat at the Snake Pit's bar, you would put your drinking money right in front of you on the bar. As you ordered your drink, Preacher would slide it over to you and often start up a conversation. One of his trademarks, however, was that while you were engrossed in your discussion with Preacher, he would often proceed to drink your shot of whiskey. I almost always drank beer, so he couldn't pull this on me. If you were so lucky to have him do this to you a second time, Preacher would buy you a drink on the house. Now some of the people who frequented the Snake Pit were not exactly mental giants. To

✝ ✝ ✝ ✝ ✝ ✝ ✝ ✝ **✝** ✝ ✝ ✝ ✝ ✝ ✝ ✝

them it felt good to get the free drink, not really comprehending that they had to pay for two in order to get one.

While it is also true that my brother Jamsie and some of my closest friends would allow Preacher to get away with his two-for-one drink routine, we had a motive in mind that I swear to this day Preacher never suspected. It was almost a ritual with Jamsie, Allie, Waxy, Joey Pig, Ernie Onions, and me that we would help Preacher close down the bar at 5 a.m. Saturday morning and then travel to Chinatown for a sumptuous four-course meal.

By now Preacher would be totally intoxicated from all the extra drinks he had consumed, and it almost inevitably turned out that he would pay the entire bill for the whole gang of us. Sometimes he would pay because he wanted to prove he was the big sport. Other times he paid because when the bill came, he was the only one with any money on him. Once Preacher got so drunk that he fell right in his bowl of soup. When he woke up, he found the bill right under his face.

This Chinatown feast was my main meal for the week, and I looked forward to all the antics that surrounded the entire experience almost as much as the food. Now if it wasn't for this free meal in Chinatown, chances are that none of my friends would have allowed Preacher to get away with his drinking-our-drinks game, for it would have been an insult if we allowed him to pull one over on us.

Back in the early '60s, I can vividly remember that while my friends and I didn't have much money or future to look forward to, we did have a lot of pride. It was very important to project an image of being tough and smart. If we felt we were in control and manipulating the situation, it helped bring a sense of importance and accomplishment into our lives. While I secretly knew that it was all a game, it didn't matter because for that moment I felt good about being in control.

Life back then for me was centered on constantly keeping busy, doing things and going places to stay one step ahead of having to face the realities of life. In this way, I tried to create my own fantasy world to escape into. The only responsibility I had was to myself and my circle of friends. Back then, I didn't know what it meant to reach out to others who had real needs. So, by getting by on Preacher, I was able to keep my façade and continue to travel on my own road to nowhere.

While in the bar, Preacher maintained a dual role. When he wasn't serving drinks, he acted as a front man for the mob. In this role, he often took numbers for the organized crime element that inhabited our community. He would also take sports action and keep law and order in the bar.

This was the backdrop behind the man who was now faced with the

✝ ✝ ✝ ✝ ✝ ✝ ✝ ✝ **✝** ✝ ✝ ✝ ✝ ✝ ✝ ✝ ✝

prospect of having his kneecap blown off if he didn't follow the instructions of the man behind the mask. Preacher had his hands up and was very frightened as the robber told him: "Give me all of your money or I will blow your kneecap off." Although his face was covered, there was no doubt in my mind that this was Bobby BeBop sticking up the bar. Bobby BeBop spoke exactly like James Cagney. He had that same distinctive voice and Cagney accent. In view of the gun in his hand, I was not about to say or do anything except put my hands up along with the bartender.

BeBop jumped over the bar and went right to the cash register. He took all the money in the register and then came back to Preacher, threatening to blow off his kneecap if he did not give him all of his personal money. As Preacher handed BeBop all of his money, I said to myself, "There goes Chinatown tonight."

When I did not come out of the bar, my friends and gang members became concerned. As all of this was going on, about thirty people came into the bar looking for me. As each of them entered the bar, the guy in the front with the mask on directed them to the back of the bar, where Bobby told them to put up their hands. Ultimately we had over fifty people standing in the back of the bar holding up their hands! At this point, the guy in the front came into the back and told Bobby: "Let's get out of here—the whole neighborhood is coming in." At this point, they both ran out of the bar.

BeBop was an ideal candidate for the job. First, he wasn't from the immediate neighborhood. This was important because the mob had a rule that you couldn't rob a store in your own neighborhood. If you did, they would either break your legs or give you the beating of your life. In addition, they would make you return the money. Second, BeBop needed money to support his heroin addiction. His agreement with the mob was that he could keep all the money he stole. And, finally, he was willing (and crazy enough) to go back again and rob the bar if the owner still wouldn't sell.

Now, we were not supposed to know who was robbing the bar and nobody really cared, although most of us knew who it was. However, two days later, everybody was drinking in the bar and once again here came the same two men in masks, waving their guns at us. One of them jumped over the bar and slapped Preacher in the face. With a gun pointed at the kneecap of my bartender friend, we were once again directed to the back of the bar.

As BeBop proceeded to take the money out of the cash register, we were all by now a little annoyed to have this repeat performance so soon after the first stickup. As BeBop always idolized James Cagney, he decided he would add a little flare to his escape the second time around. This time, as he was leaving the bar, BeBop turned around and fired a single bullet into the clock

✟ ✟ ✟ ✟ ✟ ✟ ✟ ✟ **✟** ✟ ✟ ✟ ✟ ✟ ✟ ✟

that was hanging from the ceiling by a string, incapacitating the clock. BeBop got a big charge out of this. Even some of the guys were impressed with this melodramatic act, not to mention his accuracy.

As he was fleeing the Snake Pit, he accidentally took his mask off, allowing everybody to see that it was BeBop. The real reason for this foolish action was that BeBop was so high on heroin that night that when he got near the door, he thought that he was already outside of the bar, not still inside.

If this were not enough action for one week, two days later a third robbery was about to commence. By now, we knew exactly the pattern that BeBop and his friend (who we subsequently found out was named Patty, another drug addict) were going to take during the robbery.

BeBop again jumped over the bar, hitting the cash register. Once again he pointed his gun right at the bartender's kneecap and then proceeded to play traffic cop, directing everyone to the back of the bar. By now, these robberies had begun to take on a certain air of entertainment. We all knew that BeBop was the man behind the mask and by now were looking forward to see what would happen next. It's hard to imagine how a bunch of guys being held at gunpoint, in the middle of an armed robbery, could actually be enjoying the whole bizarre crime. But, as a frequent regular at the Snake Pit, I had by now come to expect the strange as well as the wild.

On Bebop's third visit to the bar, he happened to encounter one of my dearest friends, Fat Wax. Richie Wax was a butcher by trade who stood 5'11" tall and weighed almost 250 pounds. He was all muscle and a true powerhouse in the neighborhood.

One thing that everybody from the Snake Pit knew was that when Waxy was in a bar drinking, he didn't want to be disturbed. On this occasion, as Bobby was directing everyone to the back of the bar, Waxy turned around and told Bobby BeBop (with his mask over his face), "I am not moving from this seat and if you keep on bothering me, I'm gonna take your gun and shove it right up your rear end." BeBop chose to back down because he realized that Waxy's threat was no idle one. He told Waxy: "All right, Waxy—you can sit there. Just relax and don't get excited."

I can still picture the scene in my mind. While everybody was standing in the back of the bar with their hands up, Waxy was sitting at the bar, right in the middle of a robbery, relaxing and drinking his beer. After taking all of the money from the cash register, BeBop also started to take the money that was lying on the bar.

Waxy, without raising his voice or getting up from his seat, told Bobby not to take the money from the bar because it belonged to the patrons. He then added: "If you touch that money, I'm gonna beat the crap out of you." Bobby

☩ ☩ ☩ ☩ ☩ ☩ ☩ **☩** ☩ ☩ ☩ ☩ ☩ ☩ ☩

not only refrained from taking the money from the bar, but he also took money out of his own pocket and offered it to Waxy if he needed it. Waxy declined the money, and BeBop left the bar. This was the third time that BeBop held up the bar in a six-day period.

On a side note, besides the great Snake Pit robberies, BeBop had one other claim to fame in South Brooklyn. He was, without a doubt, the greatest Kings player around. Now for those of you who have never played this wonderful street game, let me explain the rules. First, the equipment: the three things needed to play Kings are an apartment building wall, a sidewalk, and a Spalding ball.

Usually, three to six people play. Each player stands in his own square on the sidewalk and faces the apartment building. All the other players stand in their own squares adjacent to one another. The object of Kings is for the player in the first box to hit the ball with his hand so that it bounces once, hits the wall, and then bounces off the wall and lands in any of the other player's boxes. Each person then hits the ball as it comes into his box, so that after one bounce to the wall it lands in another player's box. Play continues until someone fails to hit the ball before it bounces more than once as it comes off the wall into his box.

If a player misses the ball, he has to go to the last box in the line and everyone before him advances one box. The object is to continue knocking out players to your left until you can advance to the first box and be called King.

Well, it was at this game that Bobby BeBop excelled. He had a great serve called a "killer," which was almost impossible to return. A killer (also known as a slicer) is when you hit the ball with a spin, causing it to bounce in some wild ways. One of BeBop's habits was that just before he would apply a killer, he would look you straight in the eyes and say, "In your mother's eyes." Kings was a very popular street game, and in between the three Snake Pit robberies we would play Kings with Bobby and act as if nothing was wrong. We never mentioned the heists to BeBop, although all the Kings players knew he was the one who had pulled them.

The reason we never spoke to Bobby about the robberies was because it had come across the grapevine that the mob had put BeBop up to the crimes in an attempt to get the Snake Pit owner to sell out. If we let Bobby know that everyone knew what was going down, word might get back to the owner of the bar and thwart the mob's intimidation tactics. And we knew that if the mob found out that word leaked out, the one who was the talebearer would have their tail bared.

As we kept silent, BeBop allowed his string of successful crimes to go to his head. I guess he must have felt like he was on a roll because two days later, with his confidence riding high, BeBop decided that he would expand his horizons and make his take a little more profitable. He tried to rob the bowling alley on a league night. On that fateful night, there were over 300 people in the bowling alley and BeBop put them all up against the wall. However, on this particular night, the owner of the bowling alley was tipped off that a robbery might occur. As BeBop had everyone against the wall with their hands up, the owner pulled out a gun and blew Bobby's head off.

The tragedy that befell Bobby BeBop was, sadly, one of many that I would encounter while growing up. Many of the people I knew who were like BeBop got hooked on drugs and either wound up in jail or the grave. Often the pressures of a dysfunctional family would turn people onto drugs as a way to escape their constant despair. Others turned to gangs to find the acceptance they couldn't find at home. This route also often led to a life of crime and jail.

However, in other cases, people's lives would be destroyed because of some of our old crazy codes of behavior. One such incident involved Bobby BeBop's brother, Vinny Bop. In our neighborhood, there was an unspoken rule that you never spoke against someone's mother. To swear against someone's mother was an incredible offense. We literally believed that if you did, you would go to hell when you died. It was a solemn thing to hold our mothers in high esteem.

As I mentioned earlier, Bobby's brother Vinny was also a drug addict and a bank robber who had spent hard time behind bars. Before he went up to the Big House, someone had said something quite offensive about his mom. Vinny told everybody that when he got out of jail, he was going to kill the person who had insulted the character of his mother. Well, it became public information that Vinny Bop was looking for this guy. When he did come out of jail, he found the guy who threatened his mother, shot and killed him, and was sentenced for murder in the second degree. Vinny went back to jail and spent the remainder of his life there.

It was just three months after the three Snake Pit robberies and some additional scare tactics that the owner finally threw in the towel and sold the Snake Pit. By now BeBop was dead, the Snake Pit was sold, and the mob had again gotten what they wanted. Once again, evil seemed to triumph over good. It would not be until many years later that I would learn what was really happening: in the last analysis, evil may temporarily prevail, but when it comes time to finally settle up accounts with God, evil invariably loses.

✝ ✝ ✝ ✝ ✝ ✝ ✝ ✝ ✝ ✝ ✝ ✝ ✝ ✝ ✝

5 The Lighter Side

While growing up brought with it much pain and sorrow, there were times when my friends and I did some very insane and funny things. Our foolish pride often led us to do things that, looking back, are hard to believe. And, on more than one occasion, I tried my hand at being a young entrepreneur. Raising money was something that I learned to do out of necessity in whatever way my mind could devise. There was indeed a lighter side to growing up in poverty and pain that brings back a host of feelings and memories.

My brother Anthony was, at this time, the leader of the South Brooklyn Boys, a very big and dangerous street gang in Brooklyn and the toughest crew in the 1960s. Anthony envisioned himself at the time as a "visiting prince on the earth." If he was not treated as such by others, there could be serious repercussions. As a visiting prince, Anthony mysteriously came into the possession and ownership of an absolutely beautiful Persian cat, which he named Maha La Mew. The name had some relation to Pepe Le Pew, the famous French television cartoon character in the 1960s, '70s, and '80s. The name always mystified me, but it wasn't something to which I gave deep consideration. The obvious fact was that Maha was a beautiful specimen of a cat. Anthony would let everyone know it by walking Maha on a leash up and down the block and throughout the neighborhood. It was certainly an odd and curious sight to see. Since Anthony was tough and the leader of the South Brooklyn Boys, everyone would only watch and marvel at the sight but not comment on its strangeness.

One Friday Anthony was going away for the weekend, and requested that my brother Jamsey and me watch and take care of Maha. We did not relish or welcome the responsibility, but we had no choice. That Friday night, unfortunately for Maha, my mother had prepared and cooked some bad food. Jamsie and I had decided not to eat it but instead gave it to Maha. Maha ate it and eventually fell asleep on the parlor floor. Jamsie and I noticed that Maha did not wake up all of Saturday or Sunday. We had assumed he was just sleeping and needed his rest. When Anthony returned home on Sunday afternoon, he asked us how Maha was doing. Jamsie and I told him that he had a sleeping problem or sickness. We were quite surprised, shocked, and fearful when Anthony petted Maha and found that Maha was hard as a rock. He picked him up and was quite dismayed to discover that the whole right side of his face and body, which he had been sleeping on, was completely cratered and caved in.

Yes, Maha was dead. He had been dead for two days and Jamsie and I didn't know about it. Anthony demanded to know how that happened. We had to confess that Maha ate my mother's leftover food and that had caused his death. Anthony had to believe us. I couldn't say anything to my mother. So he promptly demanded and coerced Jamsie and I to go with him to our backyard, and we had to listen to a two-hour sermon by Anthony on the beauty and essence of Maha before he was buried. It was a shame that such a beautiful animal died so tragically. Out of respect for Maha, Anthony decided that no one in the family could ever own a cat again. He said that this was the right thing to do. Jamsie and I clumsily agreed.

I vividly remember hanging out on the street corner on Friday nights in South Brooklyn, back in the summer of 1965—not just as a way to pass the time, but as a way of life. It was as American to us as baseball and apple pie. The corner of President Street and Fifth Avenue took on a life of its own whenever Friday night rolled around. That street corner represented freedom and a sense of belonging, and provided a home away from home to the group of fifty or so who faithfully met there every Friday night.

While the group was mostly Italians, we did allow a few Spanish and black people to join us. We drew young people from as far away as New Jersey and Long Island to this fellowship. Funny how our parents often didn't get too uptight when we didn't return home until six or seven the next morning. I guess it was because at least they knew where they could find us if they needed to.

There was many a lively discussion about gang activities, sports, and a million and one other things that young people are prone to talk about. We drank lots of alcohol, smoked some pot, played loud music, danced, and generally felt a great kindred spirit with one another.

However, amidst all this comradeship there existed a tremendous amount of competition between the Italians and the Puerto Ricans. We were constantly fighting one another, and intense jealousy existed between us. As I reflect back, I can now see how a jealous spirit can lead to some incredibly insane and hilarious events.

One of the reasons why hanging out on Friday nights was such a big thing was due to the many different personalities on the scene. There is one person who immediately comes to my mind. BaBa was a Spanish drug addict who would suddenly and mysteriously appear every Friday night at the corner of President Street and Fifth Avenue. His appearance was as bizarre as his speech pattern. BaBa was about fifty years old, walked with a hunched back, and had gray hair that looked like a giant bush. His clothes were old and ragged, and soap and water never seemed to make contact with his skin.

Almost like clockwork every Friday night, this strange little Puerto Rican drug addict would stand on our corner for three to four hours, yelling, "BaBa—BaBa." He would do this the entire time he was on the scene, and then mysteriously vanish into the darkness until the next Friday evening.

As odd and deranged as he was, BaBa became kind of a celebrity in the neighborhood. People flocked from all over Brooklyn, and even New Jersey, to see this man chant the only word anyone had ever heard him utter.

We Italians had our pride hurt because of all the attention and publicity this non-Italian was getting, so we held an emergency meeting to figure out how we could get one up on the Puerto Ricans. Our plan was ingenious. We figured that the only way to top BaBa's act was to come up with our own Italian BaBa who could out-BaBa the Spanish BaBa.

The leaders of the Italian gangs, including myself, put out the word throughout the community that we were looking for an Italian BaBa. The great BaBa search was now in full swing. Each prospective candidate was put through a series of interviews to determine if he could meet the requirements that an authentic Italian BaBa would have to possess if he was going to give the other BaBa a run for his money. He would, of course, have to be Italian, as well as a drug addict, someone who was on in years, and someone who had been shooting drugs for quite a long time. After an extensive search, we finally located the person we felt was ideal for the job.

Our Italian BaBa had just been released from prison. He was six feet tall and had a solid build, rotten teeth, a big nose, very drawn cheeks, messy hair, and, like the other BaBa, old worn-out clothes. In addition, he had been shooting drugs for over twenty years. We offered to pay him five dollars every Friday night to appear on the corner of President Street and Fifth Avenue, and to yell out "BaBa" for the same three to four hours that the other BaBa was out. He needed the money, and a simple handshake sealed our bizarre employment contract.

It was truly a sight to behold to see the Spanish Baba on one corner of the street and our Italian BaBa on the opposite corner. They would then both proceed to shout out "BaBa—BaBa—BaBa," each trying to out-BaBa the other.

We felt, in a strange sort of way, that our dignity and pride had somehow been restored through our Italian BaBa, and that the corner of President Street and Fifth Avenue was once again known throughout the community as our turf.

For almost two months, this battle of the BaBas was waged until one day the Puerto Rican BaBa overdosed and was no longer able to come around on Friday nights to do his act. The final victory was ours. While the BaBa chant would no longer be heard, we will always remember the sights and sounds of that bygone era, and that certain enchantment our old street corner possessed.

Another pastime that we loved to indulge in was having Italian ices during the long hot summers. Back in the early '60s, neighborhoods still had a regular ice cream man who would travel with his truck, and everybody knew who he was. Our ice cream man was an Italian man in his fifties named Mike, who spoke

✞ ✞ ✞ ✞ ✞ ✞ ✞ ✞ ✞ ✞ ✞ ✞ ✞ ✞ ✞

in broken English and sold Good Humor ice cream.

Unlike today, when big businesses seem to make so many things impersonal and large scale, we enjoyed a lot of personal services and small-town amenities, even though we lived in a giant city. In addition, people like Mike took pride in the simple jobs they performed. Mike always prided himself on keeping a spotless truck.

Back then he proudly wore his Good Humor uniform, which he also kept spotless. I can still picture his all-white uniform with a gold sash diagonally crossing his chest. On his head he wore a white cap, and just one look at him gave you the impression that he was far more than an ice cream man. Perhaps by today's standards it might be considered a menial job, but when you took pride in what you did and everybody knew who you were, a sense of dignity, purpose, and belonging made for one content ice cream man.

We enjoyed buying Italian ices from Mike not only because they were a great treat but also because you always had a chance to win a free ice cream. If you pulled the top off and there was a star stamped on the ice, you got a free ice cream. While there was always a chance to win, my friends and I never came up with the star.

Only certain kids would get the star, and we decided to see if Mike was playing favorites since we kind of felt he didn't really like us. One day when he wasn't looking, I opened the freezer door and saw an ice on the top shelf all by itself. We then knew why only certain people got the stars—Mike knew their exact location and therefore was in control of who he gave them to.

To get even with Mike, Allie, Waxy, Sammy, and I decided to place a dozen eggs on the roof and leave them there for a whole week until they became rotten. Our intention was to give Mike one last chance. We decided that if one of us didn't get a star on our ices that day, we would bomb Mike's truck. Well, we didn't get a star, and the four of us began to launch an attack of eggs at Mike's truck.

As we hurled the eggs, we were quick to duck so that Mike wouldn't see who was bombing him. Unfortunately, Sammy wasn't too bright or fast, and as Mike looked up to see who was firing the eggs he saw Sammy standing with an egg in his hand, ready to hurl it at the truck. Later that day, Mike went to where Sammy lived and told his mother what had happened. As a result, all four of us were punished for two weeks. However, oddly enough, Mike the ice cream man began to give ices with stars on their covers to my friends. It was nice to be "lucky" and get a free ice. Even Mike seemed to be happy with our "luck."

I could usually find the money to buy ice cream, but anything more expensive was beyond my financial means. In order to remedy this situation, I needed

✝ ✝ ✝ ✝ ✝ ✝ ✝ ✝ ✝ ✝ ✝ ✝ ✝ ✝ ✝ ✝ ✝

to think up ways to make spare money.

One idea I came up with to make extra money was our "haunted house ride." Back in the early '60s, Coney Island was a very popular amusement park in Brooklyn. People would flock to the rides in droves throughout the spring and summer, both day and night. One of the most popular attractions was the spook house. While the amusement park was a lot of fun, it was also far too expensive for many of my friends. We decided to build our own spook house and charge people just ten cents a ride. We found the perfect spot right on my block in an apartment house at the corner of Fifth Avenue and Carroll Street.

About fifty families lived in the building and, like most large apartment buildings, this one had a big basement with many separate rooms in it. Jamsie and I happened to find one room in the basement that had a ramp leading from the ground floor right to the entrance of a room. We broke the lock on the room's door and went inside to see it.

As I was standing in the room, looking up the ramp, I mapped out the entire ride in my head. I told Jamsie, "All we have to do is get a supermarket shopping cart and push people down the ramp into this room. We can then have people dressed as ghosts and have them break bottles against the walls and make scary sounds. It's perfect." With this, our spook house was born.

At first, the ride proved quite popular. Nicky Egghead and I, after collecting the admission fee, would sit our customers in a shopping pushcart and start them on their journey down the ramp into the basement. As they were pushed into our spook house, they found themselves in a room with no lights and were greeted by the sound of shattering glass as we threw bottles against the walls. People also appeared with sheets over their heads, making strange noises to give the effect of a haunted house.

This really scared people, and for the first few weeks we made a lot of money. But after a while, people got too familiar with the spook house and its scare appeal lost much of its value. With business down, I began to think of ways to make our ride scarier. I even began to seriously pray to God, asking: "God, please send somebody to help us make our spook house scarier." My prayer was quite sincere, and just two days later a man named Lumpy appeared on the scene.

He seemed to come out of nowhere, and I firmly believed that he was sent from God in answer to my prayers. To me, it was a real miracle. One look at Lumpy convinced me that he was just the person who could revitalize our haunted house ride.

Lumpy had a tooth about five inches long that grew sideways out of his mouth, pressing against the inside of his cheek to the longest limit possible without breaking the skin. He was five feet tall, stubby, and about fifty years old. His face looked deformed and was quite red and rough. If he was this scary to look at in the daylight, I thought that if we put him in the dark basement he would scare the daylights out of anyone who came down our ramp.

As we found out later, Lumpy had escaped from the G ward of Kings County Hospital, and while he was harmless he was definitely a mental case. I immediately asked Lumpy if he would like to make some money by joining our spook house team. I told him that all he would have to do is to stick his face into our customers' faces as they came by him in a shopping cart. Lumpy, who had no money and no means of making any, agreed. We offered him three cents for each person he scared. With Lumpy as our new added attraction, we raised the cost of the ride to twenty cents.

In order to make the ride authentic and super-scary, I decided to give Lumpy a short training course in how to scare the people he would encounter. Inside the basement room, there was a large brick column that I instructed him to stay behind until the shopping cart passed right in front of him. I then demonstrated how he should jump out from behind the column and exactly how he should stick his tooth into people's faces to maximize the scare value that Lumpy naturally possessed.

Lumpy became an instant hit. He made a small fortune with his tooth, and so did we. It could only happen in Brooklyn—that someone could put on his résumé that he was employed in a basement haunted house, making his living sticking his tooth in people's faces!

Granted, the way I was making money was totally illegal from start to finish. I had stolen the supermarket shopping cart. We had broken into a locked, private room. We had disturbed the people who lived in the building, and we broke bottles and made a mess of private property. But it kept us off the streets and from having to resort to more violent types of crime to raise money, as many of us did in later years.

We were also fortunate that the super of the building took a liking to us and allowed us to continue giving rides as long as we didn't destroy the place. His name was Joe, and he thought of us as family. He lived all alone and had no family of his own. He actually thought that the haunted house ride was a lot of fun, and he felt kind of happy to play a part in helping us make some extra spending money.

On one occasion Nicky Egghead, who was often known for his insanity, decided to put grease on the ramp and not tell anyone about it. He greased up the entire ramp and floor. Nicky then asked Jamsie if he would like to take a free ride into the spook house. Since Jamsie was always one of the ghosts, he jumped at the opportunity. If there is one thing I can say about my brother, it is that he always seemed to be in the wrong place at the wrong time.

✟ ✟ ✟ ✟ ✟ ✟ ✟ ✟ ✟ ✟ ✟ ✟ ✟ ✟ ✟ ✟

With Jamsie in the cart, Egghead gave the cart a big push and let go. As the cart speeded down the ramp, it picked up speed and flew right into the spook house and crashed into a brick wall. When Jamsie fell out of the cart, he banged his head and started to bleed. Jamsie was lying half-unconscious on the floor, covered with grease and groaning in pain. With no lights on, who should appear but Lumpy to stick his tooth in Jamsie's face. Lumpy didn't know what was happening and thought that this was all part of the haunted house ride.

Egghead was standing next to Jamsie, telling him, "Jamsie, hold on and I'll get you something to make you feel better." Nicky bolted out of the spook house and kicked down the door of another room in the basement that was being used as a storage room for toys. Egghead found an old toy chest that contained a ukulele. He returned two minutes later, and began to serenade my brother with an old favorite: "I'm an old cowhand from the Rio Grande. . . . I never learned to laugh. . . . I never learned to cry." As he sang, my sides started to bust out with laughter—with my brother lying there in pain and covered with grease, Lumpy sticking his tooth in Jamsie's face, and Egghead playing the ukulele and singing his song.

About a month later, our haunted house business came to an end. Somehow the people from Kings County Hospital found out that Lumpy was living in the spook house basement. They came with a straitjacket and took Lumpy away. By now, we had come to love Lumpy and consider him part of the family. It was indeed a sad day when we watched him go. Without him nobody used our haunted house ride anymore, and Joe the super felt sad that his basement reverted back to its normal quiet use.

Another way that I made money revolved around a street game called Skelzy or Skully. Skelzy was played with discarded soda bottle caps. We would take the liners out of the bottle caps and melt crayons right into the caps, allowing them to stand until they got hard. Skelzy caps were quite colorful because we made them in a great variety of colors.

Skelzy was normally played right on the street. We would use chalk to create a Skelzy board, which consisted of eight square boxes numbered from one to eight. All the boxes were adjacent to one another but not in numerical order. The object of the game was to shoot your cap with your finger from one box to the next until you went from box one to box eight, all in order. If there was another Skelzy cap in the box you needed to enter, you could fire your cap and knock the other cap out. Then the other player had to get his cap back into that square before he advanced to the next numbered square.

It was a lot of fun and required skill. The way we made money at it was to hold a monopoly on the block in Skelzy caps. The only way you could play with us was if you purchased your crayon Skelzy cap from us, at a cost of three cents each. If you didn't, you couldn't play.

This moneymaking scheme was short-lived, however, since several kids told their parents what we were doing. When my dad found out about it, he was quite upset and told me to stop. I loved my dad, and when he told me not to continue selling the caps I knew it was best to listen to him.

When my dear father died in December 1963, my mother continued on her downward slide into the dark abyss of paranoid schizophrenia, and I was just beginning my "illustrious" career as vice president of the gang I helped create, the Little Gents. As I headed further down the road to antisocial behavior, I started to attract many interesting and entertaining individuals. One such individual was a friend called Tommy. Tommy came from a family whose father was a good man but had a career as an "undistinguished gambler." Unfortunately, Tommy was beginning to follow in his father's footsteps. One Saturday during the summer of 1964, Tommy graciously invited me to go to the Belmont Racetrack with him. I didn't completely understand why he would want me to go with him, but felt it would be interesting and entertaining. After Tommy picked me up in his father's car, he insisted on paying my way into the racetrack. He informed me that he was doing so because he felt that I would be "good luck" for him. He asked me to look over the program and the telegraph racing newspaper (the telegraph tells the reader the horses' past performances, latest workouts, and other details) and pick nine specific horses for the nine races. I was inclined to pick favorites. I was what was known in horse racing terms as a "chalkie," a player who always picks the favorites.

I did as Tommy instructed and picked nine favorites for the nine races. It was amazing that each favorite I picked, without fail, lost. Nine picks for nine races and nine losers. I felt bad for Tommy since he paid my way into the racetrack. However, he seemed to be in a good mood considering. He even insisted on buying me dinner at a fancy restaurant, and I obliged him. I thought the whole thing seemed suspicious, since I had learned early that "we don't get something for nothing."

I obviously concluded that this would be the end of my brief horse-racing career. However, much to my surprise Tommy called me early the next morning and was very excited, insisting that I come with him to the racetrack again. He insisted on paying for everything, including lunch, dinner, and going to the trotters that night. He was becoming extremely strange. Why would Tommy want to do all this for me when I picked all losers? Maybe my luck would change on this day.

Again, when we got to the Belmont Racetrack, Tommy asked me to pick specific horses for "chalk." Again, all my picks lost. I was beginning to get depressed, but Tommy was ecstatic. He asked me to the trotters that night, and

✠ ✠ ✠ ✠ ✠ ✠ ✠ ✠ ✠ ✠ ✠ ✠ ✠ ✠ ✠ ✠ ✠

again I picked all losers. Again, Tommy bought me dinner and insisted I go to the racetrack with him the next day.

In good conscience, I could not go with him the next day since I was picking all losers and he was spending so much money on me. But the next morning Tommy insisted that I come. He would again pay for everything. After picking three more losers, I confronted him and insisted that he tell me the truth. He said it was quite simple: I was the "eliminator" in that every horse that I picked he would automatically eliminate.

Consequently, he was making a profit on me. Naturally, I was very relieved and happy since I was performing a valuable service and enabling Tommy to make a profit on the horse races, and I was eating filet mignon and living the good life. How could I ever imagine that I had this God-given talent of being the eliminator, or the so-called handicapper, in the sport of horse racing?

One thing I do know is that amidst the many sad and strange things I did while growing up, I will always treasure the times my dad and I spent together. I looked forward eagerly to the times we would go crabbing or to the driving range to hit golf balls. I was his caddy and felt so proud to carry his golf clubs.

My dad loved people, and one of the things he enjoyed most was to gather seven or eight of my friends together and take us to the park. We always had a great time doing this. Today, thirty years later, I practice the same thing with my son and his friends. I guess the park is a Gelormino tradition that I hope I will be able to pass down to my son as well.

My dad was the backbone of our family, and when he died I was only fifteen years old. It was at the time of his death that I really started to get heavily involved in the gangs. Perhaps my involvement in gangs would never have escalated if my dad had not passed away, but I guess I will never know for sure.

My dad was also a very gentle man. In fact, I can remember him hitting me only on one occasion. When Tommy Onions moved into the neighborhood, I wanted to hit him but had no legitimate reason for doing so. But I knew that if I just hit him, my dad would find out and punish me. I told Tommy to call me a name so that if I did hit him, I could tell my dad I had a good reason for doing it.

As I continued to provoke Tommy to call me a name, he finally gave in and called me "Crazy Louie." I hit Tommy, and he cried all the way home. Tommie told his dad, who then told my dad the whole story. When my dad found out about it, he asked me why I had hit Tommy. After I told him it was because he called me a name, my dad hit me. When I asked him why, he said, "You got hit because you lied to me." My dad apparently found out how I had provoked Tommy and knew I had told a half-truth. This incident left a lasting impression

✟ ✟ ✟ ✟ ✟ ✟ ✟ ✟ **✟** ✟ ✟ ✟ ✟ ✟ ✟ ✟ ✟

on me, and I find lying very distasteful.

Of all my family members, it was my dad who really had a positive impact on my life. I regret it had to end when I was so young.

✝ ✝ ✝ ✝ ✝ ✝ ✝ ✝ **✝** ✝ ✝ ✝ ✝ ✝ ✝ ✝ ✝

6 Organized Crime

The Mafia, the mob, and organized crime are all synonymous with power, greed, and crime. All three terms can be used interchangeably to represent that sector of the population that, though small by percentage, yielded great influence in all areas of life—not only in South Brooklyn but all across our nation. It was no secret in our community that a small band of Italian families were the policy-makers and authorities that literally ran the way we lived.

While it is true that politicians were supposed to run the communities we elected them to, several had strong mob ties themselves. Many others were very careful not to alienate the organized crime element, which had either helped them get elected or made them realize that they stood to lose a great deal, including their lives, if they came down too hard on the mob and their activities. The Mafia intimidated people very effectively through fear.

The psychology of fear is a great weapon in the hands of people who know how to use it. As I was growing up, I learned to live with all types of fear. I was often full of thoughts of inferiority and low self-worth. At other times, my fears centered on the difficulty of having to live with a mother whose mental condition was so very fragile. Living in poverty brought with it the constant fear of having to live my entire life with very few of the things I so desperately wanted.

As I struggled through the early years of childhood and then adolescence, fear and I became constant companions. Whether it was in school or the gangs, or even when I was just relaxing by myself, fear never seemed to leave my side. Fear had stripped away my self-esteem and helped to keep my potential for success in a place of neglect and inactivity.

Later in my life, I began to learn one of the greatest secrets in the world concerning fear. Only then was I able to break the chains that had kept me a prisoner for so long. And that secret was that God loved me! When I began to see that God is my heavenly Father and that He loves me just because I am His child, I began to see that fear can only exist when we view ourselves though faulty eyeglasses. I am so grateful that I now know that I have a God who loves me and cares for me. If I had only known that earlier, I wouldn't have had to live with the constant emotional pain I had to endure.

But the fear that the Mafia had mastered was the constant subtle pressure of intimidation. Early on, we learned an unwritten rule of conduct: that the mob was entitled to a large piece of the action in a wide variety of neighborhood activities. We knew that they had this right by virtue of their ability to project a belief system that stated that if you didn't follow their rules, you ran the risk of getting either beaten up or worse. They periodically carried though on their threats to demonstrate to the community that they meant business.

Throughout the years, the Italian mob etched this tough-guy concept into the minds of an entire generation right from birth. As a result, my generation was born into an environment where the Mafia was an integral fabric of the community we lived in. We really didn't question their presence but just accepted it as part of the way we lived.

Back in the '50s and early '60s, the Mafia was involved in a great range of activities. They ran numbers and controlled betting on horses. Loan sharking was a major part of their income base. Extortion of both small and large business owners, and prostitution, rounded out their core business ventures. One noticeable difference between the Mafia of that time and organized crime of the '80s and '90s was that the Mafia didn't really deal in drugs back in the early days.

One of the reasons why the Mafia began to deal heavily in drugs was their explosive use in the '70s and thus the huge potential for incredible profits. Another reason was that Spanish and Caribbean people began to heavily traffic in drugs, thus taking potential profits away from the mob. Innately greedy, the mob quickly entered this lucrative market and, as with everything they got involved with, became the dominant player.

It was kind of strange that despite their obvious greed and evil character, many people in our community looked up to the Mafia and actually idolized them. In fact, many of the members of the Little Gents wanted to be just like these men of evil.

I had no such love for the mob. I always felt that they were very selfish, had no compassion, and were takers and never givers. I saw right through their phony PR, which they often used to try and give the impression that they were helping the community. They often gave sizable donations to the local churches and even helped with food drives for the poor. But I viewed this as just a smokescreen to try to cover up their true nature, which was totally evil.

I had little respect for the churches that were willing to take a Mafia donation and then turn a blind eye to the evils that prevailed in our community. And the politicians who also ignored the corruption around them drew little praise from me either.

But for other people, the mob represented status, power, glamour, and a way out of poverty. Seeing a mobster driving around in a big fancy car, living in a home that we could only dream about, and being surrounded by beautiful women were things that had a huge appeal to many of us who had nothing.

Several of the activities that the mob engaged in were not considered that evil to many of the people in my neighborhood. In fact, many people who I knew played the numbers and the horses. With this already going on and many of my friends already in the gangs, it isn't so hard to see why many of them were prime targets for the lure of mob life.

✟ ✟ ✟ ✟ ✟ ✟ ✟ ✟ ✟ ✟ ✟ ✟ ✟ ✟ ✟ ✟

It is only by the grace of God that my eyes were opened to the true evil of the Mafia and that their glamorous appeal never sucked me into their lifestyle. I say this because many of my friends in the Little Gents eventually wound up entering the ranks of the Mafia. Today, a good 80 percent of those who went this route and idolized the mob are either in jail or dead.

It may seem strange that the mob would allow the Little Gents to stay in business since we engaged in many similar, though smaller-scale, activities. The reason was a selfish one. The Mafia viewed the Little Gents as providing a valuable service. We were viewed favorably for helping keep the blacks and the Spanish out of the neighborhood. The Mafia was very happy with this since they had no love for these people.

As long as we didn't make much money, they were content to let us to keep our small (in fact, tiny by comparison) piece of the action. If, however, we were to exceed this small piece of the pie, rest assured that our leaders would have been somehow persuaded not to get too greedy. When greed is the driving force, even apparent acts of kindness are little more than façades aimed at self-interest and not the interest of society.

Another factor that led many young men into employment with the mob was the widespread ownership of television sets in the early '60s. Despite their poverty, many families owned TV sets. As more and more youngsters started to see the glamorous life so often portrayed on TV, they became desirous of this lifestyle. The powerful visual stimulus of the so-called good life fueled many into wanting more in their lives.

Since we felt that there were no other positive role models to look up to, the Mafia became our role models by default. Society often seems to place little value on the average hard-working individual who provides for his family and is honest and caring. These are the real heroes in life, but they often go unsung. Since they lack glamour and fame, they get lost in the shuffle when it comes to providing a suitable model for the youth of America to admire.

It's a sad reality that fame, glamour, and bad news seem to dominate the spotlight, and the common everyday person who is really worthy of respect and admiration attracts little if any attention. Since we were looking for the superstars to emulate, many of my friends foolishly chose the wrong ones.

To many of the Little Gents, the gang life provided the support and protection they didn't receive at home. However, it didn't provide any means of truly bettering their lives or escaping their poverty. You couldn't stay in a gang all your life. As we grew older, the day came when each of us had to make a choice about what we were going to do with ourselves upon leaving the gang.

My choice was to try to better myself through honest means—getting a good education and making something of myself. Those of my friends who

✝ ✝ ✝ ✝ ✝ ✝ ✝ ✝ ✝ **✝** ✝ ✝ ✝ ✝ ✝ ✝ ✝ ✝ ✝

chose a similar path are still around to talk about the wise choice they had made back in the '60s. Others chose to promote themselves into the ranks of the mob. Those who chose this road often found out that living in the fast lane had short-term blessings, but they were only that: short-lived.

At first the lure of quick, easy money led many of my friends into the mob. There was, however, a heavy price to pay in order to advance among the ranks. You basically had to sell your soul to evil and strip away all moral values.

Several people I knew decided they wanted to make the big time in the mob. In fact, two of my friends even became what is called "made men." In order to become a made man, you had to kill somebody for the mob. After performing this act of faith and loyalty to the mob, they would take you under their wing and groom you to advance up their hierarchy. You would then be entitled to a piece of the action.

Another group that the mob counted on heavily to maintain law and order were the "hit men." This small group of elite killers would, for a fee, kill people for the mob. These hit men represent the lowest level of all humanity. They could kill someone in the morning and then relax over a nice meal at lunchtime without the slightest feeling of sorrow or remorse for the murder they had just committed. In essence, they had no conscience at all. To them it was just business.

The easy life was often short-lived because many of my friends got caught and several of them were sentenced to very long prison sentences. Others were shot and killed by the police. And, except for the hit men, those who happened to escape jail and death never really experienced any joy in life since deep down they knew that their success in life was made possible by inflicting pain and harm, both physical and financial, on others.

If there is one thing I learned firsthand from being on both sides of the fence, it is that crime doesn't pay. Perhaps it does in the short run, and sometimes even in the long run financially, but there is a heavy cost for this. Having to hurt others and morally bankrupt one's conscience in the process is too high a price for fame and fortune. I truly thank God for steering me away from this lifestyle that so many of my friends chose to enter.

There was a shining star amidst all the crime, gloom, and poverty that enveloped South Brooklyn—her name was Mary Sansone. To many, she was an angel sent from God who attempted the almost impossible—to reach the youth of South Brooklyn. Mary is the executive director of the Congress of Italian American Organizations (CIAO). Unlike the politicians, she was not a bullshit artist. She was a very sincere person who has devoted her life to helping troubled people, both young and old alike.

Mary came into our neighborhood and began to win our hearts through her tireless efforts of love. She opened up a storefront on Fourth Avenue and Carroll Street and instituted a high school equivalency program in English as a Second Language. And she was always working with the youth, trying to assist them in any way she could.

It was at this time that my brother Anthony was trying to rehabilitate himself. He cleaned himself up from his heroin habit, and I guess Mary saw his potential because she appointed him assistant director of the CIAO program. Sadly, as the program evolved, Anthony turned to drugs again.

One incident in my life that helped convince me that the mob lifestyle definitely wasn't for me involved my older brother Anthony. If there was one word to characterize Anthony, it would have to be "crazy." He was one of the toughest people I ever knew, and was heavily into drugs for many years. Anthony was a born leader and later in his life would go on to lead in a very positive way, but for several years he headed the South Brooklyn Boys.

Right next door to the storefront was a bar where all the Mafia guys liked to hang out. One particular gentleman, who shall remain nameless, was a mob hit man. I was about fifteen at the time and remember this guy coming into the CIAO office one day and seeing Anthony selling drugs. He didn't say a word to my brother—just turned and walked slowly out of the store back to the bar next door.

Anthony said to me, "Let's go next door and have a drink." As we sat at the bar drinking, Anthony started talking about how certain people in the neighborhood had a greedy spirit. These people, he said, often took things that did not belong to them, and they would have to be put in their place. For the life of me, I didn't have any idea what he was talking about. To my shock, Anthony pulled out a gun, put it on the bar, and repeated that certain people had to be straightened out. I had no idea what he was talking about. I only went with him to get a Coca-Cola.

Sitting right next to my brother was the hit man who had been in the CIAO office. Anthony apparently was addressing his message to this hit man and strongly implying that if he continued to interfere with his drug business, he would have to be taken care of. Anthony obviously felt that it was only a matter of time before the Mafia would be insisting on a percentage of his business.

After my brother finished delivering his message, we finished our drinks and left the bar. As we began to drive home, a car pulled up alongside our car, carrying the hit man from the bar and another hit man. They started shooting into our car. Anthony pulled out his gun and fired back. They were really trying to hit each other. It was amazing that with all of this shooting, none of us got shot. I was scared to death, stepping on the gas and fleeing for our lives. The gun duel lasted for about six blocks, and we finally shook them off.

✟ ✟ ✟ ✟ ✟ ✟ ✟ ✟ ✟ **✟** ✟ ✟ ✟ ✟ ✟ ✟ ✟ ✟

Driving home with a car full of bullet holes, feeling the shock and fear of nearly being killed, I began to worry about what my father was going to do to us. My poor father, God rest his soul, with all the other things he had going against him, was about to see his only car riddled with bullet holes.

When he asked me where the bullet holes had come from, I told him to ask Anthony, who would be able to explain. To this day, I still do not know the explanation my brother gave to my dad.

This incident only helped to confirm the very low view I had of the Mafia. Once again, they had shown their true colors. Their goal was to obtain a piece of whatever action there was in the community, regardless of the cost to human life.

If there was ever any doubt about my embarking on a career in organized crime, those bullet holes in my dad's car became a symbol to me of just what kind of people the mob was composed of. The expression on my dad's face after he took one look at his only car, now full of bullet holes, was enough to convince me that I wanted no part of a lifestyle that thrived on hurting others.

✟ ✟ ✟ ✟ ✟ ✟ ✟ ✟ ✟ ✟ ✟ ✟ ✟ ✟ ✟

7 High School Days

Back in 1960, a transition took place in my life that was as radical as any I have ever experienced. It was in that year that I said goodbye to the Franciscan Brothers, who had ruled over me with an iron hand, and hello to a four-year term of almost total freedom at Manual Training High School.

The contrast between the strict discipline that accompanied my education at St. Francis Xavier Grammar School and the almost total anarchy that seem to reign at Manual Training High School was something I can't say I didn't welcome. In grammar school I had been taught reading, writing, and arithmetic by a group of Catholic brothers who tolerated little if any disobedience to their strict teaching style. They were famous for using what they called "the board of education," which was a wooden yardstick, to speak on their behalf whenever their vocal command failed to gain our attention. One rap on the back of a student's hand was usually enough to bring most of us immediately back to order. When this wasn't enough, they took the problem pupil into a closet and literally worked them over to drive home their point. Within this atmosphere learning may not have been the most fun, but learn we did.

Wearing the school uniform was painful to those of us who had an eye to fashion. For many years, I had to wear a white shirt and a red tie with the school initials SFX boldly displayed for all to see as I walked to and from school. All of this regimentation and structure, however, had its benefits. With my home life in such constant turmoil, it was kind of nice to be in an environment where I knew what to expect and where I knew I would be learning a great deal. I was always a good student and graduated near the top of my class at St. Francis Xavier.

As I look back, I am grateful for my grammar school days because they helped instill within me good learning habits. Although I was about to suspend them for the next four years, they would prove invaluable to me during college and my future career. The reason why I let go of my good habits was not so much my desire but the circumstances that my new school environment brought with it. It is no great secret that circumstances have a way of altering our plans and desires in life. In my case, the circumstance was called Manual Training High School (now John Jay High School).

My parents wanted me to continue my education in Catholic school, but the cost was just too much for them to bear. With all the expenses my dad had for my mom's hospital bills, there was very little money left for essentials, let alone private high school. As a result, I left my red SFX tie to hang forever in the closet and enrolled in John Jay.

✝ ✝ ✝ ✝ ✝ ✝ ✝ ✝ ✝ ✝ ✝ ✝ ✝ ✝ ✝ ✝ ✝ ✝

During the summer before I changed schools, I felt apprehensive about the switch. I really didn't know what to expect since all I had known was Catholic school. Catholic school was a safe environment for me; I knew what to expect there. Although some of my friends went to public school, it was going to be brand new to me. This fear of the unknown made me very anxious.

During my first week at John Jay, I began to see things I had never encountered at St. Francis Xavier. Students talked in class and oftentimes were not told to stop. Hanging out in the hallways was permitted, and I soon learned that you could cut classes and not be afraid for your life when you returned to school. The teachers were different, too. Many of them were not really very good in my opinion, and certainly not strict in comparison to what I was used to.

At this point in my life, my family problems were mounting day by day. Not only was my mom's mental condition not improving, but our financial situation was getting desperate. On top of this, my brothers Anthony and Jamsie were both on drugs. For my part, I was really struggling to find out who I was in life. I had no sense of identity or self-worth. Both St. Francis Xavier and John Jay in large part provided me with an escape from the problems of the home front. The discipline at SFX helped put me on the right path in life. Unfortunately, the freedom at John Jay led me down a different road that almost caused my destruction.

I enjoyed the lack of structure at John Jay, and my involvement in gang life became full-blown during high school. But I believe that, despite my straying from the clean and honest ways of life, God had a plan for my life and His grace placed several key people in my path that would prove instrumental in helping to transform my life into one of productivity instead of destructiveness.

But these were to be future blessings—at the present, I never thought they would come my way. At this time, I was only interested in getting by and being popular in school and in the newly formed Little Gents.

As my first year at John Jay progressed, I began to learn the ropes of living the easy life at school. I saw some of my friends cutting classes and still passing their courses; I thought this was cool and decided to do the same. At first I didn't cut too many classes, but as time passed I found myself less and less in class and more and more in the pool hall on Seventh Street and Fifth Avenue, just two blocks from school. Now don't get me wrong—I still spent most of my time in school, but whenever I had a desire to shoot pool or just take a breather from studies, I had no problem cutting class. At that time there was little security in schools and, unlike at SFX, cutting classes brought little if any punishment.

Shooting pool became one of my favorite pastimes. I picked up the game really fast, and some said I was a natural. The people I hung out with between classes at the pool parlor were not the most respectable pillars of the community. My pool buddies were high school dropouts and a wide variety of schemers and hoodlums. As I progressed in the game, I even began to hustle others. Like the haunted house ride and Skelzy, this became a way to make a little extra spending money.

By the time my sophomore year at John Jay began, I had made the transition from SFX to public high school with flying colors. While I really didn't enjoy my classes, I did enjoy the social life there. The only subject I found interesting was social studies. Learning about what was going on in the world around me always held a certain fascination to my curious mind. Math and science never got me very excited, nor did English or language.

One reason why I never really got motivated to study hard was the teachers I encountered. While some were actually very good, they seemed too boring for my taste. Others were okay, but seemed to have attitudes toward me and my friends that immediately turned me off. And some were just downright weird.

Take, for example, my second-year science teacher, Mr. Zutler. His nickname was Zut the Nut, and it was well deserved. During my four years at John Jay, Mr. Zutler's science class was the only course I ever passed without ever attending a single class. It was Zut the Nut's habit to greet his students on the first day of class with either a smile or a screwdriver. As each student passed by Mr. Zutler for the first time, he would immediately size up that individual to determine if they had the potential to be antisocial or a troublemaker. To those who he labeled antisocial, he would take a screwdriver, place it right up to your neck, and quietly tell you your options concerning his class.

When I passed by him, he shoved his screwdriver just a few centimeters from my neck and said: "Listen, you punk, you have two choices in my class. You can either stay out of class all year and I'll pass you, or you can come to each class and learn some biology and watch films." I had never received an offer of this kind before and didn't hesitate in my response. I shook Mr. Zutler's hand and told him, "You got yourself a deal. I'll see you at the end of the semester, and I expect to get a B." It's hard to believe that at the end of the term, most of my friends who attended Zut's class saw a film almost every day while I learned absolutely nothing about biology and still got my B. Though Mr. Zutler taught me nothing about biology, he was responsible for sharpening my pool skills during my second year of high school.

Zut clearly felt that if you didn't plan to learn and were going to be a troublemaker in class, he didn't want to see his other students suffer. Several other students took Zut up on his offer, and as a result those who remained in his class had a very good atmosphere for learning. It's a sad commentary on our society that while Mr. Zutler's teaching beliefs back in 1960 were very unorthodox, they have quite a large following these days.

As the public school system in America continues to go through what some call a meltdown, many teachers are throwing in the towel and leaving the profession because there are just so many problem children in the schools. And, I might add, the problems of today are much different than those of 1960. Back then, the main problems we had were students talking in class and the hallways, smoking cigarettes, and chewing gum in class. Today the problems are kids bringing guns and knifes to school, breaking heads in the classrooms and hallways, and cutting throats instead of classes.

I have often wondered whether, if I was growing up today with my dysfunctional family background and life, I would survive the pressures and problems I would encounter. It's funny and also sad that Mr. Zutler, while an oddity in 1960, would blend right into the stream of things today (except, perhaps, for the screwdriver).

Later on in my life, while I served in public service as a deputy commissioner in Honorable Mayor Rudolph W. Giuliani and Honorable Mayor Michael Bloomberg, I did see a significantly improved public school system. Mayor Giuliani held the board of education strictly accountable and wanted to do away with it; he wanted the school's chancellor to be directly accountable to him to improve reading, writing, mathematics, and scores and to improve the overall quality of education for all New York City schoolchildren. Mayor Michael Bloomberg accomplished this, doing what no other mayor in the history of New York City could do. He made history and our schools and its teachers and students are much better off, to the benefit of our great city of New York.

By the time I started my junior year, school started to really be a lot of fun. The reason for this certainly was not my courses, which I took little interest in, but because by then I had become one of the most popular and respected kids in the school. In fact, I had my own following of students who really admired me. Some would even do my bidding and follow me wherever I went.

Having such a low self-image made it all the more essential for my emotional well-being for people to like me and want to be around me. I certainly didn't like what I saw in the mirror each morning. Having the adoration and respect of many of my peers helped me feel important and like I was a somebody—at least while I was in their presence. Of course, when I had to go home and be by myself, depression and anger would set in. Having to face the harsh realities of my home life was something I could never cope with back then. Thus, my high school years were an emotional roller coaster.

I guess you could say that I had a certain charisma and charm, even though the person I saw in the mirror each day didn't impress me very much. I definitely tried to project a tough-guy image, but I was not your typical tough guy. Some of the things my friends always said about me were that I had a heart and was kind and understanding. This combination of tough but tender was kind of unique and made me a big hit with both the guys and gals. In addition, a lot of my friends knew of the tremendous trials I faced each day at home, and they respected me for hanging on despite the abnormal lifestyle I had to live with every day when I left school. My life was one that radiated courage and perseverance to many.

Throughout my high school career, I was fortunate to be surrounded by a great crew of friends who were really more like family to me than my blood family. The need to feel like you belong is such a fundamental human need that without people like Big Wax, Buzzy Ubotz, Joey Heart, Allie Boly, and several other special friends, my life could well have taken a tragic turn during those very trying teen years.

These guys were my family and support structure. We did everything together. We were all members of the Little Gents, we all went to the same school, and we partied together, hung out together, and played stickball and Kings together. The only thing we didn't do much together—or individually—was our homework.

Let me introduce you to some of these special guys. First there was Big Wax or, as I affectionately called him, Waxy. Waxy was my best friend in high school and was so attached to me that he would often fight some of my fights for me. Waxy was a gentle giant. He was kind and really quite lovable. But he was like a volcano. When he was calm, he was great fun to be with. But if you ever got him mad, he would erupt without warning, and all 5'10" and 225 pounds of solid mass could destroy you in an instant. His dad died while he was starting high school, and in order to help support his mom and younger brother he went to work in a butcher shop. His trademark was his love of potato chips. He literally consumed five or six bags a day. Having a man like this on my side was a valuable asset whenever trouble broke out at school. Waxy ended up marrying a lovely Italian lady, and he is a wonderful father to four children.

Another good friend had a most peculiar lunchtime habit. His name was Buzzy Ubotz. Whenever we sat down to have lunch in the cafeteria, Buzzy could be found playing his drumsticks on the top of one of the metal lunchroom tables. Several of the girls thought he was cool and enjoyed his rhythmic beat. Others wanted to shove his sticks right up his you-know-what. Buzzy beat up a few people who questioned his musical talents as well as the shape of his drum. His beat became a fixture and in a way enhanced our dining experience at John Jay. Who could have imagined that one day Buzzy, whose real name was Thomas, would rise to become one of the most decorated and highest ranking detectives in New York City?

Then there was my dear friend Joey Heart. We used to go out to the discos on Friday night, and we always seemed to attract the pretty women. Joey really idolized me, and our friendship has lasted to this very day. One thing that really intrigued me about Joey was his understanding of the stock market. He used to brag about owning stock in AT&T and IBM. Today, Joey is a millionaire—climbing all the way from repairing air conditioners to managing some of the biggest office buildings in Manhattan.

Another friend who was an integral part of my inner circle was Allie Montello. Allie rarely came to school. His passion was the horses. While the pool hall was my escape, the racetrack was Allie's place when school was in session. Though he was not a very strong or tough-looking guy, he did command a lot of respect at school due in great part to the fact that it was well known that his uncle was a "made man" in the mob. Allie ended up being a good and decent citizen and a wonderful father to his stepson.

These were my closest friends and, although we were very different in many ways, there was a certain chemistry that bonded us together. Some of my fondest memories revolved around our after-school activities. During the spring months, we would often head to the old railway—our gang headquarters—and just enjoy hanging out and being in one another's presence. The great thing about the railway was that it attracted people from all over the neighborhood. We drank and swapped stories. Even the girls would come to be part of what was then "the in crowd." Several of these ladies were uninhibited and if you were lucky sometimes you would score an unexpected surprise.

One of the great highlights was the gang fights we used to have on Friday nights. Whenever a bunch of us assembled and had a few drinks, mixed with a lot of pent-up emotions and frustrations, it was only natural back then to rough it up with another group of guys who were like-minded.

A typical Friday night would begin with us sending Danny the Phantom down to the corner of St. Marks and Fourth Avenue. Danny was a member of the Little Gents and his sole job was to incite a fight with our arch-rivals, the Soviet Lords. He would often instigate a fight by smashing a bottle right in the heart of Soviet Lord turf and yell out a few choice words, skillfully chosen to infuriate a group of guys more than anxious to pick a fight. This was the signal that the battle was about to begin. Danny would then run for his life with his target audience chasing him in hot pursuit right back to our headquarters.

Our fights were held mainly to help feed our egos and prove that we were tough and real men. We fought to help gain dignity for ourselves—in a strange sort of way. It was also another form of entertainment for us. Our primary weapons were our fists. Guns were not used at all, and only an occasional knife was flashed. We did employ car aerials a lot, but more often than not they only served to scare away our opponents rather than seriously hurt them.

✟ ✟ ✟ ✟ ✟ ✟ ✟ ✟ ✟ ✟ ✟ ✟ ✟ ✟ ✟ ✟

Although on occasion someone got hurt pretty badly, it was rare for anyone to be hospitalized.

And if someone came looking for us at the railway and didn't find us, the chances were pretty good that we could be found at Zorro's. Zorro's was a famous old candy store located on Sackett Street and Fourth Avenue. We would often have a soda or malted at the counter and then retire to the back of the store, where we would play records and dance. We enjoyed the music, and trying to make out with one of the chicks was always something we had on our minds.

Back then the most popular sport was stickball. During the summer months, we played stickball almost every day. While I was a fair player, Nicky Egghead was perhaps the best hitter I have ever seen. He was a three-sewer man—when he got hold of a ball, he could sail it a distance of three city sewer covers away. It was good clean fun and helped pass the time during the long hot summer months.

Reflecting back on some of my teachers, two stand out in my mind but for very different reasons. One was my music teacher, the other my typing instructor. As freshmen, we were required to take a music appreciation class, which I didn't appreciate at all. The main reason was a little old lady named Miss Hessian. She must have been sixty years old and, though kind, was most irritating. Buzzy, Waxy, and I really hated her morning ritual of having us listen to her play the piano and requiring us to greet her in song: "Good morning, Miss Hessian. How are you, Miss Hessian?"

Each morning for a whole month, we would have to sing this greeting to her as she played her theme music on the big piano that stood by the window. Not only was it corny, but it was quite embarrassing and bad for our image. Being a freshman meant that we would be teased by the older students who knew that we were singing this sissy song. With each passing week, we grew more and more upset at being forced to perform at her bidding.

We finally got fed up and took an informal vote among our classmates as to whether we should protest this ridiculous custom. Most of the class agreed to stand with us in the revolt. I am sure that most of the students would have been happy to just tell Miss Hessian about our dislike of having to recite the good morning chant and hope she would consider abolishing it. However, Waxy, Joey Heart, Buzzy, and I felt we had to get our frustrations out in a more demonstrative way. We felt that since this had been Miss Hessian's practice for many years, she probably wouldn't go for abandoning it. Therefore, we figured that if we could just get rid of the musical accompaniment, we would be free to enter class in a nonmusical way.

Early one morning, before Miss Hessian came to class, Waxy, Joey Heart,

Buzzy, and I decided to get rid of the villain. We calmly, at least outwardly, went over to the window where the big black eighty-eight-key piano stood and pushed it right out of the third-floor window into the alleyway below. The sound was like a giant explosion, causing quite a stir at John Jay that day. Students and teachers alike ran to the windows to find out where the bomb blast had occurred.

When Miss Hessian arrived, the look on her face caused us to do our best to hide our laughter. She knew we had been up to no good and immediately brought the principal into the picture to try and find out who the culprits were. When it was our turn to be interrogated, we all said the same thing: that when we arrived at class, the piano was already in the alleyway. The other students knew what had happened, but none of them would dare tell. They were scared that if they ratted on us they would get beat up, and for the most part they were glad not to have to sing the good morning song anymore. It went down as an unsolved mystery. For the rest of the term, we didn't get a replacement for the piano, and there was no more singing.

As result of our boldness, we became more popular than ever. I felt kind of sorry for Miss Hessian, but having my popularity increase at the expense of having her feelings hurt was something that I really didn't correlate too well back then. Nor did it bother me that much. I regret now all the people that got hurt when I allowed my pride to get in the way of my compassion. It would take me more than a few years to learn that pride and compassion can't really exist at the same time.

Whenever the name Miss Lepore comes to mind, I always get a special feeling inside. She was my typing instructor in the tenth grade. She was young, Italian, and very beautiful. I was fifteen and she was twenty-six. Right from the start of her class, there existed a strange sort of chemistry that attracted Miss Lepore to me. Not only did I find her very attractive physically, but I also felt an attachment to her in a mother/child sort of way. I hated to type, but couldn't wait to get to class to see her and listen to her speak and just move about. I wanted to stay in her class so much that I intentionally failed typing in order to be able to spend one more semester there. This would prove to be the only class I ever failed.

I can't explain exactly why I felt these dual feelings of girlfriend/mother toward her, but they were real. I loved it when she came over to me and placed her hands on mine to instruct me on how to properly hold my hands on the keyboard. Miss Lepore was gentle and sweet but not overly sexy. Always polite and compassionate, she possessed a motherly instinct that often made me feel comfortable and warm inside. I just enjoyed being in her presence, even if it meant failing typing. While I hated typing, Miss Lepore's charm and beauty were

✟ ✟ ✟ ✟ ✟ ✟ ✟ ✟ ✟ ✟ ✟ ✟ ✟ ✟ ✟ ✟ ✟

well worth the monotony of banging one's fingers on a bunch of metal keys. Miss Lepore, wherever you are, I'll always have a special place for you here in my heart.

By the time my senior year rolled around, I had to make up my mind what course my life would take. Making a career in the gang really didn't have much appeal to me. Moving on to a life of organized crime had even less appeal. My only two choices were to go to work at some menial job, since that was probably all I would qualify for, or maybe shoot for the moon and go to college and law school. After hearing the Gent's Prayer and being represented by a Legal Aid lawyer, I promised the Lord Jesus that I would become a Legal Aid lawyer and do for other indigent and poor people and defendants what the Legal Aid lawyer had done for me. It was a mission and calling from the Lord Jesus. As luck would have it (although I now know it to be the hand of God), a very interesting series of events made it possible for me to go to college.

Despite the fact that I cut many classes and went to school more to have fun than to learn, I managed to do fairly well at John Jay. I felt like it might be worth a shot to try college, since I knew that a good education was one way to get out of the poverty I was living in. While I thought I was college material, our family had no money for it. With all the medical expenses for mom's hospitalizations, my dad ran out of money. There was just enough to buy food and clothing. With no money, college seemed like an impossible dream.

During my last year at John Jay, a gym teacher named Vinny Riccio was appointed the new dean of boys. Vinny was a kind and caring man who really tried to improve our school. Unfortunately for him, in his first year as dean, the now-famous John Jay riots broke out. For a period of two weeks, the students from Boys High would pile into buses and come down to John Jay to fight the youth from our school. Boys High was an all-black school, and somehow they just got it into their minds that they wanted to beat up on the white students at John Jay. It was entirely a racial thing, with both sides wanting to prove they were the toughest.

These riots were pretty vicious, and several guys from both schools got hurt very badly. There was plenty of press coverage, and this was proving to be a huge source of embarrassment to our school management. As the riots entered their third week, Vinny Riccio approached me and offered me a deal. He liked me and thought that I had a lot of intelligence. He also knew I was a leader in school who was well liked and respected—someone who had influence with the students.

Vinny called me into his office and said, "Louis, I know you carry a lot of weight in this school. If you can convince the Italians to stay away from school and not riot for just one day, I will personally get you into college." He knew my father very well, and Vinny wanted to help me get ahead in life. He also needed my assistance in putting a stop to the riots.

I told him I would accept his offer, even though I knew I wouldn't follow through on it. I couldn't stand up for school management at the expense of my classmates. This would cause me to lose face in the eyes of the people I counted as most dear to me. That same day, though, the bus that was carrying the students from Boys High down to John Jay never arrived. I found out subsequently that it broke down en route due to mechanical problems. Well, they never made it, and for the first time in two weeks there were no riots at school.

When I went up to Vinny's office the next day, I was greeted with a hero's welcome. Vinny told me that what I had done was fantastic and a miracle. The real miracle, of course, was that the bus broke down. But I now decided that I would remind Vinny of his promise of getting me into college. With the chance to go to college now staring me in the face, telling Vinny the truth was not a very appealing option. So, in one of my best acting performances ever, I began to relate to Vinny the difficult speech I had delivered to my classmates.

"Mr. Riccio," I said, "I have made a lot of enemies today. It wasn't easy but somehow I was able to convince my friends to stay away from school. There was quite a bit of flak and criticism dished out as I told them that in this instance I felt it was important to side with school management." I told Vinny that it was one of the most difficult talks I had ever given, but was glad they agreed not to riot that day.

After I related all of this to Vinny, he seemed even more impressed with my intervention skills and leadership potential. True to his word, Vinny somehow pulled a few strings and got me into college on a special scholarship program called the College Discovery Program. This was a special program aimed at helping black and Puerto Rican kids get into college. Very few whites got into this program. In fact, I was the first Italian American to ever be admitted.

As a result of the John Jay riots and a broken-down bus, my life would never be the same again. What I was now about to embark upon was a chance to change and channel my energies in a positive and constructive direction. What I needed was a break to get me on my way. I feel strongly that God sent Vinny Riccio into my life to assist me. To this day, I am humbled at the great mercy of my heavenly Father. Despite the lies I told Vinny about how I stopped the riots, God somehow didn't hold this against me. Vinny was the instrument that God used to get me into college, and college was the stepping stone I would use to begin my real transformation from a kid with no purpose or direction to a man with a burning desire to make our world a better place.

✜ ✜ ✜ ✜ ✜ ✜ ✜ ✜ ✜ ✜ ✜ ✜ ✜ ✜ ✜ ✜ ✜

8 Farm Cadet

Vinny Riccio was also responsible for getting me into a program called the Farm Cadet Program. As my junior year at John Jay approached its end, I began to eagerly await summer vacation. I was all set for an exciting summer of hanging out, playing stickball, and mixing it up with the Soviet Lords. However, thanks to my dear brother Anthony, I was soon to discover that instead of chasing fly balls, my summer vacation would revolve around chasing cows.

When my dad passed away, family problems became even more difficult to handle for the Gelorminos. I loved my dad, and his dying opened up a giant void in my life. Dad represented the only real stable element in our household, and with him no longer at the helm we were all headed for more troubled waters. It was against this background that Anthony stepped in and more or less tried to fill a pair of shoes he was not very equipped to fill.

While Vinny was still a gym teacher, he became aware of a new program being made available to students called the Farm Cadet Program. He handed Anthony some literature on it, and before I knew what happened I was signed up for this summer farming experience in the Catskills. As a farm cadet, you traveled upstate to work at a farm for an entire summer, helping the farmer wherever he needed assistance.

Anthony knew of all the trouble I was getting into at school and in the Little Gents, as well as the destructive course my life was taking. He felt that this program would help me to get away from all the headaches at home and give me a chance to experience a new way of living. He tried to paint a positive picture of all the benefits I would gain from this experience, but I had no desire to go away from my friends for so long or to an environment—farming—I knew nothing about.

When Anthony saw that the wonderful picture he was painting of farm living was not making too much headway, he made me an offer I couldn't refuse. His offer was simple: "Louis, if you don't go into the Farm Cadet Program, I am going to have to break your head." Since my brother was a lot stronger and tougher than I was, and I was in no mood to have my head busted, I reluctantly conceded to go. So, on a hot summer day near the end of June, I packed my bags. Destination: Madoosa, New York.

The car ride lasted almost four hours, but it seemed like an eternity to me. I suffered from carsickness, and the combination of my anxious heart and queasy stomach made my arrival at Madoosa quite auspicious. As I got out of the car I immediately vomited right in front of my new boss, farmer Fink. Mr. Fink took one look at me and told the person from the program to take me back home because I was not equipped to be a farm cadet.

To make matters worse, the farmer and my driver were now discussing my future in a way that made me feel like a used car. My driver was telling this complete stranger, "Why don't you try him for three days? If you don't like him, I will come back and take him away." With the taste of vomit in my mouth and my new boss reluctantly agreeing to use me on a trial basis, I was officially welcomed to Madoosa, New York.

Louis Fink was a sturdy old German who must have been in his late fifties. He spoke with a heavy German accent, which took me a little while to get used to since I was used to hearing mostly Brooklyn and Italian accents. In addition, farmer Fink was quite a miserable person. He was so miserable that his wife did not want to live with him and only visited him once a week. My new boss had no personality at all and apparently no friends. In fact, during my two months at Madoosa I hardly saw any people anywhere.

If the discipline and harshness of the St. Francis Xavier brothers were bad, I soon learned that living a disciplined life was a relative term. When farmer Fink told me to get a good night's sleep because work started early, I soon learned what "early to bed, early to rise" meant. When I asked him how early, he said work started at 5:30 every morning. I told farmer Fink that I went to bed by 5:30 on occasion, but getting up at that time was impossible. When he told me that we would also be working seven days a week, I thought it would be better to be dead than endure sixty straight days of slave labor. And when he informed me that my salary was going to be $15 a week, I knew that I was indeed little more than a slave. When I sat down to figure out what my hourly wage would be, it came out to about twenty-five cents an hour!

Right before going to bed that first night, my new boss began to outline my duties as a farm cadet. My job each day would consist of walking half a mile into a big field to round up and bring back about forty cows. I had to help shovel the cow manure, help transport cow milk in big metal pails, cut and bale hay, and put the bales of hay away for the winter.

Somehow I managed to get up the next day at the prescribed time, although I was half-asleep. I can remember saying to myself that this was ridiculous. Here I was walking in the middle of nowhere in the pitch dark, having no idea what it was like to be on a farm or close to nature. Farmer Fink told me to take along his faithful dog Bosco, who would help me to round up the cows. Bosco was a fifteen-year-old black-and-white collie who I prayed knew more about rounding up cows than I did.

Farmer Fink told me to relax, since Bosco would help me round up the cows. He told me that I just needed to call out, "Cow-boose—cow-boose," which the cows would respond to. You had to first walk over a little bridge before you hit the field, but it was pitch dark at 5:30 in the morning and I was scared stiff. When I finally got into the field, I told Bosco to go gather up the cows. As I yelled at Bosco to get up and run, he just lay there and did nothing. So I decided to try yelling, "Cow-boose," expecting the cows to follow my voice. They took the lead of Bosco and just lay still, not bothering to heed my call.

I decided to look for the cows and try my best to get them all together. I looked behind trees and all over, and somehow finally managed to round them all up and start marching them back to the farm. What was supposed to take about fifteen minutes took me two hours. As I approached the farm, I could see farmer Fink walking toward me. All of a sudden Bosco started running like crazy around the cows, as if to say, "Look what a good job I did rounding up the cows."

"Farmer Fink," I said, "this dog is useless. He didn't do anything but lie around while I went hunting down your cows." He looked at me and said that Bosco had been rounding up cows for fifteen years and he had never had any problems with him. He said that if I hadn't come back when I did, he was going to call the police, thinking that I had been killed. He said he would come with me the next day to see if what I claimed about his prize cow dog was true.

So here I was again, with the farmer and Bosco at 5:30 in the morning, slowly walking across the bridge into the field. As soon as we got into the field, Fink yelled for Bosco to get the cows. To my amazement, Bosco instantly got up and like a bullet ran all over the field, corralling all forty cows in just about five minutes. For the remainder of my two months on the farm, Bosco never repeated this performance for me and I had to learn the fine art of yelling, "Cow-boose."

During that first week on the farm, I wrote letters back to my mother, telling her that I had contracted some kind of rare disease and that I should come home to be examined. I also shared with her that I was very homesick. Anthony wrote me back and told me, "If you keep bothering Mommy, I will personally come up there and beat you up." From that point on, I had no alternative but to resign myself to a summer of farm work.

After two or three days of this routine of gathering the cows, shoveling their excess, cutting and baling the hay, and a host of other farm chores, I asked farmer Fink what type of social activities there were up here. He said that the big night out was Friday night. So for the next eight weeks, my only social event was to travel to the local pizza store with farmer Fink in downtown Madoosa and buy a pizza pie and a bottle of soda.

During the first few of these Friday night rituals, we exchanged very few words. But by the end of the first month, we actually got to like one another and began to share our lives in a friendly, caring way. He began to share his personal life with me. He told me that the reason he avoided people was that

✞ ✞ ✞ ✞ ✞ ✞ ✞ ✞ ✞ ✞ ✞ ✞ ✞ ✞ ✞ ✞

he didn't trust them very much. And to avoid the pain and disappointment they would cause him, he chose to stay by himself. As I began to share my hurts and fears, we formed a kind of friendly bond that made Friday nights a time I looked forward to. When it was time for me to return to Brooklyn at summer's end, farmer Fink actually cried as I was leaving. I felt sad, too, since I knew he had no children and I guess in a way he was starting to view me as family.

The only other time we had to relax a little was on Sunday, when Mrs. Fink would stop by to spend a few hours with us. She always brought us a cherry pie, which was delicious. After she left, it was back to the daily grind. I might add that farmer Fink was quite a good cook, and we ate well all summer long.

As the summer progressed, so did the frustrations that were building up inside of me. My experiences during those two months at Madoosa were like night and day. The first month was a time to let my pent-up frustrations all out, while my second month was devoted to taking some very positive steps in dealing with my life.

I was all alone in the Catskills and quite homesick. I felt like my brother had sold me into slavery. Instead of appreciating all the beauty of the countryside around me, I chose to focus on the hate and anger I held within. I hated missing hanging out with the gang and going to Zorro's. And most of my ego was deprived by missing out on all the praise my friends gave me. All I could think of, besides the cows that I hated, was that this experience would be bad for my reputation and that someone might step into my leadership position back in Brooklyn. I resented being forced to do something I didn't want to do, and that was being in this miserable farm town.

Most of my thoughts were about how rotten my life was and how hopelessly trapped I was, regardless of whether I was in Madoosa or Brooklyn. I was cursing the unfairness of life and felt that someone would have to pay for this gloomy life I was leading. Since there were no people around to take my frustrations out on, I chose to make the poor cows pay.

I must admit that I was quite mean to the cows on farmer Fink's farm. I would often take the heavy bales of hay to the top of the barn and hurl them down onto the cow's heads below. When I got tired of bombing them, I used to get a real charge out of sticking the cows with a pitchfork. Another animal that I really abused was farmer Fink's bull. Fink would let his bull out of the barn for a couple of weeks during the summer to mate with the cows. What I didn't do to this bull. I hit him in the head with the end of my shovel, stuck him in every place imaginable with the pitchfork, and dropped the heaviest bales of hay I could find on his head. Little did I know that this bull was soon to get his day in court.

Although the bull was tied up and couldn't do anything, one day the farmer let him out without telling me. While I was picking up rocks in the field, all of a sudden this giant bull with horns down started stampeding toward me as if to take care of some unfinished business. Fortunately, there was a tree within running distance. I raced for my dear life and climbed up that tree just before the bull arrived. I literally had to stay in that tree for five hours awaiting the return of good old farmer Fink. When he arrived, he was shocked to see me in the tree but glad he had found me. To this day, farmer Fink has always said, "I wonder why that bull chased you." Of course, my answer is, "I have no idea."

Even though the cows and bull got the brunt of my outward hostilities, it proved to be good therapy for me. By the middle of my stay on the farm, I had succeeded in getting quite a bit of anger and hatred out of my system. To this day, I am grateful that it was animals and not people who suffered while I was letting off steam. Thank God the cows and bulls were not seriously injured.

One thing I began to do regularly for the first time in my life was to spend a lot of time talking to God and praying. With no people or companionship, I began to turn to God and had some wonderful conversations with Him. At nighttime, I would often look up at the stars and stand in awe at God's magnificent universe. Back in Brooklyn, even on a clear night you rarely saw more than a few stars. But up in the Catskills, what a show the stars put on.

As the days passed at Madoosa, I could see changes in my makeup. No longer was I hating my situation here. I was learning to appreciate the beauty around me and the fact that I was doing good, honest work. By summer's end, I had helped put almost 5,000 bales of hay away for the winter. I felt proud of myself and happy that I had accomplished something that I viewed as meaningful. Even my talks with God began to take on more and more substance and sincerity than they had in the past. Even though I felt an emotional loneliness, for the first time I began to feel a spiritual awakening in my soul. I didn't understand what this all meant back then, but I knew it was something I wanted to keep with me when I went back to Brooklyn.

As I continued to get more of my hostilities and frustrations out, I began to think in a constructive direction. I started to ask God for direction about what path my life should take. Thoughts of leaving the gang and going to college, then law school, became distinct possibilities for the first time since I had joined the Little Gents. Getting away from family, friends, and school was the best thing that ever happened to me because for the first time in my life I had a chance to think clearly about who I was and where I was going.

Now, while a lot of positive beginnings were taking place in my heart and soul, I still had a long way to go in working out all the hurts and fears in my life. Even though I was beginning to appreciate some aspects of farm life, I still resented my brother Anthony for forcing me to go away for the summer. And, to be very honest, one of my main motivations for working hard all summer long was to build myself up so that when I finally did go home, I would be physically able to take care of my brother.

As farmer Fink and I parted ways in early September, I packed my bags and said farewell to Madoosa. In addition to my suitcase of clothes, I took a body that was in great shape and my entire summer earnings of $105 back to Brooklyn. It only took that first night back home for me and my friends to drink up my entire summer's wages. When I finally got home that night, it was three o'clock in the morning and my brother was fast asleep.

I woke him up and told him that it was not nice of him to send me away to the farm and that he should have consulted more closely with me before making up his mind to enlist me in the Farm Cadet Program. It was now time, I said, to straighten things out and for him to pay his dues. Anthony got up and put his arm around me, saying, "Louis, I want you to understand one thing. With Daddy having passed away, I felt that as your older brother it was my responsibility to take care of you. I felt that sending you away to the farm would be for your own benefit. You may feel that this was the wrong thing to do, but it was done out of love."

I thought to myself, maybe this guy is not a bad guy after all. As I started to reconsider my position, Anthony gave me a shot to the stomach that doubled me over, then another fist to the head. This was followed by a very short sermon: "Don't ever forget that I am still your older brother, and I'll always be able to beat you up." I never did exact my revenge on my brother, and on that night I abandoned the idea of doing so. Looking back, I owe a lot to Anthony for the courage he had to stand up for my well-being, even at the cost of hurting my feelings.

✝ ✝ ✝ ✝ ✝ ✝ ✝ ✝ ✝ ✝ ✝ ✝ ✝ ✝ ✝ ✝

9 Mary Sansone

I first met Mary Sansone in a small storefront on Fourth Avenue and Carroll Street. It was 1964, after my slicing and court case and hearing the Gent's Prayer. I was still sixteen. Little could I have imagined that this diminutive woman would have such a monumental impact on helping me chart a new and bold course for my life.

Mary Sansone is one of those rare individuals who lives by principle and is guided by a vision to help others no matter what the cost. When she came into South Brooklyn, she brought with her one of the most precious gifts imaginable: the gift of hope. Mary offered us hope for success in life despite the odds that were stacked against us.

She came to us with a heart of compassion and a will to make a positive impact no matter what. While that small storefront is long gone, the work that Mary Sansone started thirty years ago lives on, and I am just one of the fruits of her labor. Mary, God bless you for seeing the potential in me and helping me see it too!

Before Mary came into my life, I was living a very unproductive existence. I had no real goals or desire to excel in anything, except perhaps in the Little Gents or in popularity with my peers. My life revolved around hanging out and just getting by from day to day. I was going nowhere and doing a great job of just marking time. What I needed was a chance to see what I could become and accomplish in life, and not what little I had done in the past.

After hearing the Gent's Prayer while in the bullpen, I said it daily. The Lord had spoken to me and told me that I would become a Legal Aid lawyer. Mary was the answer to my prayer, and I knew it immediately after meeting her.

I believe that everyone has locked within them the potential to excel in some special way. The key is to find someone who knows how to help unlock and tap into that potential. One of the great gifts that Mary has is the ability to spot that potential and the desire to bring it out. A lot of people can spot it, but very few are willing to take the time and caring needed to offer a helping hand. Mary is one of those few.

When someone asked Mary what she saw in me that was worth pursuing, she answered: "When I first met Louis, I thought he was a snotty little kid. He struck me as a little con artist. But despite being rough, he was adorable. I saw how he was heavily influenced by his peers, but felt if I could get him away from them I could deal with him." Mary was the first person in my life who was willing to go that extra mile and challenge me to make something of my life. While her methods may have been unorthodox, her sincerity won the hearts of those who crossed her path.

When she first came into our neighborhood, Mary knew that we would be a tough bunch of kids to reach, so she decided to establish a very innovative program that was calculated to help us learn and have fun at the same time. With a few dollars and a lot of determination, she opened a small storefront on Fourth Avenue and Carroll Street with the intention of helping poor Italian kids earn their high school equivalency diplomas.

What was unique about this program was that in the front, two teachers conducted classes geared to help the neighborhood youth gain the knowledge needed to earn their high school equivalency diploma. And in the back, when we weren't studying and learning, we shot a great deal of pool and hung out in a place where love was all around us instead of deadbeats and losers.

It would not be proper or complete if I did not finish this chapter by describing how Mary Sansone first met the Little Gents and me. It was in early 1964 or thereabout that Father Anthony from Our Lady of Peace Church came to me and informed me that this little lady named Mary Sansone from CIAO (the Congress of Italian-American Organizations) wanted to meet the Little Gents. Apparently, according to Father Anthony, she was directed by the new mayor of the City of New York, Honorable John Lindsay, to meet with us and discuss the Neighborhood Youth Corps Program. This program was designed to get some of the Italian gang members working legitimately. In so doing, the goal was to stop the gang warfare among various ethnic groups that was blemishing and tarnishing the image of the Big Apple, New York City.

Since I wanted to get out of the gang and go on to college and law school, I thought it would be a good idea to meet with this "well-meaning" individual. So Father Anthony scheduled a meeting in the storefront on the corner of Carroll Street and Fourth Avenue in Brooklyn. I scheduled the meeting with a few members of the Little Gents and Mary Sansone. The Little Gents were "Sally Fotz," "Sickness," Nicky Egghead, Hornsey, and me, Crazy Louie. We designated Hornsey to speak for the gents. Hornsey was mean and nasty, and surely would put this lady Mary Sansone to the test. He wanted to see what they could get out of her. I wanted to see if she could help me get into college, then law school, and help me reach my prayer and dream of becoming an attorney. I was expecting a lady with a fur coat in a limousine to drive up to the storefront; when a little lady in a house dress came in instead, I assumed she had made a wrong turn. I asked her what her name was and who she was looking for. She said her name was Mary Sansone and she was looking for the Little Gents.

Needless to say, I was surprised by her modest and humble appearance. I told her to come in. She sat alone opposite the table from the five of us. Hornsey started to dig into Mary and accused her of making false promises and being just another no-good social worker or some kind of politician who would actually not do anything for the Gents. I was amazed at this lady's calm demeanor, apparent self-confidence, and serenity. When Hornsey finished criticizing her, Mary spoke. She asked Hornsey if he was finished speaking, and he said yes. Then she pointed her finger at Hornsey and called him a son of a bitch. I thought for sure that Hornsey was going to try to hit her, but he was just as startled as the rest of us. Then Mary said that she wasn't going to do anything for us unless we truly wanted to help ourselves. She began to explain the Neighborhood Youth Corps Jobs Program. She said that if we were interested, she would work with us 100 percent. She gave us her card and said if we were interested to call her.

When she left, we discussed our participation in the program. After much discussion we all agreed, but for different personal reasons. Some wanted to try to go legitimate, while a couple saw it as an opportunity to get paid without doing any work. My reason was that I wanted to know this lady better. Maybe if I participated in this program, she would help me get into college and then law school. Little did I know then that I would know this wonderful human being for the rest of my life.

We successfully executed this program under Mary's guidance and my directorship. The Neighborhood Youth Corps Program became a model for me to institute the Nova Ancora Program when I later became deputy commissioner for the New York City Department of Probation in 1994.

It was ironic that when I eventually became an attorney and was in my own practice of law in the 1980s, I received a collect phone call from Hornsey, who was on his deathbed dying of AIDS in a hospital in Florida. He wanted me to help get social services for his wife and son, who lived in New York. It was my pleasure to help an old friend. I will never forget that at the end of that conversation, Hornsey asked me how Mary Sansone was doing. I said she was fine and still helping many people. He said to me, "You know the difference between you and me? You listened to Mary Sansone and I did not." I said that was true to a tremendous extent. This was also true with Sickness and Sally Fotz, who died of unnatural causes three years after our first meeting with Mary Sansone. After the phone call from Hornsey, he died two days later. We helped his wife and son get the required social services.

At first we were very skeptical about Mary; we had a hard time believing that someone would want to help us without having some selfish motive in the back of their mind. But within a matter of two or three weeks, Mary Sansone had won not only our hearts but also our respect. She was so real, and most of us had never felt that a stranger would want to help a rough and tough bunch of lost souls like me and my friends.

I think that one of the real secrets of success that Mary had in winning our trust was that she understood the real problems we faced. As poor Italians, growing up we felt like we had no true identity as individuals or as a group.

✝ ✝ ✝ ✝ ✝ ✝ ✝ ✝ **✝** ✝ ✝ ✝ ✝ ✝ ✝ ✝

The blacks and Puerto Ricans, while also very poor, at least were viewed as minorities and had a host of programs designed to help provide them with basic essentials and acceptance in society. As a group, we felt like misfits—we had no programs or any real sense of belonging. Mary immediately understood this, and she felt that it was extremely important that we knew that Italians also had an important place in society. With her faith, Mary Sansone founded CIAO to help the poor and needy, regardless of race, color, or creed.

CIAO is the brainchild of Mary Sansone. One of the first CIAO programs was our school/pool hall storefront in South Brooklyn. The purpose of CIAO was and still is to help to create a positive image of Italian Americans, both in the eyes of all Americans as well as in the eyes of the Italian Americans themselves. It was this dual goal that made CIAO such a wonderful success in our small community and in hundreds of other Italian communities over the past thirty years.

Aunt Mary, as we affectionately called her, almost from her initial arrival into our neighborhood began to make things happen. Before Mary came, the Italians and the Puerto Ricans were arch rivals that had little to do with each other except to fight and exchange hatred with one another. Within only a few months' time, this little lady had initiated meaningful dialogue between these two camps of opposites for the first time in my memory. While we still didn't love one another, at least we were willing to tolerate and understand one another. And also, as a group for the first time, we felt that our storefront program was uniquely Italian and made us feel special and no longer left out.

It's strange how governments spend millions of dollars trying to help fix societal problems, holding countless debates about the best course of action to solve these difficult issues, when all that is needed is to allow people like Mary Sansone to show us what a little love and determination can accomplish.

If there is one lesson that I have learned from my thirty years of association with this remarkable lady, it is that the only reason why people and situations remain hopeless is lack of vision and love. Of all the organizations that I have come into contact with from the time I participated in that tiny storefront until today, CIAO stands at the top of the list in terms of its vision for making our world a better place.

In addition to Mary's love of people, she also proved to be a great catalyst for change. And if anyone was in need of a change, it was me. One incident that demonstrated the unique flair Mary brought to working her magic with the youth of South Brooklyn involved a fundraiser dinner dance.

In order to help raise funds for CIAO, Mary decided to hold a gala dinner and dance. She invited people from all walks of life, including many local businessmen and politicians. She invited ten of the youth from our storefront program. Mary

✝ ✝ ✝ ✝ ✝ ✝ ✝ ✝ **✝** ✝ ✝ ✝ ✝ ✝ ✝ ✝ ✝

felt that learning shouldn't be confined to the classroom. It was her strong belief that we should be exposed to other ways of life—things that kids like us would not normally be able to see.

Since this was a formal affair, Mary helped us rent ten tuxedos. Unfortunately she forgot about the shoes, and we all came in our sneakers. We certainly were a sight to behold, and we felt quite out of place. To my amazement, though, Mary had come up to me a week before the dinner dance and asked me to deliver a speech to the gathering. Needless to say, a host of emotions flooded my soul. I felt flattered that she was willing to give me a chance to be the center of attention in front of such an important group of people. My only speech up until that time had been to the gang members in the Little Gents.

My heart was also excited to think that someone had enough confidence in my abilities to let me deliver the keynote address at such an important event. And I was also very nervous since Mary told me there were going to be about 300 people at this affair. With an eager heart, I began to prepare for this event. After thinking a lot about what I should say, I decided to write my whole speech out and show it to Mary for her comments.

To my great surprise, when I asked Mary to look it over she refused, saying that she had confidence in me and knew that whatever I had written would be fine. I can't tell you how special it made me feel to think that she would risk possible embarrassment in order to show her strong faith in my abilities. Little did I realize back then that what Mary was doing was instilling confidence in me and providing me with the incentives I needed to prove to myself that I was special, had talents, and could make a success of myself if I only applied the gifts that God had given to me.

Mary chose not to look at my past and why I was living in defeat. Instead, she chose to look inside my heart and where I could be if given the proper training and the chance. Over 2,500 years ago, King Solomon penned these immortal words: "Where there is no vision, the people perish" (Proverbs 29:18). In this respect, Mary Sansone is clearly a modern-day Solomon because she is truly a lady with a vision. She saw where Louis Gelormino could go in life and knew that this speech could play a key role in challenging my negative and faulty belief system. Mary saw clearly that for many of us, our biggest ambition was to be like the bookie in the corner. She felt that providing us with opportunities to experience new things, and believing in our ability to succeed, would inspire us to do good.

The big day finally arrived. Though I was very nervous, I managed to deliver a speech that moved quite a lot of people that night. Mary told me it was a great speech and that she was really proud of me. Unfortunately, I also made several enemies that night by delivering a rather stinging series of accusations

✝ ✝ ✝ ✝ ✝ ✝ ✝ ✝ ✝ **✝** ✝ ✝ ✝ ✝ ✝ ✝ ✝ ✝

condemning the behavior of our local politicians. In fact, several of these political bigshots were so insulted by my unkind words that they walked out of the hall right in the middle of my speech. All things considered, though, this event was one of the major turning points in my life. That night I was on top of the world, and something inside of me began to say, "Louis, you have a future ahead of YOU."

Our storefront program will always hold a special place in my heart because it was in that caring environment that I saw, for the first time, that there was another alternative in life. Mary boldly came into a hostile neighborhood where a lot of bad kids hung out. She took the bull by the horns and brought us something we had never had before—hope.

While this storefront remained in operation for only about one year, it did more for the people who participated in the program than the schools, the politicians, and clearly the gangs ever did. I was always helping Mary organize things in the storefront, and she made me one of her main helpers in the program. Unfortunately, our operation did such a good job in the community that the politicians became very jealous of our success. Sadly, after just one year of operation, a terrible fire hit the store and burned it to the ground. Even a casual observer could see all the positive benefits of this CIAO-sponsored program, and Mary and the rest of us were convinced that the local politicians and another enemy were responsible for the fire.

Needless to say, I was devastated by this loss. But a blessing emerged—CIAO began to establish senior centers and day care centers all over New York City. In 1964, CIAO incorporated as a nonprofit organization and earned its reputation as the first real catalyst for change in the field of social services in the Italian community. Throughout the '60s and '70s, Mary, acting as the executive director of CIAO, was instrumental in opening more and more senior, day care, and community centers around the city.

Since that time long ago in 1962, Mary and CIAO have been a very important part of my life. On numerous occasions through the years, Mary continued to help me along my path in life. Her life touched mine in so many ways that it is safe to say that without her, I may very well have fallen through the cracks like so many of my friends from school and the gangs. I know today that God had a plan for my life and that Mary Sansone was an integral part of it.

Now don't get me wrong—my changes in life didn't happen overnight. It would take more than the influence of Mary to break down a whole lifetime of negative thinking about myself and to establish a positive identity—both of which are so crucial for anyone's success in life. But she gave me hope and a beginning. While my involvement in the gangs didn't cease right away, I knew that something was beginning to change in me, and it was my outlook on life.

✤ ✤ ✤ ✤ ✤ ✤ ✤ ✤ ✤ ✤ ✤ ✤ ✤ ✤ ✤ ✤ ✤

Mary was a possibility thinker. From the first day we met, she began to work with me. She got me involved over time in other community organizations and social service programs for the youth in the community, and slowly but surely started to bring out my true abilities. I started to form my own identity and began to leave all the bad memories of my home life and the pain and suffering of my community behind. For the first time, I was maturing and developing as a human being. After I graduated from high school, I went on to college, and during my college years I continued to work with Mary on CIAO programs and other things in the community. I became a county committeeman, became politically active, and with Mary's assistance began to get the youth of South Brooklyn involved in various programs.

But before I continue with my story, I would like to give you a little more background information about this very special love of my life—Mary Sansone. One of the greatest joys in my life is reminiscing about this special friend.

If there was one thing that Mary loved to get involved with throughout her life, it was the challenge of helping make things better for people. And this trait was clearly something that was passed down from father to daughter. Mary's dad was born in Italy. As a young man, he became fascinated with the idea of becoming a priest. But with only one month to go before he would receive ordination, he became disillusioned and decided that instead of entering the priesthood he would set sail for America and start a new life.

Right from the start, Mary's dad became a social activist and joined the Industrial Workers of the World (IWW). This young Italian dynamo became heavily involved in setting up various union shops in New York City. From women's clothing to the train workers and everything in between, it became his passion to champion the working class.

"Whenever my dad would give a speech at Union Square in Manhattan, I would go with him," Mary proudly boasts. To Mary, her dad represented more than just a great father. He was a man with a vision and a mission of making society a better place for the working people. When he spoke, you could sense the compassion in his voice and the love in his heart. It would be safe to say that Italy's loss was America's gain. Not only did Mr. Sansone have an impact on the people he came in contact with, but he also left with his daughter a belief system and a set of values that would help ensure that a future generation would also become blessed.

So as a young girl, Mary was exposed to the plight of the American poor and working class. Like her dad, Mary began to experience firsthand all the hurts and social injustices many of her fellow Italians had to endure. And, like her dad, she refused to just sit back and allow what she felt was wrong to continue.

As Mary grew, so did her desire to follow in her father's footsteps. What

✝ ✝ ✝ ✝ ✝ ✝ ✝ ✝ **✝** ✝ ✝ ✝ ✝ ✝ ✝ ✝ ✝

made her work even more noteworthy was the fact that she was one of the first women in the Italian community to organize union shops. She was a forerunner in bringing women out of the kitchen and into the battleground of social activism. Her long list of involvement in various nonprofit and quasi-governmental organizations had prepared Mary well for launching CIAO many years later.

If you were to examine her résumé, it would be filled with public service activities. During World War II, for example, Mary worked with the Red Cross and quickly earned a reputation for efficient and caring humanitarian service.

After World War II, as Mary's reputation for getting the job done spread, she was approached by the Italian consulate in America to represent Italy in an organization called the United Nations Appeal for Children. This was a wonderful organization set up to help raise funds for the orphans of Europe. Mary's assignment entailed traveling around America with two children from Italy, with the purpose of appealing to hearts to donate money.

Right from the start, Mary fell in love with this precious brother and sister, six and eight years old, whose mom graciously allowed her to take them on tour across America. Wherever Mary went with her two tiny traveling companions, they were given VIP treatment. When the tour was over, they had visited twenty-three states in a little over four months and were instrumental in raising thousands of dollars for a group of children they would probably never meet. And if I know Mary, these kids must have been treated like a little prince and princess. Mary kept in touch with her new friends and is proud to say that both of them went on to college. Those four months spent in Mary's presence surely left a strong and positive impression on those young minds.

Another organization that was fortunate to have Mary on board was the American Medical Committee. Mary went to the pharmaceutical companies for donations and medicines, particularly penicillin. She did this for one year, and thousands of poor and sick people were helped.

In 1949 she married and, when she became blessed with her new title of mother, Mary decided to temporarily retire from active duty and devote her time to raising her family. However, I could never imagine her not helping people and, even as a mother and homemaker, Mary somehow found time to do social work right out of her home.

When she made it known that she was willing to help out in community affairs, the local schools and churches began to enlist her aid in a variety of activities. Mary helped people get Medicaid, welfare, and medicine, and became one of the most valuable information resources in the community.

In addition, every year Mary volunteered her time and services in the political arena to help elect those politicians she felt would make for a better society. She would often open up the basement in her home and set it up as a local

✝ ✝ ✝ ✝ ✝ ✝ ✝ ✝ **✝** ✝ ✝ ✝ ✝ ✝ ✝ ✝

political headquarters where meetings could be held and strategies planned.

So when Mary Sansone and CIAO came into South Brooklyn in the early '60s, she brought with her not only a desire to help the troubled kids that were all around her, but also a wealth of experience in dealing with people of all different ages and types of problems.

To me, Mary Sansone is an unsung American hero. Her influence in terms of helping people and initiating positive change may never fully be quantified, but those who have been privileged to know her can attest that their lives have been enriched from their association with her.

I believe that the reason why many people from the old neighborhood never amounted to much is because, sadly, they were not as fortunate as I was to have a Mary Sansone or Vinny Riccio take an active interest in them. The same situation applies today to a large extent. People are wasting away not so much for lack of social programs but from lack of truly caring individuals. What this world needs more than ever today is not more programs and funds, but more compassion and truly caring people who are willing to spend the time and make the commitment that so many people—young and old—desperately need. True love, the type that radiates from Mary Sansone, is what this world needs.

While Mary often affectionately referred to me as her problem child, I am so grateful that she never treated me like one. She was always there for me. She always pushed me to do better and, even though I still got into trouble after we first met, my life slowly started to turn around. And when Mary saw that I was interested in going to college and doing something positive with my life, she went to bat for me all the way. One thing she always said about me was that I was a very determined kid who had a good head on his shoulders.

As my story continues to unfold, this special lady will continue to play a pivotal role in many areas of my life. Mary always told me that she expected me to become a success. How grateful I am to God for sending Mary Sansone into my life and how grateful I am to you, Mary, for sending life into my heart.

✟ ✟ ✟ ✟ ✟ ✟ ✟ ✟ ✟ ✟ ✟ ✟ ✟ ✟ ✟ ✟ ✟ ✟ ✟

10 College

What if? As often as I reflect back on my life, I wonder, "What if this didn't happen?" What if Mary Sansone had never come to South Brooklyn? What if the Mafia hit men had had better aim when they were chasing Anthony and me after we alienated them in the bar next to the CIAO storefront? And what if that bus carrying the students from Boys High during the John Jay riots hadn't broken down? Well, I thank God that the bus did break down, because if it hadn't I might never have gone on to college and might have ended up either behind bars or in a pine box.

Even though I told Vinny Riccio, then dean of boys at John Jay, that I would intervene to stop the riots during my senior year, I really had no intention of doing so and losing face in front of all my friends by siding with the school administration. While some may say it was coincidence, I believe it was truly the hand of God that caused the Boys High bus to break down, so that no riots ensued that day and Vinny Riccio viewed me as the master peacemaker. As a result of this good fortune, Vinny kept his part of the bargain and pulled a few strings that enabled me to get into college on the College Discovery Program.

Since college cost a lot of money and my family had very little of this commodity, I needed some kind of miracle to bridge the gap. The College Discovery Program proved to be that miracle. This scholarship program was mainly for blacks and Puerto Ricans. I was one of the very few white people to be accepted into this program. Vinny was somehow able to convince the people from the College Discovery Program that I too was from a minority neighborhood—South Brooklyn—and that it was also a poverty-stricken neighborhood. Since my grades were decent and Vinny's arguments quite persuasive, I was granted a full $1,000 scholarship to attend Manhattan Community College.

From day one at Manhattan Community, I always felt a great deal of academic pressure. There was no doubt in my mind that a good education was my only ticket out of poverty and the only way to avoid winding up like so many of my friends—on drugs, in jail, or dead.

There were other pressures too. Going to college was uncharted waters for a Gelormino. I was the first one in my family to go to college, as well as the first person in my circle of friends. Again, my fear of failure and my inferiority complex made me always feel like I had to prove to others as well as myself that I could succeed.

As I began to attend classes, it was as if I was suddenly thrust into another world. Though we were the same age, I was surrounded by students who had in most cases a totally different cultural, intellectual, and emotional makeup. I was downright scared and felt overwhelmed and intimidated by my new group of peers. As I rode the subways each day back and forth from Brooklyn to Manhattan, I had plenty of time to think about this brave new world I had gotten myself involved with.

Within my heart, I felt as if I was being torn apart. One side of me felt totally unable to compete and do the work that college was immediately demanding of me. The other side of me kept speaking back, "Louis, you're gonna make it." Little did I realize that this inner struggle I was having was quite common among many of my freshman classmates.

But along with this inner conflict came something quite refreshing. As I became more adjusted and comfortable with college, I began to really enjoy the whole atmosphere of free thought and the give-and-take exchanges that a college experience offered. College course work didn't come very easily to me and, although I managed to maintain a B to B– average during my freshman year, I had to study hard and devote a lot of my after-school hours to homework.

At first it proved very difficult to gain the discipline that was needed to handle all of my course work, especially since I basically took a four-year vacation from serious study habits once I started John Jay. Fortunately I was able to quickly recall the eight years of discipline I had been used to at St. Francis Xavier. During my first few months at Manhattan Community, I was feeling my way and pretty much making the necessary adjustments that would allow me to continue this new four-year experience.

By the time my first year of college ended I had made no real close friends, but I can honesty say I enjoyed myself. Being around intellectual people proved to be a valuable stimulus to my own intellectual development. Participating in the radical '60s also provided me with even further culture shock. It was the time of the Vietnam War, a return to talk about moral values, student uprisings, and even the flower children. The Beatles and the Stones were turning the music world upside down, and all of these movements and changes were turning me in the same direction. But through it all, I was growing and maturing as a young man and learning a great deal about people, places, and things. I had been given a wonderful opportunity to experience a new and different world, and I was beginning to enjoy the possibilities.

But, at the same time, I wasn't completely letting go of my old world. I still enjoyed hanging out with my friends back in Brooklyn—though only on the weekends since my studies took up all my weekday evenings. In the future, this ability to relate to all kinds of people from different walks of life would prove to be a tremendous asset in both my civic and business endeavors.

Another companion that traveled with me during my college days was loneliness. There were many times when I would feel lonely, but one way I found to relieve this feeling was a new habit I was just starting to form—reading

✝ ✝ ✝ ✝ ✝ ✝ ✝ ✝ ✝ ✝ ✝ ✝ ✝ ✝ ✝ ✝ ✝

the Bible. There just was something very special about this book that drew me to it. I knew that it was a great book, but until my college days I never really spent much time within its pages. I owned a Good News New Testament, and over the next four years I could often be found reading many of its passages.

The parts of the Bible that I enjoyed the most were the parables. These words of Jesus seemed to present in very compact form tremendously deep spiritual truths. The principles they taught and the codes of conduct these parables spoke about would one day be the very basis for the way I would live my life. The spiritual food that the Holy Scriptures were nourishing me with was beginning to develop character and integrity in my life. Though I often strayed from following many of these wonderful ideas, I knew that the Bible had the answers to how to live a happy and successful life.

At first, I turned to reading the Bible as a crutch. My loneliness drove me to it, but the more I read it, the more peace I received and the more strength I gained. And I started to see God in a completely new light.

In my childhood, I had thought of God as being very harsh and demanding, always angry at me whenever I did something wrong. I had a very negative concept of God. In fact, I felt like God was always putting me on a guilt trip and was very disappointed with me. But just before I started college, a five-minute talk radically altered my concept of God.

I had just committed a pretty bad sin (I don't remember what it was) and decided to go to church to confess it. I wasn't sure whether God would forgive me. At that moment, God decided to send another special person into my life: Father Donald Kenna. This Catholic priest was, like Mary Sansone, destined to become a wonderful and powerful influence in my life.

In just five short minutes, Don Kenna shared with me that God was always willing to forgive me, no matter how bad my sin was, if I was truly sorry and repented from it. He told me, "Louis, you are being too hard on yourself." Those few moments with Father Kenna made me feel so much better and had a profound impact on how I looked at God. It was this fresh and positive concept of a loving and forgiving God that I brought with me to college, and how I thank Don Kenna for opening my eyes and heart to understanding this simple and beautiful truth.

Meanwhile, back in South Brooklyn, I was still enjoying my friendship with Fat Wax, Allie, Buzzy, and the rest of the old gang. Although my gang days were rapidly coming to a close as I clearly focused on who I was becoming instead of on my past hapless life, I could see the changes in how my old friends viewed me. While they still admired me, the reason why was shifting. In the old days, I was looked up to because of my insanity and tough but tender heart. Now they were viewing me with great respect because of my courage and determination

✝ ✝ ✝ ✝ ✝ ✝ ✝ ✝ ✝ ✝ ✝ ✝ ✝ ✝ ✝ ✝ ✝

to succeed and because I was doing something—going to college—which no one in our circle of friends had ever done.

I was living in two different worlds, enjoying both my old friends and some of the new ones I was starting to make in college. By the end of my second year at Manhattan Community I had done even better, getting mostly B's and B+'s. My philosophy, psychology, and social studies courses were proving fascinating to my always inquisitive mind. All of my hard work finally paid off, and at age twenty I received my associate's degree from Manhattan Community College. I was a graduate and felt proud of what I had accomplished. With these two successful years of study under my belt, I decided that I wanted a four-year degree and that the following September I would enroll in City College. However, the lure of the almighty American dollar almost ended my college career.

During the previous summer, I had worked as an ironworker to earn money for school and other living expenses. My uncle Buddy was a foreman in the union, Iron Workers Local 40, and got me a great job as an ironworker. What was great about this job was the fact that I did very light construction work and spent a lot of my workday doing coffee runs for all the men on the job. The other great thing was my salary, which was $400 a week. This was an unbelievable amount of money for me and a far cry from the $15 a week I had earned as a farm cadet two summers earlier.

While I wanted to go to City College in the fall, I felt that making $400 a week was a more attractive alternative. So after I had worked for just one week during this second summer, I approached Buddy and told him that I had decided not to go to college in the fall and wanted instead to have my summer work become my permanent career.

Uncle Buddy was not too pleased with this decision since he, like the rest of my family, wanted me to continue in college. He had done me a big favor by getting me the ironworker job. But I didn't fully understand that Buddy was also doing me a bigger favor by giving me such an easy workload. Most of my coworkers had to bust their behinds to earn the money they were making. I foolishly thought that I could just continue to relax on the job and make good money. In order to wake me up to the real world Buddy, within a week after hearing that I was quitting college, changed my work assignment from delivering coffee to humping sheets.

When Buddy told me what humping sheets would entail, I immediately saw why ironworkers earned such a good income. My first job was traveling to Manhattan and helping to build One Penn Plaza in midtown. We worked in teams of three. It was really wild. Here I was, a skinny Italian kid with no experience at all, working with two American Indians who between them had sixty years of experience in the construction business.

✝ ✝ ✝ ✝ ✝ ✝ ✝ ✝ **✝** ✝ ✝ ✝ ✝ ✝ ✝ ✝

To me, it was like being in the circus. The three of us would in unison have to lift these huge 1,000-pound sheets of steel and then slowly walk out onto steel beams some thirty stories above ground. Each of us walked on our own beam as if we were on a tightrope. When we had reached the end of the beam, we had to drop this huge sheet of metal, again in unison, onto the beams we were standing on. This maneuver was called "planking off," and I soon understood that the first mistake you made would also be the last. Once I forgot to drop the sheet and almost went overboard. I quickly decided to end my career as an ironworker and return to the safe world below as a college student. I knew what my uncle was up to by changing my job and I can only say thank you, Uncle Buddy, for looking out for my future.

One especially bright spot in my days at Manhattan Community College was Mrs. Garnett. One of the nice things about the College Discovery Program was that every student in the program had their own guidance counselor. Mrs. Garnett was mine. She was a wonderful fifty-year-old black lady who possessed a gentle and caring maternal instinct. Not only did she counsel me on school matters and career choices, but she also acted as a psychologist, social worker, and friend. She was always there for me when I felt depressed about my home problems, and she always seemed to have just the right words to pick me up. Of all the people I met at Manhattan Community, she was the most special.

City College was located right in the heart of Harlem. While Harlem might have been an area on the decline with lots of crime and danger, my new campus was like a fresh oasis in the middle of a neighborhood in turmoil. The campus of CCNY was so beautiful and the buildings so majestic that I instantly fell in love with my new daytime home.

I was now beginning to blend in with the students. Though I still viewed them as quite intellectual, I now felt as if I could participate in school discussions instead of just absorbing this incredible flood of new knowledge, and contribute my own input and ideas. Having great professors and challenging coursework made every day an exciting learning experience. We studied everything from the great thinkers of the past to the great problems of the present.

Plato, Aristotle, and Shakespeare became my new mentors. What I found most exciting was the fact that I was able to integrate all this new knowledge with my old background; instead of dropping the old and taking on the new, I could assimilate the two and become a more well-rounded and useful member of society. What I think was happening was that instead of severing my early family and background roots, I was transplanting them into new and better growing soil. It was as if my college experiences were helping to dig up a lot of the weeds I had grown up with and replace them with the sweet aroma of roses. There were still lots of weeds in my makeup, but I was beginning to bloom.

✝ ✝ ✝ ✝ ✝ ✝ ✝ ✝ ✝ ✝ ✝ ✝ ✝ ✝ ✝ ✝ ✝ ✝

As my life continued to unfold, I could see that all of the poverty and pain I lived with for so long were valuable additions to the book knowledge and wisdom I was now accumulating. And people like Mary Sansone, Father Kenna, and Mrs. Garnett were the stirrers who mixed all of these different ingredients together, molding me into the person I was destined to become. Life was no longer boring, and I was now glad to be a part of it.

One example of how I managed to combine elements from both my past and present involved a paper I wrote entitled, "Shakespeare, the Gang, and Me." This paper was one of the highlights and proudest moments of my college career. What I had endeavored to do was equate Shakespearean characters with the members of the gang I knew. I knew that Shakespeare was a master at bringing to life, through the medium of the stage, the real-life dramas we all live. My contribution to the world of literature would consisted of replacing Falstaff with Big Wax, Othello with Buzzy Ubotz, and Shakespeare with me, and allowing the Little Gents to perform on a Shakespearean stage of today. I wanted to demonstrate that the inner struggles and conflicts that Shakespeare was able to brilliantly bring out through his characters exist to some degree within all of us. I used the people I knew best to bring Shakespeare a little more up-to-date. While I could never replicate the beautiful Elizabethan poetry of this timeless master, I did try to inject a little bit of my own Gelormino flair. I don't really know what my professor thought of my literary style, but I know that he found the concept quite novel and said it was a truly unique literary work—enough to give me an A+.

As time traveled by, I could see that my relationship with my brothers was deepening in the sense that they were now looking at me with respect and admiration. My mom was so proud of me, too. She enjoyed telling her friends that her son was a college man. Having this respect from the people I loved most had a big impact on me.

My favorite course at CCNY was called The Philosophy of Law. It was taught by Professor Pavis. This guy was such a blessing to me. It was not so much because he was a good professor, which he was, but because he was a regular guy. He had been a construction worker and now was traveling all around the world. His background made it easy for me to relate to him. So many avenues of thought that I never had been exposed to were discussed in this class; I savored each and every moment of his lectures and our talks.

My college days put me right in touch with the hippie movement of the mid-1960s. While my hair was always short and my skin clean-shaven, I was quite liberal in my thinking and rebellious in my spirit. In order to help put some of the ideas we were learning into action, a group of us decided to hold a major protest at CCNY. We felt strongly that the Vietnam War should be ended and that our course curriculum should be changed. We wanted more courses on philosophy, and black students wanted more on African American history.

With these noble ideas in mind, we closed down South Campus, which was the liberal arts part of CCNY. For three days, the main gate was shut and we slept in the administration building in order to make our voices heard. TV crews were on campus to help moderate and report on the dialogue we were having with the college administration. After our three-day uprising, we were 50 percent successful with our demands. While our troops didn't come home from the war at that time, we did manage to get some changes to our courses of study. It was an exciting time to be participating in a cause, and I was learning firsthand that there was often a price to pay to change the status quo.

By the middle of my third year at City College, I had completely withdrawn from all gang activities and was replacing this part of my life with helping the youngsters in the gangs to get out, and helping those who were not in a gang to stay that way. As I looked at all the blessings in my life, I felt deep within my heart a strong desire to help return something positive to society. As I meditated upon receiving a four-year scholarship, my friendship with Mary Sansone, my good health, and the way God was constantly turning negative situations in my life into positive outcomes (despite my not-so-honest behavior), something within my soul kept saying, "Louis, don't you think it is time to give thanks and return these blessings to others?"

From that point on, my life was never the same again. Throughout my life I had always prayed that God would use the abilities and talents He had given me in a constructive and positive way, and maximize my effectiveness as a human being. This was the same prayer that I prayed the night I was stabbed and arrested. But it wasn't until this time that I seriously wanted to have this prayer answered. My early involvement with Mary Sansone and CIAO in our small storefront back in high school had given me a taste of community work. Now I knew that what Mary had helped plant in my heart way back then was ready to become an integral part of my life's work.

Mary had often told me that I possessed good leadership qualities, the capacity to understand and relate to people with all kinds of problems and hurts, and the compassion to lend a helping and loving hand. So it was only natural that I would again turn to Mary and get involved with other CIAO programs. Mary and CIAO had just received a grant from the Lindsay administration to establish in South Brooklyn a new program. Mary appointed me as the overall coordinator of job placement. It was my role to help thirty or so youngsters, who were mostly poor and antisocial, to find summer employment. These kids wouldn't work for anyone but me. They felt that I was one of their own and respected me. My background was already starting to pay dividends. These summer jobs consisted of opening and closing youth centers each day, supervising sporting events, organizing field trips, and other recreational activities involving schools and gyms.

Another innovative program I was involved with proved to be not only fun but also life-changing, at least for three young people. Mary, myself, and a public relations officer from American Airlines, Hank Boerner, came up with the idea to give a group of kids the opportunity to experience their first airplane flight.

American Airlines had generously agreed to allow our Youth Corps kids to take a free forty-five-minute plane ride around New York City. Mary, Hank, myself, and Mayor Lindsay would be their chaperones. We had a glorious time seeing New York City from a vantage point most of us had never experienced. The kids loved chatting with the mayor, and so did I. The idea behind the trip was to expose the youth to private industry and give them an experience they would never forget.

As a result of this flying tour, one black girl decided to become a stewardess and two of the boys went on to an engineering school for American Airlines to learn airplane repair and maintenance. All three eventually landed jobs with American Airlines. Civic fever had definitely grabbed hold of me, and I'm glad to say twenty-five years later that it hasn't let go. I was happy to hear from Hank Boerner that this program was duplicated throughout the country, and over 300 young people had acquired good jobs.

My community activities added a wonderful balance to my schoolwork. By now, time was passing quickly and it was almost time for my graduation. During my first semester at Manhattan Community my college career as well as my life almost ended when I received those forty-eight stitches at the hand of a razor-blade-wielding Puerto Rican. But it was also at that time that God brought a young Legal Aid lawyer into my life. It had been approximately three and a half years since that incident, but the memory of how impressed I had been by this sissy-sounding lawyer advocate on my behalf was still strong. Through his efforts, instead of going to jail I was free, and I again began to seriously entertain the thought of one day becoming a lawyer as I did that night I was stabbed in my back.

While my enthusiasm about becoming a lawyer had died down somewhat after that incident, the thought never completely left my mind. By my senior year it started to gain momentum, and I decided that law school would be my next stop on my journey through life.

I submitted applications to five different law schools. The big day finally arrived when I was to graduate from City College. Even though I was very proud to graduate, I chose not to attend the graduation ceremonies. For one thing, the ceremony really wasn't that big a deal to me. And with my father now gone, my mom still not well, and Anthony and Jamsie still on drugs, I felt somewhat ashamed. Nonetheless, it was a great day when I received my B.A. in political science from City College.

I had officially graduated from college but still hadn't been accepted into law school. I had been turned down by three of the five schools I had applied to when I graduated. My friends were really proud of me, but began to ask what I was going to do if I didn't get into any of the law schools I had applied to. I was secretly doing a lot of praying because I had no idea what I would do if these law schools all rejected me. A few days after my graduation, I received word that the fourth school had turned me down also.

As the days of summer marched forward, my nervousness increased. There was only one more law school on my list of possibilities, and if they said no I was finished. I had applied to the CLEO Institute at Temple University in Philadelphia. This was my last hope. In early July, a letter came in the mail from the CLEO Institute. As my eyes read the words of rejection, my heart sank. All hope was gone—or was it? I knew I had only one hope, and her name was Mary Sansone.

✞ ✞ ✞ ✞ ✞ ✞ ✞ ✞ ✞ ✞ ✞ ✞ ✞ ✞ ✞ ✞ ✞

11 Law School

Although I had good grades in college, I knew it would be very difficult for me to go to law school because it was expensive. College had become a reality only because of the scholarship I received from the College Discovery Program. My prayer was that some law school would also grant me a scholarship. One scholarship program I had heard about at City College was the Council and Leader Education Opportunities (CLEO) Program. CLEO was directed to get minorities (especially blacks and Puerto Ricans) into law school since there was a shortage of minority lawyers.

I had conferred with Mary about the CLEO Program and decided to apply. After receiving my rejection letter from them, I decided to seek Mary out and see if I had any recourse. We both knew that the basic reason why I had been declined admission was because I was not black or Puerto Rican. Mary decided we should pursue the matter on the basis of possible reverse discrimination. Mary and I took a very hard position. We stated that I came from a poverty-stricken area and background and that I, too, was a minority, just like the blacks and Puerto Ricans. We contended that their rejection of me constituted reverse discrimination, and we threatened to file a lawsuit if they didn't reverse their position. By mid-July, just two weeks after I was initially rejected, another letter came from the institute welcoming me to CLEO.

I have learned that not knowing what to do in a situation is not that big a problem if you know where to go for help. Fortunately, I knew where to go, and thanks to Mary's subtle threat of a lawsuit I became the first Italian American to be admitted to the CLEO Program. This was the second time that I had received a scholarship and the second time unorthodox methods had been employed to secure it. With my bags packed, I was ready to travel to my new home in Philadelphia, Temple University, and tackle the world of law.

Another incident during this time involved a different rejection I received during my last semester at City College. With graduation only two months away, I got the bad news that my birthday was picked as number sixteen out of a possible 365 in the draft. With our three-day sit-down demonstration against the Vietnam War fresh in my mind, I knew that any demonstration against fighting in Vietnam would only land me behind bars or force me to flee to Canada.

Disbelief filled my soul at the mere thought of having to fight in a war I was so strongly opposed to. And having such a low draft number made it virtually certain that I would be called to fight in the Vietnam War. It was indeed a tense and lonely day when I went to take my military physical.

I knew that I was in good health, except for my nose, and when they passed me I would be shipped out to Vietnam. I never liked taking orders, and when I

was ordered to take my shirt off, move from here to there, and what seemed like a hundred other things, I almost lost my temper and almost got into several fistfights. When the doctor told me I had passed the physical, I protested, stating that I was unfit to serve since I had a severe nasal problem. "Doc," I said, "ever since my nose was broken twice I have had a lot of problems breathing with excessive nose bleeding and dizzy spells." While he didn't buy my story although it was true, he reluctantly consented to let me see a nose specialist at Fort Hamilton Army Base.

Right before going to see this nose specialist, I went to talk to my own personal physician in the hope that he knew this specialist and could provide me with some background on how best to approach him on this controversial subject—the Vietnam War. Amazingly, he knew all about this military nose specialist and told me that I was in for big trouble since he hated draft dodgers and people trying to avoid going to war.

I had enjoyed taking psychology courses at City College and felt this was the perfect time to put into action some of the book knowledge I had learned. The approach I decided upon was quite daring, and if I miscalculated I was on my way to the other side of the world. So as I traveled down for this second physical, I was determined to use reverse psychology and my acting skills to convince this doctor that I really wanted to serve my country in battle.

As I stepped into his office, the Doc looked up at me after staring at my chart for a minute. He said: "What are you doing here? I see from your record that your health seems to be quite good." Since there was no turning back, I began to play out my cards. With a very calm voice, I replied: "I have no idea why they sent me to see you. I feel physically fit and I'm eager to go fight in the war. I don't understand why they would send me to another doctor since I already passed the physical."

He repeated that there must be some reason they had sent me to see him. I replied, "Except for the fact that my nose bleeds frequently, and that I can't breathe properly through it, and I suffer from dizzy spells and have trouble running long distances, I feel fine."

He once again looked at my file and commented, "I see you will be graduating from college this June. Could you tell me what your future plans are?"

My response was instant: "I first want to go and fight in the war, and after I return I want to become a prosecuting attorney." When he came back with, "Why?" I walked up to him and slowly put my arm around his shoulder, looked him straight in the eye, and told him, "The only reason I want to become a prosecutor is because of all the guys who are evading the draft and skipping out to Canada. These lawbreakers deserve to be put in jail, and I want to be the man who handles these cases."

✟ ✟ ✟ ✟ ✟ ✟ ✟ ✟ ✟ ✟ ✟ ✟ ✟ ✟ ✟ ✟

I had played out all my cards and wondered if he would call my bluff or perhaps buy another card. To my great surprise, this fifty-five-year-old, gray-haired doctor flashed one of the biggest smiles I had ever seen. He placed his arm around my shoulder and said in a most friendly voice, "Son, I've got bad news for you. I have to exempt you from going to war because of your nose. Besides that, we need guys like you in the system." He never once examined my nose, and I stood outside his office in a state of bewilderment. This was one of the most exhilarating experiences of my life, and for the next two days I partied and celebrated my exemption from the draft.

Back in April two of my good buddies, Joey "Hercules" Castagna and John Horan, also took their physical with me. Both of them passed and went on to fight in the Vietnam War. As elated as I was that day when I was excused from going to war, my spirits took a nosedive when later both of these good friends were killed in action. Oh, how fragile and uncertain life can be. Now that I was exempt from the draft, I was able to attend the CLEO Institute at Temple University Law School.

Allie's dad graciously consented to let his son borrow his 1962 Ford and drive me out to the law school in northern Philadelphia. So one very hot and muggy morning in early August, Allie and I left our comfortable Brooklyn surroundings to journey to what was for me another world.

The last time I had traveled this far from home was when I joined the Farm Cadet Program in Madoosa, New York. Even though I was quite nervous, I felt pretty good since this time I didn't get carsick like I had in the Catskills. Our car, however, was the one that got sick this time. Just as we pulled up in front of the law library, the car started to smoke something fierce. People came running out of the law school thinking that it was a fire. I was, needless to say, extremely embarrassed by the whole incident. Allie had to have the car towed away, and his dad drove all the way out to Philly to bring him home. When Allie left, I could feel deep within the pit of my stomach a very tight and gripping feeling as reality set in—I was all alone!

Everything was happening so fast. In one day, I had said goodbye to my mother and family members, driven all the way to Philadelphia, had the public embarrassment of a broken-down car, and was about to bid farewell to one of my dear friends, and I still had to face my first law class at 4 p.m.

The CLEO Institute was a very unique program. There were four CLEO Institutes in America, each housing a famous law school. This was the Northeast Regional Institute and was held at Temple University. In order to be formally accepted into the three-year law program, I had to successfully maintain a C average during the CLEO Institute's intense six-week probationary summer program. If you failed to achieve a C average on the three courses that everybody had to take, you were gone from CLEO and law school. I managed to get a C+, a C, and a D+ on the three courses, which worked out to exactly a C average. I had passed by the skin of my teeth. The pressures I felt during those first six weeks were like none I had ever experienced. All I did was study and pray.

Looking back, I think that what made the difference between my passing and flunking out was Allie's smoking 1962 Ford. You see, when our car started smoking, one of the guys who came running out of the law library to see what was going on was a young black man named Ronald Harvey. When my first class started at 4 p.m. later that day, Ronald Harvey came up to me and said, "Weren't you the guy who was in that broken-down car I saw earlier today?" After I said yes, we began to share a little bit about our backgrounds. I told him that I was from Brooklyn, and he asked me if I had found a place to stay yet. When I told him no, he invited me to his house after class for dinner. So after class we went back to Ronald's house, where he lived with his parents and grandparents. During dinner, I shared a great deal about my life growing up in South Brooklyn. Whatever I said must have really touched Ronald's mom because she more or less insisted that I stay the full six weeks at their house. I was grateful for this most generous offer and immediately accepted the Harveys' hospitality.

The Harveys were all so warm and kind toward me; I felt like they considered me part of the family. During that time I learned a lot about brotherhood, sharing, and loving from the Harvey family. Here I was, an Italian American from Brooklyn, and this black family from Philadelphia took me in and treated me, a total stranger, like they would treat a son. Without the love and support of this precious family, I don't think I would have made it through this emotional and challenging probationary period.

If Allie's car hadn't broken down, I might never have been invited to the Harveys'. If I hadn't met the Harveys, I would have missed their love and support. And without this love, I am sure that the pressures would have been too much for my very fragile state of mind to handle. Once again, the hand of God was at work. Four years earlier, a broken-down bus had proved instrumental in getting me into college, and now a broken-down car proved critical in keeping me in law school. On a sad note, though, after completing his first year of law school, Ronald decided to drop out and pursue a different career path.

On my first day of law school, the dean of the school assembled the incoming freshmen and delivered these sobering words: "As you know, law school will be perhaps the most difficult and challenging experience you will face in your early lives. I want you to take a good look around you, and especially at the person next to you—because next year at this time one of you won't be here."

✟ ✟ ✟ ✟ ✟ ✟ ✟ ✟ ✟ **✟** ✟ ✟ ✟ ✟ ✟ ✟ ✟ ✟

In a joking spirit, I turned to the guy right next to me and said, "Sorry to hear you won't be here next year." Deep inside, I felt that I was going to be the one who would flunk out. However, also deep inside, another voice was saying, "No matter what it takes, I am going to make it."

With these discouraging words echoing in my ears, I braced myself for what I envisioned as three years of hell ahead. For the first two years of law school, I became known as the class bookworm, a social recluse, and a secret member of the Mafia since I was an Italian American from Brooklyn, New York, a rare sight to see.

Over 70 percent of the student body was Jewish, but most of the people I became friends with were the blacks and Hispanics from the CLEO Program. With a name like Gelormino, and being the only Italian in the CLEO Program, almost the entire school thought I must have some strong connections and relatives with the Mafia. Only two or three of my good friends and Ronald Harvey believed me when I told them this wasn't so.

Nobody studied harder or longer at Temple Law than I. After I moved out of the Harveys' home, I took an apartment with a roommate in northern Philadelphia, one half hour from the law school. For the first two years at Temple, I commuted to school almost every day on the subway to school. When I wasn't in class, I was inevitably in a corner of the law library studying away. While I was quite fortunate to receive a living expense stipend of $1,000 a semester from the CLEO Program, I still had to supplement my income, which I did by working nights at—where else?—the law library.

One of my few diversions from the grind of studying was watching the football games on Sunday at 4 p.m. after a long day at the library from 9 a.m. to 3 p.m. The only other time I took a break from the law books was when I went to visit my family, which turned out to be almost every other weekend. My roommate for the entire three years at school was a man named Ed Silvers. He was one of the smartest guys in the law school and, like myself, came from New York City. It worked out well for me since I couldn't afford my own place and Ed was a nice guy. In addition, he also went home to New York City to visit his folks on the same weekends I did, and he drove me to the city each time.

Traveling home so frequently helped me stay in touch with my family and friends. However, this continuous contrast between my old and new surroundings brought me face to face with the intense inner conflict that was being waged in my mind. As I went back and forth from Philly to Brooklyn, I began to feel out of place in both of these two very different worlds.

At home among my longtime friends, I could see that they hadn't changed one bit. Hanging out at the Snake Pit, playing stickball, and getting high on alcohol and drugs were still a way of life for them. They were stagnating. I had left this lifestyle far behind and was in the process of growing and maturing as a person. It was very difficult for me to relate to many of the guys I had grown to love over the years, since our ways of viewing life were now diverging.

My first year at law school was the most difficult time of my life. After putting in a solid year of intense study I found myself on probation because, despite my efforts, my grades didn't follow suit. Discouragement was the word for my first year at Temple. Not only did I have the pressures of the scholastic challenge, but I was also going through a tremendous reevaluation of who I was and trying to establish a positive self-image for myself. Having to constantly see my friends going nowhere in life and my family problems worsening (by now, Anthony was starting to do hard time in jail), I was fighting to just survive. I started to ask myself if I really belonged in the world of law school.

The intense competition and dog-eat-dog atmosphere at school were not my cup of tea. Although there were no guns, knives, and car antennas, students' mindsets were the same as if they were fighting on the street. Often, I felt overwhelmed by the level of intelligence of the students and the professors. I had given it my best shot. I worked and studied as hard as possible, but my grades said I wasn't good enough. I was at a crisis state in my life. Feeling out of place in both my old and new surroundings left me with no place to go.

Emotionally and intellectually I was burning out, but something inside said I must go on and find my place in society. While my gut feeling said, "Drop out," the spirit within me rebuked this devil of doubt and despair with words of power and purpose. As I began to reflect back on all the people who felt that I was a special person, with many God-given talents (like Mary Sansone, Vinny Riccio, Father Kenna, and Professor Peter Liacoris, the director of the CLEO Institute), a burning desire took hold and right then and there convinced me that God cared for me and had a special plan for my life, and that Temple Law was to be a part of it.

This burning desire, which I now characterize as the spirit of the Lord, began to show me that I did indeed have special abilities and talents and that God would one day use them to help improve the lives of many people. While my emotions often still got the best of me during the rest of my time at Temple, I felt very strongly that I would be cheating myself if I did not develop my own personality and identity and become the person I now knew that the Lord wanted me to be. In addition to this powerful revelation from God, a book, a course, and a person helped provide me with the added confidence I needed to let me know that I was going to make it no matter what.

Throughout my law school days, I often turned to the Bible for words of encouragement. Opening my Bible at night, after a long day of looking at technical law books, proved to be a welcome relief from the daily grind. Just knowing that God was thinking about me and cared for me meant a lot, even though my intensely fluctuating emotional state often seemed to show a lack of trust in God. As I kept reading the Bible, God continued to show me that I was special and that He had a wonderful plan for my life. Yet I still was living with heavy doubt about myself and my abilities.

It would take several more years before I would learn the reason the Bible possesses such power and can generate such incredible peace in the hearts and minds of those who read it. During those long and seemingly endless days at Temple, my Bible was the one companion I could always turn to for comfort of my troubled heart.

What I was doing was tapping into its incomparable inspirational nature. And oh, how I needed words of comfort and inspiration! But back then, I was viewing God as an outsider and just admiring His words of comfort and wisdom. Yet, even as an outsider, His words had a very positive effect on my life. It would only be much later in my life that I would bring God to live inside of my heart and begin to truly experience His explosive peace and joy in a wonderfully unique and intimate way. For now, the Bible was definitely helping me to cope with the rigors of law school.

Despite being placed on academic probation, there were two courses I enjoyed and got B's on during my first year at Temple Law. These were Constitutional Law and Criminal Law. Since I found the other courses very difficult and unenjoyable, these courses helped me to realize that not all law was boring, and that there were areas of study in which I could excel. So all was not doom and gloom in the classroom for me.

Professor Peter Liacoris, who as I mentioned was director of the CLEO Institute, subsequently became the dean of the law school. During my time at the school he served as my mentor, father figure, and friend. He always found it quite amusing and had a hard time understanding how an Italian ever got accepted into the CLEO Institute and law school. He always asked me, "How did you get into this program? You're not black or Puerto Rican." Mr. Liacoris greatly admired and respected me because I had managed to take advantage of the scholarship and demand my rights under the CLEO Program.

We became good friends right from the start. He took a genuine interest in me and tried his best to help me make it through the school. He invited me to his home and introduced me to his wife and children. They, like the Harveys, sort of adopted me as their son. He even assigned me a tutor to work with me during my first year at the law school.

And as I was learning about law, I was also learning some wonderful things about people. Growing up in an Italian neighborhood and always fighting with the black and Puerto Rican gangs, I didn't view non-Italians in the best way. But

✚ ✚ ✚ ✚ ✚ ✚ ✚ ✚ ✚ ✚ ✚ ✚ ✚ ✚ ✚ ✚ ✚

the Harveys were black and they loved me, and Mr. Liacoris was Greek and he loved me too. Love has a wonderful way of breaking down false views about people. With all of this kindness and love coming my way, my concepts of race, color, and creed began to radically change. I was no longer judging people based on how they looked, but on the size and contents of their hearts. Temple Law was providing me with a well-balanced education in more ways than one.

As my second year of law school began, new pressures were added to the old ones. They had a rule in law school that if you were on probation for the second year, you would be dismissed from the law school. I think that during my second year at school, my social life consisted of going to one party. Being a social recluse and bookworm didn't make me the most popular or best-known guy on campus, but it did help me get off of probation and make it to my third and final year at Temple. Getting off probation felt really good, especially since I was told that 90 percent of the students who make it to their final year graduate.

With the knowledge that I had such a good chance of graduating, a lot of the pressure was taken off me. As a result, I got all A's and B's during my third year, and for the first time I started to socialize and loosen up a bit. Even the way I viewed my professors changed. Before, I had viewed most of them as cold and impersonal; now I got close to two of them and found them quite warm and caring. My two favorite courses that final year were Criminal Procedure and Evidence, both of which I aced.

As I was nearing graduation, I really started to believe in the vision I had, way back in the bullpen at 120 Schermerhorn Street, that one day I would become a lawyer. God somehow was able to use my getting arrested as the means of introducing me to the Legal Aid lawyer who became my inspiration for pursuing a career in law. Somehow, God turned this very negative situation into a tremendous blessing in my life.

As I was contemplating what type of law to practice upon graduation, everything seemed to point to becoming a Legal Aid criminal lawyer. With all the studying I had to put in at Temple, I was left with very little time to get involved in social causes like the ones I participated in during my college days. I felt that working for Legal Aid would afford me the opportunity to work closely with the disadvantaged and poor, which since my high school days I had enjoyed doing so much. I was grateful for all the blessings I had received in life and felt that as a Legal Aid lawyer I could help repay society. In addition, as a Legal Aid lawyer I would have a steady income and far less pressure than if I opened my own private practice. At this point in my life, I didn't need any added pressures, since I felt like I was burning out before I even started my legal career.

Once again, when graduation day finally arrived I decided not to attend the ceremony, for the same reasons I had bowed out at City College. Instead, my diploma reached me through the mail. When I arrived back home, the whole neighborhood threw a big party in my honor. Everyone was so proud of me and I was once again, for that moment, on top of the world. One of the first things that I did when I got home was send Mary Sansone a half dozen red roses with a note saying, "I wish I could have sent you more." Her "problem child" was truly growing up.

My criminal law professor was able to set me up with a Legal Aid position in Philadelphia, subject to my passing the bar exam, but my heart wanted to practice law back in Brooklyn. I graciously declined the offer and traveled back to my beloved Brooklyn. While my Temple law degree gained me tremendous respect wherever I went in South Brooklyn, I still couldn't practice law until I passed the New York State bar examination. My entrance into the field of law rested solely on how well I did on a two-day, sixteen-hour test. This became my newest hurdle in life.

Being told that 50 percent of the people fail the bar examination the first time was not the type of news I wanted to hear. In addition, if you failed the bar three times, you could never practice law in New York State. Needless to say, when I got the news that I failed the bar examination on my first try, I became extremely discouraged. The rule was that you had to wait six months before you could sit for the exam again.

For the next six months, it was back to the daily grind of hitting my law books and reviewing for my next attempt at the bar. Joey Heart, God bless his soul, knew how difficult a time I would have if I had to live at home and study for the test. One day he just came up to me and told me to move into his Brooklyn apartment for the next six months. He said he would move back in with his mother and allow me to use his place as a study hall. Once again, I assumed the role of a recluse and channeled all my energies into preparing for the bar. Peanut-butter-and-jelly sandwiches and I became very good friends during this period, and Joey Heart became my friend in need and in deed.

In order to support myself during these nerve-racking months, I was fortunate to land a part-time job as a Legal Aid investigator. I only had to work two to three hours a day, doing mostly clerical work. The income was good and the pressure was low. This was just what I needed while I was studying for the bar. When the two days of testing came, I gave it my best shot. I thought I had done a better job this second time around, but only time would tell if I passed.

Shortly after taking the bar, Joey gave me a call at his apartment and said, "You can get out of my apartment now." I asked him what he meant by that. He said, "I saw your name in the paper." I was now quite anxious to know why my name made the paper and asked him, "What did I do?" And to my amazement,

Joey said, "I have a copy of today's *New York Times* right in front of me. It has a listing of all the people who passed the bar exam—and your name is on the list!" So right then, at one o'clock in the morning, I flew out of Joey's apartment and bought a copy of the *Times*. Seeing my name there brought feelings of indescribable ecstasy to my soul. Words cannot describe the accomplishment and liberation I felt. The long journey had finally ended—Louis Gelormino was now a lawyer!

There was just one small technicality I had to go through before everything would be official. For most people it was a mere formality, but I felt quite nervous about it. Like everyone else passing the bar, I had to go before the Character and Fitness Committee of the bar. The role of this committee was to determine if you were morally fit to practice law. I, of course, was very concerned since I had previously been arrested three times for fighting. Even though I was never convicted and had all three cases dismissed, I had no idea how the committee would view my record.

Mary Sansone told me that it was very important to fully disclose everything to the committee. She also got several people to write strong letters of recommendation as to my moral character. Mary Sansone, Nick Pileggi, Peter Liacoris, and several local politicians, all of whom were well respected in their fields, came to my aid with glowing letters of praise on my behalf.

As I stood before the committee, they reviewed all of my arrests and the letters of recommendation. After just two minutes, one of the members from the committee rose to address me. His words, even today, still ring in my ears: "Mr. Gelormino, after reviewing your entire file it is quite evident that you have come from a very difficult and adverse background. You should be commended for how far you have come. After reviewing your letters of recommendation, it is also quite evident that you have a lot of people who believe in you. Mr. Gelormino, my only advice to you is that in the future if you are going to fight, don't do it with your hands, but with your mouth." It now was official!

✠ ✠ ✠ ✠ ✠ ✠ ✠ ✠ ✠ ✠ ✠ ✠ ✠ ✠ ✠ ✠

12 A Tale of Four Brothers

Just what is it that separates a good lawyer from a great one? Well, before I officially launched my career as a lawyer, I got involved in a case that taught me the incredible secret that separates goodness from greatness. During my last year at Temple, my mom called and told me that my brother Jamsie had gotten himself arrested and was sent to jail.

She didn't exactly know why he was in jail, but she told me that it was serious. I immediately made arrangements to come home. Upon my arrival, Waxy told me that Jamsie had been arrested for hijacking a fish truck. My heart was breaking as I traveled to Rikers Island to visit my brother. Jamsie and I had always been very close. While growing up, we had done everything together—from playing stickball to just plain hanging out. But now our worlds were about to be radically separated. While success and the good life were just around the corner for me, I knew that if Jamsie got convicted for hijacking, which was a very serious crime, a long jail sentence was all he could look forward to.

When I got to Rikers Island, Jamsie told me he had already been there a week. As he began to relate to me the details of the crime that brought him to this miserable place, I could see that he was dead scared at the prospect of not making it out this time. He had previously been arrested but always managed to escape incarceration. But he knew that this time was different.

Jamsie had gotten involved with drugs, and although my brother was basically a good and decent person, he couldn't break the habit. At this point in his life, he needed money for his habit and decided to be the stickup man in the hijacking of a fish truck. Jamsie told me that he was really uncomfortable about the whole idea but there had been another powerful force driving him on, which at this time in his life he couldn't control. As Jamsie and his companion in crime sped off with the fish truck, they suddenly stopped three blocks from the entrance to the Manhattan Bridge and decided to bail out and make a run for it on foot. With the police in hot pursuit, it took only a minute before they were caught and arrested.

As he concluded his sad story, I knew that Jamsie was in real trouble. Since stealing a truck doing interstate commerce was a federal offense, I knew that probation was probably out of the question. Jamsie pleaded with me to get him out on bail. He said that he wouldn't be able to last in jail, and he was scared they might rape and hurt him in there.

In the past I had gotten Jamsie out on bail, but I felt that since he hadn't learned his lesson yet, this time I would leave him there. I told him that I couldn't come up with the bail money, which was $10,000. While this was certainly beyond my means, I knew that if I went to my grandfather I might be able to convince him to come up with the money since he has real money. But I felt that it would be in Jamsie's best interest to stay right where he was. He then begged me to get him a good lawyer—which I did.

The lawyer we got to defend my brother was one of the best criminal lawyers in New York City, Joe Fontana. Since his retainer fee was quite high, I felt that this time I had better pay a visit to my grandfather.

My mom's dad was quite an interesting man. Born in Italy in 1885, he came to America in 1902 and began working for Con Edison. For the next eighty-six years, he lived in New York City. From the time of his arrival at Ellis Island to the time of his death in 1988, at the ripe old age of 103, he never learned to read or write any English, and spoke very few words in his new country's language.

His job at Con Ed during the early part of this century consisted of pushing carts loaded with coal. When he was twenty-eight years old, one of the carts he was pushing backed up on him and pinned him up against a wall, causing a severe back injury. To compensate my grandfather for being permanently disabled, Con Edison offered him his choice of a lump sum payment or regular monthly payments with cost-of-living increases. He chose the latter and during the next seventy-five years, until the time of his death, he collected approximately 900 checks from Con Edison.

On one occasion, he called me and said that he had a legal problem. He knew I was going to law school and thought I could help him. Apparently, he had a whole bunch of checks that were uncashed. He didn't know how to sign his name in English and as a result they had gone uncashed. He explained that he had asked a relative to sign his name for him in the past, but he had decided a while back that this was wrong and thus began accumulating the uncashed checks.

In order to help solve my grandfather's problem, I took a small three-by-one-inch card and wrote his name in English on it. We then practiced writing his name until he was able to do it by himself. Shortly thereafter, he signed and cashed his checks. Up until the time he passed away, the only thing he could write in English was his name on the back of a check.

Over the years, my grandfather had accumulated a lot of money. In fact, he owned the brownstone apartment building we lived in on Carroll Street. He had allowed our family, seven of us altogether, live in the four and-a-half room apartment for very low rent. In exchange, my mother cooked for him practically every night. So it was to this man that I went to request and fortunately receive the money we needed to retain Joe Fontana.

I met with Mr. Fontana several times. He knew that I was familiar with criminal law, and told me that based on my brother's past record, the type of crime he had committed, and the particular judge who had been assigned

✛ ✛ ✛ ✛ ✛ ✛ ✛ ✛ ✛ ✛ ✛ ✛ ✛ ✛ ✛ ✛ ✛

Jamsie's case, the best we could hope for was a three-year jail sentence. After spending thirty days at Rikers Island, Jamsie went before the judge for a pretrial conference (which is given to determine how strong the case is against the defendant). Fontana had warned us that this judge was very tough, and felt that if Jamsie got only three years he should consider himself lucky.

When we appeared in court, they called out our case: "The People of the State of New York vs. James Gelormino." It was at this moment that Jamsie decided to bug out. He looked at his hands and all of a sudden started to act like a crazy man right in the middle of the courtroom. He jumped on the judge's bench and pushed all the books on the bench right onto the judge. He then fell on the floor and went into a seizure. I thought that he was definitely out of his mind. As he was having his seizure, two court officers dragged him out of the courtroom, feet first, into the bullpen that was about twenty feet away from the courtroom.

I was very concerned and asked if I could go into the bullpen and speak to him since I was his brother. They let me go in, and I asked Jamsie if he wanted a doctor. I thought he was actually having a seizure, and when I asked him if he was okay he winked at me and whispered that he was fine. Here we were, just the two of us, now on our knees in this small holding pen, and Jamsie was quietly telling me that he faked the seizure so he could bug out and get out in ninety days on an insanity plea. When I asked him why he thought this was true, he said someone at Rikers Island told him it would work. "You dope," I said, "that is only true of a misdemeanor and not a felony." He realized that he had made a big mistake. So much for listening to "jailhouse lawyers."

They took Jamsie to the G Ward at Bellevue Hospital. G Ward was a building where the criminally and mentally insane people were taken. It was from a similar G Ward (at Kings County Hospital) that our old friend Lumpy had come. When I went to visit Jamsie there, he really looked bad. He had long hair and needed a shave. They had him on heavy antidepressant medication, and all he did was watch television all day. He was in G Ward for about ten days, begging me to get him out. He feared for his life and felt quite out of place among so many truly "disturbed" people. Shortly after my visit, he was summoned back to court, found fit to proceed, and escorted back to Rikers Island.

Once again, Jamsie pleaded with me to get him out on bail. This time I decided that it would be in his best interest to get out, and I asked our grandfather to put up the $10,000 bail. He very reluctantly agreed, and so off I went with my eighty-five-year-old grandfather to Rikers Island. We posted the bail, and within a half hour Jamsie and I were ready to go home to Brooklyn. There was only one small problem—I had lost my grandfather on Rikers Island.

We couldn't look for him on the island since most of the areas were restricted, so we filed a missing persons report. Jamsie and I left for home feeling very dejected, not knowing if we would ever see him again. To our great relief, when we arrived home, who should be sitting there but Grandpa? When we asked him how he got home, he told us he really didn't know how he did it. To this day, I have no idea how he made it back home.

It was great having my brother back home, but I was very concerned that he might go back on drugs and skip bail. However, he was so scared from being in jail that he never got into trouble again and never went back on drugs. He literally was scared straight!

Fontana, after consultation with the judge, advised Jamsie to take a plea on a grand larceny charge. He told us that the judge had indicated to him that if Jamsie took a plea of grand larceny, he would get only three years. Fontana strongly recommended to us to agree with this plea since if he stood trial he could get five to fifteen years. Four months went by from the time Jamsie got out on bail to the time he eventually pled grand larceny. During that time, my brother got a good steady job as an ironworker, stayed off all drugs, and even used some of his income to help support our mother. One more month passed between the time he pled guilty to the time of sentencing.

After my dad had passed away several years earlier, my oldest brother Gene had called Anthony, Jamsie, and me into a room and tried to console us as well as paint a realistic picture of what the future had in store for us. He began by saying, "There is no room for children in the family anymore." He then went on to say that everyone had to carry their own weight and that everything would be okay.

While Anthony, Jamsie, and I were always getting into trouble, Gene was the only one who demonstrated a good sense of responsibility. He never did drugs or got involved with the gangs. He did well in school, and during that time was the only stable and dependable person in the house among the four of us. At the time of his little speech, we were all going through a deep depression and his words were quite inspirational to the entire family. We needed to hear this message after my father died in 1963. Unfortunately, within a short time we three younger brothers were back on the broad road to destruction.

When I had turned twelve years old, Gene, who was eight years older than me, got married and moved out of the house. Gene's way of dealing with the pressures, frustrations, suffering, and pain of our household was to move out. And when he did move out, the good example he did set for us left with him.

Anthony's way of handling our family problems was turning to gangs and drugs. He had signed himself into drug rehabilitation programs twice, but on both occasions he skipped and went right back on drugs. Two years before Jamsie's sentencing, Anthony was arrested on drug-related charges and sentenced to three years in jail (at Dannamora).

The Gelormino household was now evenly divided as far as its four brothers were concerned. Two were on the road to success, while two were on the road to disaster. Gene had made a good name for himself working for AT&T and was doing quite well. I was almost ready to enter the legal profession and had become the first Gelormino to ever graduate from college and now law school. Anthony was married and already had three children, but was now little more than a convict with a heavy drug problem. And Jamsie was about to spend the next three years of his life behind bars despite the fact that for the last few months, for the first time in his life, he had finally seemed to be putting all of his problems behind him.

The day of sentencing finally arrived. I was really scared for my brother that he might not be able to handle spending three years in jail—and that he would never be the same when he got out. Another great concern to me was how my mom and Anthony would handle the situation. I felt that Jamsie's sentencing would have a major impact on our entire family.

Even though Joe Fontana had painted such a bleak picture for Jamsie, I wanted to try one last idea in an attempt to sway the judge into placing my brother on probation instead of sentencing him to jail. I decided to get as many people as possible to write letters on my brother's behalf in an effort to convince the judge to give Jamsie probation. In law school, I had learned that a good trial lawyer often can sway a jury by the way he presents the evidence and portrays his client's character. I reasoned that if I could get enough people of high respectability to let the judge know how well Jamsie was doing rehabilitating himself, the judge just might reconsider. I had just a wing and a prayer to go on, but it was worth going that extra mile—after all, it was for my own brother.

I had Mary Sansone, Father Kenna, myself, and a host of local politicians write glowing letters to the judge on my brother's behalf. All I could now do was pray and wait to see if these letters of love would move the judge.

During the last few months before the actual sentencing, I had corresponded with Anthony at Dannamora, keeping him abreast of the details in Jamsie's case. Ironically, just one day before Jamsie's sentencing date Anthony was released on parole after serving two years of his three-year sentence, just in time to appear with the rest of the Gelorminos in court to hear the judge sentence our brother.

My heart was breaking as I entered the Federal Court Building in Manhattan. Looking at Jamsie made my heart sad, but seeing the expression on Anthony's face made it sink. Anthony was doing everything he could to stop the tears from flowing. I knew how bad he was feeling. He was twenty-eight years old and feeling very depressed because of the poor example he had set for Jamsie and myself. The realization that he hadn't set a very good example for his wife and three small children was now also hitting home. And, on top of all this, Anthony, who had always been a leader that made things happen, was now totally helpless to come to the aid of his little brother.

It was time for destiny to chart its course in the lives of a small Italian family from South Brooklyn. All the letters had been written and sent, much prayer had been offered, and we now held onto our only ally—hope. As the judge began to speak, silence filled the courtroom. And now, in open court, the judge gave us his decision and told us the story behind it.

He related how he had received many letters on my brother's behalf, from people of good position and high authority, but said, "Quite frankly, these letters meant little to me." He went on to say that he did receive one letter from Jamsie's brother, a third-year law student, which contained a very moving story.

The judge said that my letter basically explained all the circumstances that led up to the hijacking. It was a letter that I wrote from my heart and soul, stating that with our father's death and our mother's illness, my brother was not emotionally able to handle all the pain and suffering and turned to drugs as an escape. Since he had turned to drugs and had a drug problem, he had to support that habit and therefore committed the hijacking. I added that since Jamsie had been released from jail, he had begun to rehabilitate himself. He had stopped taking drugs, gotten a steady job, was helping to support our mother, and was going for therapy as an outpatient at Daytop. My letter concluded by saying that there really would be no redeeming social benefit to putting Jamsie in jail, and that he deserved a chance to continue his rehabilitation, maintain his job, and continue to help support our mom.

The judge said that he was very moved by my letter and decided to change his mind concerning Jamsie's sentence. Instead of giving him three years in jail, he gave him five years on probation. Was it possible that the few words I had placed on a piece of paper could radically change the entire future for my brother? According to the judge, the answer was—yes!

That one letter, written from my heart, had more positive impact on the entire Gelormino family than any other single incident in our lives. Not only did it change the direction of Jamsie's life, but it also changed the direction of many others. Please let me explain.

Obviously, Jamsie was overjoyed that he wasn't going to spend the next three years in jail. He did very well on probation, continuing the rehabilitation he had started before his sentencing. He eventually became a licensed ironworker and never went back on drugs. He went on to make peace with God and, like me, began to get a lot of joy from reading the Bible. "I didn't know what love was until I started reading the Bible," he once remarked. And he's still growing

✝ ✝ ✝ ✝ ✝ ✝ ✝ ✝ ✝ ✝ ✝ ✝ ✝ ✝ ✝ ✝ ✝

today. I wish him all the best as he continues to make his mark in society.

Anthony was so moved by my letter and Jamsie's release that, on that very same day, he decided to sign himself into Daytop. Daytop offered a special sixteen-month inpatient therapeutic drug rehabilitation program. And unlike the two previous times, when he had signed himself into these programs and shortly thereafter signed himself out, this time he made it through the entire program—graduating a totally new person. But this was just the beginning for Anthony. Two years after he finished the program, he became the director for Daytop in New York State.

For the next ten years at Daytop, Anthony was credited with the establishment of a powerful approach to drug rehabilitation. His creativity helped people not only get off drugs, but also earn their high school equivalency diplomas and even college degrees. His success became so well known that his name was submitted to the Vatican as a possible candidate to head up a special drug treatment program.

He met with the pope and was appointed to run Projectto Uomo, or Project Man. This was a major drug treatment program that was being patterned after many of the principles used by Daytop. For the next four years, Anthony lived in Rome with his wife and children in the pope's summer residence. As director, his job was to travel all over Europe and South America setting up drug treatment programs. It was truly unbelievable. Just fifteen years earlier, my brother was behind bars. Now he was meeting and interacting with some of the highest level public officials and businesspeople around the world. And the exciting thing was that his programs proved very successful.

After completing his work with Project Man, Anthony returned to the United States to become the director of the Promethean Institute in Milford, Pennsylvania. Major heads of drug treatment centers from around the country and the world would come to the Promethean Institute to be trained by my brother in the latest techniques on drug rehabilitation. Today, Anthony is still helping people through a very lucrative contract with a major worldwide computer company, helping to train their employees to become more motivated and more productive workers.

Gene continued on his steady course up the corporate ladder, and today is retired as an executive with AT&T. He is doing very well and has a wonderful wife and three grown children. The impact that my letter had on Gene was to make it possible for the four of us to get along really well with one another. While we were growing up, and before the time of Jamsie's hijacking, the four Gelormino brothers had a lot of differences with one another.

When I wrote the letter, I never dreamed that it would have such a powerful effect in our family. It really made me feel good to use my talents and abilities in a positive and constructive way, especially among my family. My mom was greatly relieved to have her son back home, and Mary Sansone was so proud to see me maturing as a young promising attorney even before I graduated from law school. I felt that God was looking down on me and smiling with approval at what I was able to accomplish through my letter.

Today, I am truly grateful for the wonderful relationship I have with each of my three brothers. Jamsie and I always got along well, even before he got heavily involved in drugs. Gene and I always seemed to be somewhat distant as we were growing up. I guess a lot had to do with our eight-year age difference. We didn't have many friends in common, and I always looked at Gene as the picture of responsibility and as a father figure. As far as Anthony was concerned, I was always afraid of his crazy ways and the bad reputation he had earned over the years. It has only been during the past ten years that I have learned to appreciate him and grown to love him.

There is a wonderful movie that I always enjoy watching called *It's a Wonderful Life*. The main character, James Bailey (played by James Stewart), is allowed to see what the world would be like if he had never been born. Because of his many years of unselfish love and devotion to the people of his small hometown of Bedford Falls, James has left behind a wonderful living legacy in the lives of many. Then, in an effort to stop him from committing suicide, an angel from heaven comes down and allows him to see how the history and lives of the people of Bedford Falls would have been different if he had never been born. We see the tragic life stories unfold in the scenario where James was never born, and appreciate his wonderfully positive impact on the lives of so many.

I have often imagined what life would have been like for the Gelormino family if I had never written my letter. Clearly, Jamsie would have been sent to prison and might not have been able to survive the debased and hard life that he surely would have encountered there. Seeing her youngest son sent away to prison certainly would have had a very negative effect on our mom—especially since she, for the first time in her life, was seeing Jamsie begin to do something quite positive with his life.

Since Anthony was at such a low point in his life, the added sorrow of seeing his youngest brother travel to a place he had just been released from might have been too much for him to handle. He might not have signed himself into drug rehabilitation. And the countless hundreds and even thousands of lives Anthony would touch in the many years to follow might have gone in much unhappier directions.

And if Jamsie had gone to prison, Anthony had continued to struggle, and my mom's fragile condition had gotten worse, I might not have been able to

✝ ✝ ✝ ✝ ✝ ✝ ✝ ✝ **✝** ✝ ✝ ✝ ✝ ✝ ✝ ✝ ✝

handle this added load of crushing pain, which might have resulted in my legal career ending before it ever got started. But, praise God, I did write the letter, and tragedy was averted.

Ever since this incident, I have seen the incredible power that good communication skills can play in the legal profession, as well as in every area of life. A well-written letter can be a powerful catalyst for change, and an emotionally charged summation before a jury can often decide a case. In my future legal dealings, I would prove these truths over and over again. This one letter put me in touch with one of the most important tools a lawyer can ever use—effective communication.

As I write this, my mind flashes back to an incident that happened when I was twelve years old. I was in our basement, building something made of wood. My dad came down and asked me what I was doing. I told him, "I am working diligently." He smiled and I asked him what he was smiling about. He said, "Because you used a big word." He then jokingly went on to add, "Maybe one day you'll become a lawyer and use your big words to help people!" After I wrote the letter that would free my brother, I felt that my dad's words proved to be quite prophetic, for in fact I did use big words to help someone else—Jamsie!

13 Legal Aid

It took twenty-five years of living to allow me to proudly boast that I was somebody. How I wished that my dad was here to celebrate the sense of accomplishment I was now experiencing. I was officially licensed to practice law in the most dynamic and exciting city in the world.

Like so many young lawyers, my eyes were wide open and I was all set to make our world a better, safer place to live in. I was an idealist in the sense that I wanted to help those who were from disadvantaged and troubled backgrounds like myself. And so it was only natural that I would start my legal career with the Legal Aid Society in my own backyard—Brooklyn, New York.

It's funny how impressions and memories seem to last so long. It seemed like only yesterday that a young Legal Aid lawyer had gone to bat for me when I was in danger of being sent to jail and couldn't afford a lawyer at the time. That was now eight years past. But the memory was still vivid in my mind. I was full of energy and ready to make my mark in the legal profession. My poverty background, my experiences with CIAO and Mary Sansone, my keen knowledge of the streets, and my love of the underdog had prepared me well to work with the kinds of clients a Legal Aid lawyer could expect to be assigned.

It is often thought that Legal Aid lawyers are inferior to those who are in private practice. Many allege that the reason why lawyers work for Legal Aid is because they can't land jobs with big corporations or start their own private practices. In some cases this is certainly true, but there are many other factors involved. For one, not all lawyers desire the extra pressures that private practice involves. Others enjoy the tremendous rewards that come from helping those who can't afford representation. Still others feel that Legal Aid offers a great training ground to launch a legal career.

In my case, all three of the above reasons served as motivators in helping me to choose where to launch my legal career. In addition, Legal Aid was the culmination of the dream I had been carrying for the last several years. With so many people helping me to get where I had now arrived, I felt compelled to return the favor to those who certainly could use any help they could get. Since Legal Aid caters to those people who are in trouble with the law and basically broke, I could certainly sympathize with them; I had traveled that road many times before.

For the next seven years, I put everything I had into being an advocate for the common man. By the time I left the Legal Aid Society, I had handled over 1,000 cases and had tried over thirty felony cases to completion. Looking back, I would not trade those years for anything. The lessons they taught me proved invaluable. Not only did I learn extremely important trial law skills, but my sense of compassion for people deepened with each and every case.

As a Legal Aid attorney, I had the opportunity to use all of the street smarts I had gained growing up in Brooklyn. I believe that the special ability I had to relate to juries was a direct result of the lessons I had learned growing up as a streetwise kid. It was such a great emotional high for me that the knowledge I had previously used to do harm and advance my own causes could now help those in deep need.

With each successful case, my confidence as an attorney was increasing. My acquittal rate was between 80 and 90 percent. And being a born fighter came in handy when I was trying difficult felony cases. A good trial lawyer must possess a broad range of skills, and must be part detective, part psychologist, part orator, part actor, and part politician. One of the most interesting cases I handled during my time at Legal Aid demonstrates how I used all of these skills. Also, after I relate this case, you will understand why the unexpected is something you come to live with in the world of law.

On the surface, the following armed robbery case should have been a fairly straightforward trial with an easy guilty verdict from the jury. But before all was said and done, over a full year would pass and the unexpected would occur.

While on their way to a meet, the Tilton High School track and football teams and several school cheerleaders were forcibly lined up against a wall, right before they were to board a bus. Two men proceeded to rob them of their valuables at gunpoint.

I was assigned to defend one of the two accused robbers, a young man named Joe Barnes. By now (this was my third year at Legal Aid), I had begun to earn something of a reputation as a sharp trial lawyer. Because of this, I was constantly given the most difficult cases. However, this particular case was more than just difficult; it was impossible!

During the trial, twenty-five young men and women who were robbed testified as eyewitnesses that my client and the co-defendant, Roger Flood, were the ones who had robbed them. All twenty-five pointed to these two defendants, stating that they were the ones who performed the stickup. For my part, I had no defense witnesses at all. And, to make matters worse, after consulting with the co-defendant's lawyer, I decided not to put the two accused men on the witness stand since they both had previous felony records as well as pending felony charges for other crimes.

With twenty-five eyewitnesses saying that my client was guilty and my client unable to defend himself, my only hope was to uncover inconsistencies in the testimony of the eyewitnesses through cross-examination. I felt that if I could do this, Joe Barnes might be able to get a reduced sentence or a plea bargain at best.

✝ ✝ ✝ ✝ ✝ ✝ ✝ ✝ ✝ **✝** ✝ ✝ ✝ ✝ ✝ ✝ ✝ ✝

It was a very grueling and long period of cross-examination, since I had to cross-examine to all twenty-five witnesses. The more I cross-examined them, the more I was able to bring out inconsistencies and contradictions in their testimonies. For example, one guy on the track team said that my client wore a blue shirt while one of the cheerleaders said it was brown. Another member of the track team said that the two accused robbers stood three feet away from them while one of them was holding a gun; a member of the football team said they were ten feet away. One thing that all twenty-five agreed on was that the co-defendant was the one who had the gun and Joe Barnes was the one who took the money and jewelry.

From the time this case commenced until the time of summation, six months had elapsed. Roger Flood's lawyer was an old-time attorney who had a drinking problem. He often came to court intoxicated and we agreed, partly because of his state and partly because of what a good job I was doing with the cross-examinations, that I should handle this entire phase of the trial.

While I had been able to generate a lot of inconsistencies through my cross-examination, it was another matter to convince the jury that my client should go free or serve only a minimum sentence. Throughout the entire trial, neither defendant took the stand. Thus, the entire six-month trial had come down to summation time.

I had by now given many summations and learned many techniques on how to move a jury and demonstrate the idea of reasonable doubt as an extremely important concept in deciding on a case. I had seen many cases where the balances were tipped because of the effectiveness or ineffectiveness of a summation. But before I was to deliver mine, the co-defendant's lawyer was called upon to deliver his.

I was feeling a little uneasy since for six months this old-time lawyer had played hardly any role in the trial. I was concerned that, because of his drinking problem and the small role he had played in the trial, he wouldn't do a very effective job in summation. And, of course, how the co-defendant came across would influence how Joe Barnes would be viewed. However, I was totally unprepared for what happened next. Well, Roger Flood wasn't too smart, and he decided that he wanted to sum up for himself, in place of his attorney. I guess he felt he could do a better job than his lawyer. In all my days of trial law, both before this trial and after, I have never seen this situation occur again.

Judge Sanford, who had viewed the entire proceedings, said that while this was extremely unusual, it was okay for Mr. Flood to proceed. With his entire future on the line, Roger Flood delivered the shortest and most ridiculous summation I have ever heard. His entire summation lasted all of five minutes. He basically said, "All the witnesses are lying because they said I had a gun in one hand and some said I took the money with my other hand. This is impossible because the kind of gun they say I used takes two hands to hold."

This statement was totally irrelevant and made no sense. Judge Sanford immediately asked the co-counsel if he wished to add anything to his client's summation. He apparently felt bad for Roger Flood and wanted Roger's lawyer to at least have a chance to add some legitimacy to his testimony. To my shock, Mr. Forbes said, "Your Honor, I have nothing to add. My client has covered everything."

It was now time for my summation. For the next three and a half hours, I delivered a very powerful and effective oration, bringing out the many inconsistencies and contradictions in the testimonies of the eyewitnesses. I was quite melodramatic and argued that there was reasonable doubt as to the guilt of my client. As a result of my persuasive arguments, the jury took three full days to deliberate the case. The final resolution was that there was none. The jury couldn't reach a verdict, and as a result a hung jury was all that six grueling months of trial could produce.

By now, Judge Sanford was very aggravated because this case had taken up so much of the court's time that other cases were getting backed up. After the hung jury, the judge came up to me and offered Joe a very good plea bargain. He offered a reduced sentence of two to four years for both this case and another pending felony case. Joe, however, had so much confidence in me that he decided not to take the plea bargain and requested another trial.

Judge Sanford was furious at the prospect of having to go through with the entire trial a second time. He asked my client to strongly reconsider taking the plea. I told the judge, "My client says he is innocent and wants another trial."

So back to court we went. Another group of twelve people was picked to serve on the jury, the twenty-five witnesses came back to court to testify, and Judge Sanford relived, day by day, what was by now a very distasteful trial.

By now, I knew everything there was to know about this case. After all, I had lived with it for six full months. This time, I decided to add something different to my defense. I decided that in order to give the jury a better visual sense of what really went on during the crime, we should all take a bus ride to the scene of the crime—Tilton High School. It was truly a strange sight to see myself, Mr. Forbes, Judge Sanford, the prosecuting attorney, and the twelve jurors travel by bus to Tilton High School. Judge Sanford was furious with the entire idea, but since it was proper he had to consent. It was a very uncomfortable trip for us in many ways, because the case was very lengthy and time consuming and it took up much of the judge's and court's time. Although I was right to make this request, he did not think that a mere Legal Aid lawyer would be so good, zealous, and aggressive and have such a great desire to do justice and to win. I wanted to protect all of my clients' constitutional rights under the due process clause of our state and federal constitutions. The value was to give the jury a firsthand and personal view of the details of the crime scene so they could have an exact picture in their minds and so I could do an even better cross-examination of all the witnesses, as any great trial lawyer would. Then, once again, the twenty-five witnesses were cross-examined and six more months passed. It was time for our second series of summations to commence.

Unfortunately, one slightly intoxicated Mr. Forbes decided that he too would add a different twist to his trial strategy. He decided to put the co-defendant, Roger Flood, on the stand. Based on Roger's previous five-minute speech, I was more than a little nervous at the prospect of what the DA might do to his credibility once he took the stand. My co-counsel assured me that he would prepare Roger well before he allowed him to take the stand, but I had strong reservations concerning both of them.

As the prosecuting attorney began to fire questions at Roger Flood, my fears became realities. The first question the DA asked Roger was, "Have you ever been convicted of a felony?" Roger said he never had. With that statement on record, the prosecutor pulled out three transcripts of three separate felony cases. All were for robbery with a gun, and all had his name, date of birth, and social security number on them. Yet Roger Flood continued to deny that this was him!

The DA next asked Roger Flood if he had ever met my client (Joe Barnes) before the robbery. Roger answered no. The prosecutor pulled out a lease showing that he and Joe had been roommates for six months. My heart was sinking faster than the *Titanic*. The co-defendant's credibility was going down the drain, and I knew that my client's credibility would suffer as a result.

Finally, the DA asked Roger why he had gone to the schoolyard that fateful day now over a year ago. He responded that the Tilton football and track teams had beaten his brother up so badly that his brother had spent six months in Kings County Hospital. Roger had gone there to try and settle the score, but not to rob anybody. Once again, the prosecuting attorney did his homework. He contacted Kings County Hospital and produced records showing that the co-defendant's brother had never been treated there.

During the second trial, all twenty-five of the witnesses said that the co-defendant had a black object in his hand that looked like a gun. Roger testified that he had a four-foot-long tree trunk wrapped in black tape and that all twenty-five mistakenly thought it was a gun.

During direct examination, the DA asked one of the witnesses if he had ever seen my client before the time of the robbery. He answered yes and explained that he had had him arrested on a previous occasion. I objected strongly and

✚ ✚ ✚ ✚ ✚ ✚ ✚ ✚ ✚ **✚** ✚ ✚ ✚ ✚ ✚ ✚ ✚ ✚

moved that this answer be stricken from the record on the grounds that my client did not testify and hadn't put his credibility in issue; therefore, this answer was improper and prejudicial. The judge denied my motion, and the testimony became part of the court record. Shortly thereafter, the trial moved on to summations.

Once again, Roger Flood gave another five-minute speech while I repeated my three-and-a-half-hour dramatic appeal for freedom. The jury took three full days to deliberate, but this time they came back with a guilty verdict for both defendants.

When it came time for sentencing, Roger Flood tried to attack the judge and had to be forcibly restrained. Judge Sanford gave him the maximum sentence: twelve and a half to twenty-five years for committing first-degree robbery. Joe Barnes was sentenced to a term of four to eight years. I felt that an appeal was strongly in order on the grounds that the judge allowed improper and prejudicial testimony to stay a part of the court record. Upon our appeal, the case was reversed and remanded back to the original judge, Judge Sanford, for a new trial. This time, instead of throwing a fit, the judge decided to take a more tactful approach to asking me to negotiate a plea settlement—he begged! I knew that the judge would do almost anything not to have to go on to a third trial. So I assembled both the judge and the DA and presented them with our plea.

The deal was as follows: I asked that Joe Barnes be charged with a lesser charge to which he would plead guilty. In return for his guilty plea, both this case and his other pending felony case would be combined into one sentence. The penalty for both would be a one-year jail sentence. Since he had not been able to post bail and had spent the last year in jail during the trials, the court should count this year already spent in jail toward his sentence. In essence, since he had already served one year, he would now be free to go.

Both the DA and the judge happily agreed to my terms, and that day Joe Barnes walked away a free man. Judge Sanford had mistakenly denied my motion and as a result my client, instead of having to spend at least another four years in jail, was able to walk away a free man (hopefully having learned a valuable lesson about how fortunate he was to escape so lightly considering the crime he had committed).

There were many other cases with strange twists and endings during my career at Legal Aid. Those years were a time of successfully trying many heavy felony cases. They were very rewarding years for me, and an era in my life when I had a lot of time to reflect on the American judicial system.

I saw firsthand the hard and depressing realities of crime at its lowest levels. I participated in a system that sometimes allowed dangerous criminals to go free

✟ ✟ ✟ ✟ ✟ ✟ ✟ ✟ ✟ ✟ ✟ ✟ ✟ ✟ ✟

because of some loophole in the law or improper courtroom procedure. As my trial skills grew, I saw how the quality of a defendant's lawyer and the depth of knowledge about how the human mind works (especially the jury's) play a major role on the outcome of a trial.

I also saw how a person's fate is often determined by their lawyer's negotiation skills during plea-bargaining situations. At times, I went home depressed at the things I saw in the courtroom; at other times, I went home rejoicing that my client was acquitted. But throughout it all, I always felt we have the best justice system around, even though it isn't perfect. Best of all, these were challenging times and I was glad that the legal profession was an integral part of my life.

While I was building a reputation as a skilled trial attorney, I was also gaining a reputation as a community activist. I continued to be active in CIAO and served on the Community Planning Board and various other community organizations. While I once was a part of the problem in South Brooklyn, now I was part of the solution. I had gained the admiration and respect of many former high school friends and members of my old gang. They respected my legal skills a lot but, more importantly to me, they respected me as a human being and a person who had a kind and compassionate heart. In my heart I had gone from a nobody to a somebody, a special person. How I thank God for His love and divine intervention on countless occasions in my life.

14 Deep Depression and Divine Intervention

After putting in my time at the Legal Aid Society, I felt it was time to move on with my legal career. Now don't get me wrong—I enjoyed my time at Legal Aid a great deal. However, as my success and reputation grew, so many people from my old neighborhood asked me to defend them that I felt it was time for a change.

By now, my popularity in South Brooklyn had reached an all-time high. I can't say that the chance to make a lot more money in private practice didn't also enter my mind. The money was certainly a factor. By now, my trial skills had greatly matured and my confidence in my abilities as a lawyer made me feel that private practice was the next logical step.

And so it was, with my hopes sky high, that I opened my own practice on Carroll Street between Third and Fourth Avenues. My original intent was to go into practice with a partner to help with the workload and ease the pressures of the transition from the relatively structured world at Legal Aid to the radically unstructured life that private practice would inevitably carry with it. Unfortunately, as soon as my partner and I opened our office, politics and a misunderstanding caused us to quickly part ways, and I was left in my little law office on Carroll Street to go it alone.

While I was going it alone at the law office, I was still living at home with my mom. By now everyone had moved out, and it was just me and my mom. Only two months had passed since I opened up my own practice, and I could see that my emotional well-being was beginning to falter. Fatigue, irritability, and intense feelings of loneliness were taking control of my thoughts. I felt as if I was lost and sinking under the waves of pressures both at work and at home.

Six months after I opened the doors of my practice, deep depression began to get a stranglehold on me. Looking back on this very dark emotional period of my life, the clear conclusion I have reached was that I was like an emotional time bomb awaiting detonation.

The years of intense pressure at Temple Law School and my constant striving to achieve had taken a lot out of me emotionally. The six-month period of intense study for the bar had added extra stress to my very tense emotional system. Adding to this was the difficulty of watching my mom's mental condition deteriorate before my eyes. I also believe that even though, on an outward level, I handled the stress well during my Legal Aid days, on a deeper subconscious level all of the above stresses were multiplying one on top of the other.

Having such a large workload from my new private practice, with people

constantly placing demands on my time from every direction, was just too much for me to handle. This vast load of cases and inner stresses, as my old friend Father Kenna said, caused me to just "come apart at the seams." It was now obvious to me that I was in way over my head. As hard as it was for me to admit it, I felt unfit to continue my own practice. My work was obviously suffering, and my depression was so deep that I had to swallow my pride and admit that I had no other option but to call up Legal Aid and see if they would take me back. I had stuck it out for eight long months on Carroll Street, but everything had now collapsed. My practice as well as my emotions had reached a low ebb. It was as if I had fallen into a very deep, very dark, black hole.

For several weeks I struggled with the idea of trying to stick it out in my own practice, but I thank God that I had the sense to realize that I was in a lot of mental trouble and to seek wise counsel. And I thank God that the one person I knew I could go to for help was my old friend, Father Donald Kenna. It was as if God had allowed me to reach this low point in my life to show me that no matter how hard we try, we can't make it alone in this world without the help of others and a firm reliance upon Him.

Throughout my entire life, God has always been very merciful to me and has always sent just the right person at just the right time to help me through the many challenges I have encountered and endured. His divine intervention, I firmly believe, is no accident. Once again, His choice of messenger was just the right one.

I first met Father Kenna when he came into the South Brooklyn area and was assigned to Saint Francis Xavier Church. Saint Francis had a mix of blacks, whites, Spanish, Italians, and Irish. At the time of his arrival, there were four priests in the parish. Father Kenna was responsible for starting a Spanish mass there and became very popular because of his tremendous love of people and concern for the community.

When he first arrived, there was an enormous amount of rioting occurring along Third and Fifth Avenues from Union Street all the way down to Atlantic Avenue. The rioting was between the Italians and the black and Spanish populations that were increasing and starting to infiltrate into our basically Italian and Irish neighborhood. The police and the politicians in the community wanted to do something about this because property values were decreasing and storekeepers were not making any money. However, there was so much hatred and violence in the hearts and souls of the young people that nobody was able to do anything about it.

The hostile hearts were even more intense among the rival gang leaders. Father Kenna felt that one of the reasons things had gotten out of hand was that no one had taken the time to sit down with the gang leaders and discuss how a

✟ ✟ ✟ ✟ ✟ ✟ ✟ ✟ ✟ ✟ ✟ ✟ ✟ ✟ ✟ ✟

solution to the fighting might come about. At this point, Father Kenna decided to take matters into his own hands. One night, in the middle of a riot, he just walked into it and got all the leaders of the gangs together. He brought them to the church, sat them down, and they started to have dialogue.

The gang meetings resulted in some very constructive and meaningful dialogue between the leaders of the various gangs. Eventually, a plan was made for lasting peace. It took a lot of effort and several years, but eventually a lasting and peaceful solution did come about. In my mind, Father Kenna was the key architect of this peace. He was willing to take the bull by the horns (walking into the middle of gang wars with knives and bullets flying) and sit the leaders down until a negotiated peace was finally worked out. Some may argue that peace would eventually have come about even without Donald Kenna, since people just grew out of the gangs. While this may be somewhat true, he clearly helped to accelerate this "growing out" period.

Father Kenna was a very decent priest who took an interest in me right from the start. Before coming to our parish, he served as a chaplain at Queens College in the early '60s. He was very unorthodox. He had left the rectory and gotten his own apartment. Because of his good track record as a priest, he asked the bishop if he could, as an experiment, leave the rectory and take on a full-time secular job so he would not have to be a burden and rely on the church. The bishop agreed, and Father Kenna took on a full-time position at Con Edison. Yet he was still a full-time priest! Not only that, but he was available to assist anyone, twenty-four hours a day, seven days a week. I guess the experiment really worked because, twenty years later, Father Kenna is still a full-time priest and still works at Con Edison (although because his work as a priest is now so demanding, he works only part-time at Con Edison).

Father Kenna is one of the few people I have ever met along with Mary Sansone that follows the Christian principle of being a servant to all. He was a strong believer in reading the Bible and placing its principles into practice. When he went to seminary, he sat under a great Scripture professor who was able to instill within the hearts of his students a great love for the Bible and knowledge of how to study its wonderful pages.

So, in my very depressed state of mind, I traveled to meet with this truly special man of God for help. Father Kenna worked with me during this deep depression. He gave me two very special pieces of advice that, coupled with another piece of advice I received from a counselor I had started to see, were destined to pull me through this truly difficult period of my life.

Father Kenna told me that if I really wanted to find peace, joy, and meaning in life and begin to break through the depression I was experiencing, I should begin to seriously read the Bible. I had told him that I had been reading the Bible

before, but was finding it very difficult to read while I was feeling depressed, and had during the past six months lost interest in picking it up. He stressed that how I felt was not that important, since the purpose of reading the Bible was to nourish and strengthen one's spirit more than one's emotions. Well, I took his advice to heart and began from that point on to read it very closely and very deeply. And since that time, I have never stopped reading the Bible and applying its timeless wisdom into every phase of my life. The Bible began to strengthen me in many ways, and I am so grateful for Father Kenna's suggestion to read it not with my emotions but with my heart.

The second suggestion that he made was that I should definitely quit private practice, at least for a while, and go back to Legal Aid, where the pressures on me were much less. While I felt this showed that I was somewhat of a failure, he was able to convince me that it was not a defeat but only a temporary setback. Father Kenna's love, concern, and wisdom made me feel special and helped me accept my decision to go back to work at Legal Aid.

How thankful I am to God for His great love for me. Throughout my life, I have faced one crisis after another. Each time a critical decision had to be made, God was so gracious that He sent a special messenger to bring me the needed love and wisdom to help me cope and make the right decisions. Even though I have made many mistakes on my journey through life, God has always been there to help point them out and teach me my frailties as a human being. Through all the trials of life, one lesson I have learned is that without a firm reliance and dependence upon God, we must struggle through life on our own. And I have seen over and over through my life's experiences that my best strength and efforts are just not good enough—but with God's help, we can overcome!

Another important step I took that helped me overcome my depression was to move out of my mother's home. I had started to see a professional counselor to help me cope with my depression, and he strongly suggested that it would be very beneficial for my emotional well-being if I severed the living arrangement I had with my mother and got an apartment by myself.

My mom's difficult emotional state had taken a tremendous toll on my own emotional well-being. While I loved my mom greatly, I felt that it might be better for the both of us for me to be on my own. I reasoned that if neither of us could cope very well with the pressures of life, then neither of us would be in a position to help one another. If being on my own helped me regain my emotional balance, I would be in a much better position to help my mom. So it was with much difficulty that I finally decided to move out.

Living at home had a big effect on my personal life, since it was difficult to entertain friends or have much of a social life. I did not have much privacy, either.

✝ ✝ ✝ ✝ ✝ ✝ ✝ ✝ ✝ ✝ ✝ ✝ ✝ ✝ ✝ ✝ ✝

Well, the combination of reading the Bible, going back to Legal Aid, and moving into my own apartment within a matter of six months had done the trick. These three prescriptions were just what the doctor ordered for Louis Gelormino. Each was aimed at a specific healing that I was desperately in need of.

First, the Bible was geared toward healing my inner spirit. Father Kenna knew that no matter how much my outward circumstances might change, if my inner spirit didn't receive nourishment I would never be able to truly cope with the pressures of life we all have to face. As a result, a steady diet of the Word of God became an important part of my spiritual healing.

Second, returning to Legal Aid was an essential part of the mental healing my weary mind was severely in need of. Being the ambitious and rambunctious person that I was, I jumped into private practice only to find myself eight months later in a very deep depression. While I was a good lawyer, I was just not prepared at this stage in my life to handle the tremendous pressures that private practice entails. While I had the technical knowledge needed to handle the caseload, I couldn't handle the million and one demands that people placed on me, especially with all the other emotional pressures I was under.

On this second tour of duty with the Legal Aid Society, I was assigned to work at a satellite office in Brooklyn, in Bedford Stuyvesant. This was a special program that Legal Aid had designed to help bring their lawyers into the local communities. I stayed in this office for two years, and I'm grateful that I did because the reduced caseload and pressure were just what I needed to help me regain my mental stability.

Finally, getting my own apartment was critical to my emotional healing. Coming home after a very stressful workday to a place of more mental instability was something I couldn't cope with. While I loved my mom, it was hard to deal with her difficult emotional state day in and day out. Since I was uncomfortable with having friends over, my social life was minimal. Perhaps if my spiritual and mental states of mind were stronger I might have been able to cope with my mom's illness, but this just wasn't the case. So when I moved out, thanks to the advice of my counselor Richard Falzone, the freedom from the constant pressures at home helped me greatly to establish a more peaceful home base where my mind could relax after a hard day on the job. In addition, my social life came to life, and having friends over—both male and female—brought the companionship I desperately needed and wanted. As a result, in just a few months' time, I began to live again.

Throughout this dark period of my life, I was still able to spend some time working with CIAO and several other community programs. Looking back I can see how important it was that I didn't abandon my social involvement completely while I was trying to piece my life back together again. During this

time, my involvement in these community programs did far more to help me than it did to help them. These community activities helped me feel important and needed, two things that were critical in my healing process. And when my depression had finally departed, I saw clearly that being a community activist was destined to be one of my callings in life. Until this very day, helping people has been not only one of my main desires in life, but it has also proven to be great therapy for my emotional well-being. When you help others you automatically receive, as a side benefit, help for yourself in many special ways.

✝ ✝ ✝ ✝ ✝ ✝ ✝ ✝ ✝ ✝ ✝ ✝ ✝ ✝ ✝ ✝

15 Love, Marriage, and the Lord

Some say that there is no such thing as love at first sight. But three months after I had finally put all of my depression behind me, I met my Cinderella—a delightful and beautiful young woman named Elaine.

I vividly remember this Thursday night when, at the last minute, I decided to attend a political fundraiser for Edward Koch. As I was sitting at my table I happened to glance across the hall, and my eyes couldn't help but focus on the face of a stunningly beautiful lady. I immediately said to myself, "I have to ask her to dance with me." I was a little concerned because she was with another guy whom I thought was probably her boyfriend. Fortunately, he turned out to be her brother-in-law.

Well, I knew what I wanted, so I got up from my chair and asked her if she would like to dance. It was a slow dance, and although I didn't do much talking with my new dance partner, while we were dancing I did a lot of dreaming about how I wished that this might be the first of many dances between the two of us. After we finally sat down and talked some more, I asked her very politely if I could have her phone number so I could call her in the future and take her out on a date. Needless to say, I was pleased when she smiled and gave me her home phone number.

Now that I moved out of my mother's apartment and was living in my own apartment for approximately the last three years, I was dating a number of women and had a busy social schedule. I was also in the habit of rating the young ladies that I met. Next to each girl in my little book, I would assign stars based on looks. When I entered Elaine's name in my book, I gave her four stars. While I seemed to make a very good impression with Elaine, I found out later that her dad, who was also present at the fundraiser, didn't think of me in a very positive way. In fact, he thought I might even be a gangster because of the dark pinstripe suit I wore that evening.

I let three weeks go by before I called Elaine up for a date. I thought that I would play it cool and didn't want to appear too anxious. However, Elaine later told me that she was very anxious, hoping I would call, and became concerned when I didn't for so long. It's amazing how we so often play mind games in order to try to project certain images of ourselves. I was very fortunate that she still was eager to go out with me. By the time our first date had drawn to a close, we both knew that there was a very special chemistry between the two of us.

Our first date was a truly romantic dinner at the Barge in Sheepshead Bay in Brooklyn. She was twenty-four and I was twenty-nine, and as we began to converse with each other we both knew that this was going to be the start of something special. As Elaine later commented to me, "It was like the meeting of two souls." We felt such an instant rapport and bond that we literally revealed our "souls" to one another on that very first date. We danced and exchanged stories about our lives, and the two of us experienced feelings that are just too hard to place into words.

What made this night so special was that as I shared my life story with Elaine, she began to open up and reveal that her background had many similarities to mine. Elaine looked toward me to give her the guidance and direction she was looking for. Meanwhile, I was looking for guidance and direction myself. We both were weak emotionally as a result of our backgrounds, and we were looking to each other for strength. Little by little, as we began to date more often, I crossed the other names out of my little black book until the only serious love of my life was Elaine.

Six months after we were going steady, I decided to take a trip with a couple of my male friends to Martinique to just unwind and have a good time. While I had a great time in Martinique, I didn't fully realize that I was putting a tremendous strain on my relationship with Elaine. After I returned, we were driving in my car and Elaine turned to me and in a very serious tone of voice said, "Louis, I'd like to know where the two of us stand and what your intentions are for this relationship." I guess I didn't understand that Elaine was very concerned that we had been going steady for the past six months, not knowing if our relationship was going to be just for fun or for good. She was in love with me and wanted some type of commitment that I wasn't ready to make.

I got very defensive and in a very unloving voice told her, "Don't pressure me." As soon as I spoke those three words, Elaine burst into tears. This was indeed a crisis point in our relationship. I knew right then and there that this was no time to be playing any emotional mind games. I knew in my heart that if I didn't make some type of commitment to Elaine, I would surely lose her. As I searched my heart, I clearly saw that I was deeply in love with Elaine and knew that I wasn't about to let her out of my life. My mind was racing as I looked for the right words to assure my precious love that she was the only person I wanted to be with. So even though I perhaps wasn't ready to make an immediate commitment to marriage, I told her that we would in the future strongly consider marriage.

From that point on, I knew that it was only a matter of time before we became man and wife. About one year passed from that eventful car ride to my thirtieth birthday—November 1, 1978, which just so happens to be All Saints' Day.

I always fashioned myself as somewhat of a romantic. So I told Elaine that I wanted to celebrate my birthday at the same place we had our first date—the Barge. She was excited and happy to return to the place where "our souls first

✟ ✟ ✟ ✟ ✟ ✟ ✟ ✟ ✟ ✟ ✟ ✟ ✟ ✟ ✟ ✟ ✟

met." Before our date, I told Elaine that I had to visit my cousin and pick up a gift that he had for my birthday. Our date was for 7 p.m., and Elaine had to wait until 7:30 for my arrival. She later revealed to me that she was starting to worry about what might have happened to me since I was always very punctual with her. But I finally did arrive, and off we went to the Barge. I wanted to surprise her for my birthday. I actually did not go to my cousin's but instead brought her a diamond engagement ring and wrapped it in a shirt box

While we were driving to the restaurant, Elaine began to open the gift box that my cousin had supposedly given to me. It was a pretty big box—the type you might wrap a sweater in. Elaine was all excited as she tore off the wrapping paper. As she opened the box she pulled apart a bunch of tissue paper and right in the middle of the tissue paper was a little square box. Her first response was, "He must have given you jewelry."

While she thought it a bit strange to use such a big box to wrap such a small gift, she nevertheless was anxious to see what my cousin had gotten me. As Elaine opened the little box, to her great surprise she saw a diamond ring sitting on a beautiful velvet platform. For a moment or two, she paused to try and comprehend the significance of this beautiful ring. All of a sudden it hit her that the ring was not for me but for her! I told her, "What better gift could I get myself on my birthday than to get engaged to the woman of my dreams?"

She was so excited that she started to cry for joy. By now we had just pulled into the Barge, and the valet parking attendant was looking to slug me because he saw how profusely Elaine was crying and thought I had hit her. I assured him that these tears were tears of joy and not sorrow. Both of us were so excited that we called about five people each, right from the front of the restaurant, to tell them the great news. I might add that in between those tears of joy, Elaine managed to say yes to my somewhat unorthodox marriage proposal.

It would be ten more months before we actually tied the knot. On September 15, 1979, Elaine and I were married at the Town House in Brooklyn, which was the same place where we first met at the fundraiser for Koch. It was truly a gala affair with over 450 people in attendance. In attendance were celebrities, old gang members, politicians, and of course Mary Sansone—the other lady of my life. And I was most excited to have Father Kenna officiate this both solemn and joyous occasion. By the time everybody had left, and all the envelopes that people had given us were put away, I finally took a moment to pause from all the excitement and just relax in the presence of my new and precious bride—Elaine Gelormino!

✝ ✝ ✝ ✝ ✝ ✝ ✝ ✝ ✝ ✝ ✝ ✝ ✝ ✝ ✝ ✝ ✝

16 The Birth of Louis Jr.

During Elaine's and my pregnancy, many strange and funny things happened to my body right up to our son's birth. Even after Louis's birth, I referred to it as "our" pregnancy because of various unusual facts. We both got morning sickness. Oddly enough, I got morning sickness much more than Elaine. Ever more interestingly, I noticed toward the end of the pregnancy that my breasts got bigger—that was a fact. I assumed that the morning sickness and the enlarged breasts were unusual for a man to experience during a woman's pregnancy. I was a little apprehensive about the actual birth. Elaine and I went to Lamaze classes to prepare for the birth. Since I had grown up in the streets and came out of gang warfare, I was quite confident that I would be ready, willing, and able to confront the birth of my son with grace, strength, and dignity.

I was quite surprised at what happened to me during the birth and immediately thereafter. I was told at the Lamaze class that it would take ten centimeters for the baby to pass through and actually come into this world and be born. When I took Elaine to the emergency room at the Lutheran Medical Center—calm, cool, and collected—I was quite confident that there would not be any problem going forward. I could not have been more wrong. They took Elaine to a room to put a hospital gown on her and prepare her for the birth of our son.

When I entered that room ten minutes after we were separated, everything had changed. Elaine was in obvious pain from the contractions and, although we had agreed to do natural childbirth, was demanding that she be given medication to dull the pain. We were taught in class that in between contractions I should do the breathing exercises with my wife and pat her face with a watered handkerchief. Since she was only two centimeters and we still had eight more centimeters to go, I was starting to feel the pressure in between contractions. I was at the sink putting water on my face instead of on my wife's. I knew I would not last until ten centimeters, so I prayed to the Lord that He would expedite the process so I could witness the birth. Miraculously, my wife went from two to nine centimeters in a matter of fifteen minutes. Her body went "psychedelic," or through a dramatic change. I called the doctor into the room shortly after I had demanded that he leave the room because he wanted to give my wife medication against our will. Thank God he was still available, and he came into the room and informed me that my wife was nine centimeters and we were going to have this baby ASAP. Naturally I was elated and excited. The good Lord had answered my prayers.

Elaine was taken into the delivery room, where she promptly gave birth to our beautiful baby boy. Then they took my wife and the baby to her room on

another floor in the hospital. No one informed me of this fact. I desperately and unsuccessfully searched for my wife and son on the floor where she had given birth. I thought they had been kidnapped. I had lost control and was exhausted. The security guards escorted me out of the hospital. I decided to go home and get some much-needed sleep. Oddly, I could not get out of bed for two days. I was incapacitated—I had given birth. I called Elaine at the hospital the next two days and told her I couldn't visit them until I had regained my strength and composure. I saw my beautiful wife and son on the third day after his birth, after I had recuperated.

At first we were like two lovebirds. We were so happy because even though we were opposites in a lot of ways, we felt that we could use our differences to help one another grow. Elaine was quiet and shy as a child, while I was just the opposite. Emotionally we both were quite fragile, but knew that love had a way of making things work. And our intense love for one another was something so precious that we couldn't wait to be together and express our feelings.

It was about a year after we were married that Elaine gave birth to Louis Michael Gelormino III. Our little Louis brought great joy into both of our lives, and I often tell people that he's "a real chip off the old block." Things seemed to be going well for us until about three to four years into our marriage. It was at this time when a host of difficulties began to attack the safe love nest we thought we had built for ourselves.

While I thought that we were doing all the right things, I had made one major miscalculation that nearly cost us our marriage. On the surface, and to an outsider, things appeared to be going great. We loved each other a great deal, we had a beautiful little boy, we had just bought a house, I had recently left Legal Aid and restarted my own private practice just six blocks from my new home, and financially things were going well. However pretty the outside picture might have looked, however, there was a terrible void within us, and even with all that we had going, we just couldn't seem to fill it.

My miscalculation was that I thought that we could combine our love and, though we were both weak in many ways, provide strength to one another out of that love. Well, after three to four years, this strategy began to break down. Unfortunately, the strength that we were looking for was not to be found from each other. By now, problems were beginning to surface both from within and outside of our marriage. Looking back, I still can't tell for sure if the problems Elaine and I were having with each other contributed to the difficulties outside our marriage, or if the problems outside our relationship caused those we were having in our relationship.

By now, I was not getting much satisfaction at the career I thought would bring real meaning into my life. Our new home was nice, but we were doing

✟ ✟ ✟ ✟ ✟ ✟ ✟ ✟ ✟ ✟ **✟** ✟ ✟ ✟ ✟ ✟ ✟ ✟ ✟ ✟

constant renovating that took up a great deal of time. In addition, the one thing that Elaine and I felt might be able to fill the void we were both feeling—our regular church attendance—was also not working. We were both devout Catholics, but somehow even going to church didn't seem to bring the peace and joy we wanted so much out of life.

Although I was reading my Bible a lot during this trying period in my life, somehow the words I read weren't getting into my spirit. One day as I was meditating on my entire life and present situation, I made a decision that was destined to change the course of my life forever. I knew that I was once again at a low point in my life, and I could feel the depression I had experienced four years earlier slowly creeping back into my life.

I had, for the first time in my life, made up my mind that I would seek God with all of my heart and do whatever He wanted me to do in my marriage, my job, everything! I didn't know exactly what to expect or what would happen, but I felt deep inside that this was going to be the answer—the real answer—I had so longed to find.

Well, I truly believe that God was looking down on me and when He saw the sincerity of my heart, He began to orchestrate the events that were destined to transform my life forever. I suffered from a bad back and decided to see our family chiropractor, Dr. Alfred Pecora. As he worked on my back, I began to tell him my whole life story and all the problems I was currently going through. He was a great listener and a man of great compassion. As I shared with him my new decision to seek the help of God with all of my heart, he shared with me how Jesus Christ had died on the cross in order to pay for my sins and reestablish my relationship and fellowship back to God.

I told Dr. Pecora that I was "searching for hope," and he said that Jesus Christ was the hope I was searching for. He suggested that I might like the services at the International Christian Center in Staten Island. He said it was a wonderful "spirit-filled" church that loved the Lord and could help me on my "search for hope." Well, I was very excited and decided to check it out!

While I was a regular churchgoer, I never really felt the deep joy and peace I thought church was supposed to give you. But my chiropractor had painted such a wonderful picture of this Staten Island church that I was really looking forward to the upcoming Sunday morning service.

The minute I stepped into the sanctuary, I knew that there was something very different about this place. I heard a wonderfully beautiful and tremendously anointed sister in the Lord, Nancy Liatsis, singing the hymn, "Great Is Thy Faithfulness." Nancy is now the praise and worship leader at the church where my wife and I regularly attend, New Hope Fellowship in Bay Ridge, Brooklyn. I vividly remember that Pastor Crandall preached a very powerful sermon and

✟ ✟ ✟ ✟ ✟ ✟ ✟ ✟ ✟ ✟ ✟ ✟ ✟ ✟ ✟ ✟ ✟

Nancy Liatsis sang with the voice of an angel. After the service was over, the pastor gave an altar call and asked if anyone wanted to accept Jesus Christ into their lives. Well, this time I knew that I wanted more than anything in my life to have a personal relationship with my God. I went up to the front of the church and told the Lord Jesus that I was truly sorry for all of the sins I had committed in my life and that I repented of them. I asked for His forgiveness and invited Him into my heart to become the Lord and master of my life.

Immediately by faith, the Holy Spirit came into my life and He at once made His abode within me and empowered me at the same time. It was like no other experience I had ever had before in my life. I felt such an emotional and spiritual freedom that mere words cannot describe it. I knew as I left church that day that my life would never be the same again. Jesus Christ was now in my heart, and a newfound freedom was living in my soul.

In the weeks and months to come, I began to attend the International Christian Center every week and to feed my soul by reading the Bible every day. I began to grow as a Christian by leaps and bounds, and now understood that the true strength that a person needs to cope with all the trials of life has to come from deep inside our heart and soul with the assistance of the Lord.

As soon as I came home from church that one very special Sunday, I told Elaine that I had found the Lord. I was so excited that I immediately shared with her what Jesus had done in my heart and soul. Of course I wanted her to come with me to my new Staten Island church so she, too, could find the Lord and experience all the wonderful things I had experienced. Each night I prayed that Elaine would decide to come, and one week later she told me that she wanted to see what this church was all about.

Elaine was going through her own struggles at the same time that I was searching for a way out of mine. She was truly reaching out to find a way out of her past that was keeping her in bondage and sorrow. I guess she was intrigued by the changes she saw me going through and felt that it was worth seeing why this church was so different from the churches she had attended in the past.

Later, when we spoke of her initial impressions of the church, she told me, "I knew that there was something that was simply tremendous. It was a truly beautiful and uplifting experience. That alone gave me hope and the desire to go back."

Elaine kept coming back to the church, and two months after that first visit she came forward when the invitation to accept Jesus Christ into her life was given. "It made a lot of sense," Elaine said, "since I needed someone who had strength." I have since learned that humans, although we may sincerely try to be good, are by nature emotionally weak, morally corrupt, and spiritually bankrupt without faith in Christ through the indwelling presence of God and the Holy Spirit.

✝ ✝ ✝ ✝ ✝ ✝ ✝ ✝ ✝ ✝ ✝ ✝ ✝ ✝ ✝ ✝

Both Elaine and I had found the secret of how to live a productive life, and that is not through our own ability but with the help and guidance of the Lord. As Jesus Christ became more and more a part of our lives, our ability to work through our marital problems became something we both were now confident we could do. At first we still struggled as we were learning to communicate with each other more effectively. But Jesus was slowly changing our entire internal makeup. We were now totally committed to bringing back those early romantic sparks that we had enjoyed as newlyweds. In order to heal the wounds that had begun to tear our relationship apart, both Elaine and I decided to go into Christian counseling together.

It was truly a wonderful experience as day by day our mutual faith in God began not only to heal the wounds we had inflicted on each other but also to form an even stronger bond of love than we had when we first were married. As Jesus became the center of our lives, our love for one another grew stronger and stronger. It was so exciting as we turned our lives over into the hands of the Lord, and He gave our lives back to us. Today our marriage is strong and vibrant, a testimony to the power of God and His tremendous healing power to restore that which was broken and seemingly beyond repair. This year, we will be celebrating our twenty-fifth wedding anniversary. Praise the Lord!

17 Private Practice and the Ministry of Law

It was not long after I came to know Jesus Christ as my Lord and Savior that God spoke to me about my law practice. I had been back in my own practice for only about a year when God told me that He wanted me to no longer have a practice of law but a "ministry of law."

While the focus of my practice would still be the same—helping people with legal problems—God wanted me to add the life transformation message of the Gospel, free of charge, as the opportunity arose. And as the weeks, months, and years went by, God was preparing many hearts to share not only their legal problems with me but their personal lives as well. As a result, the Lord literally opened hundreds of doors for me to help people with their spiritual issues along with their legal problems.

It was a wonderful experience ministering to my clients on both a professional as well as a spiritual level. The most exciting thing about my "ministry of law" was that most people were very receptive to the spiritual side of my assistance. Not only was I very successful in helping my clients win cases, but so many of them got really excited about spiritual matters. In fact, many became very interested in reading the Bible and gave their lives to the Lord Jesus Christ while I prayed with them in my office, and they became committed Christians.

As a result of this renewed interest in understanding the deeper workings of God, I spoke to a very dear friend of mine, Neal Emmino, about starting a Bible study in my office. I first met brother Neal at the International Christian Center. We became instant friends and spent many long hours discussing the things of God. Neal lived only four blocks away from us, and he became one of my closest friends. Well, we both prayed about it and decided that since the people we spoke to wanted a study very much, we would begin one.

For the next six months, Neal and I held a Bible study on Saturdays from 10 a.m. to 2 p.m. in my law office. At first about ten people came each week. Our study became so popular that within a very short period of time weekly attendance had grown to approximately thirty. After six months, Neal decided that because of the size of the class it might be better to hold it in his backyard. So for the next two years, we held our weekly studies in dear brother Neal's backyard.

Many of the people who attended these studies were clients of mine. Our studies got people involved in the practical side of Christianity by encouraging them to do outreach work to the needy within our city. One such program that several people from the study got involved with was working with Our Fathers

Ministry in Staten Island. We would go to Staten Island to distribute food and clothing to the homeless and share the love of Christ with many of them.

As time went by, my reputation for being a very professional as well as a good Christian lawyer began to spread throughout the entire city. People were coming from all five boroughs to have me represent them. And many of my clients were Christians. Though my caseload was heavy, I was able to handle things quite well, thanks to the help of the Lord and the valuable lessons I learned from the severe depression I had experienced several years previously. Not only did I have a lot of cases and clients, but their diversity was also quite overwhelming. I was handling criminal cases, real estate purchases, personal injuries, domestic law, and a host of other legal proceedings. I felt so excited each day as I kissed Elaine goodbye and headed out to the office. Work was not only challenging, but it was also fun and quite fulfilling and meaningful.

As busy as my private law practice was becoming, I had a full schedule of personal activities. Having pastors and Christian leaders as some of my clients gave me a broad exposure to the New York City Christian community. As I shared with many of these men how God was always with me and how He had brought me to where I was today, they often would invite me to speak at their churches and share my story. These speaking engagements took up a lot of time, but I loved sharing my testimony with them of how God spared my life and transformed me.

Despite all of the times I was either at work or speaking at a church, I still managed to find time to help out Mary Sansone and CIAO as well as get involved in a few political campaigns.

And, last but not least, I made it a high priority to spend as much time as possible with Elaine and Louis Jr. Sunday morning was always reserved for our trip to Staten Island and the International Christian Center. Going to church was an extremely important part of our weekly activities. We always felt something special as we attended the services as a family. Often, after church, I would take Elaine and our son to a restaurant to just laugh and share our love for one another, as well as talk about the week just gone by and the week ahead.

Elaine was always an important part of my life. One of the things I enjoyed the most about our marriage was the time we spent together each evening just talking, sharing, and enjoying each other's company. Elaine was a full-time mother and homemaker. All the extra little touches she added to our home made it a joy to return after work to our humble but wonderful little abode in Brooklyn. It's sad how our society often looks down on women who choose to forego a career in order to stay home, raise a family, and create a home. But being a full-time homemaker and mother is a rewarding career for many, and I thank the Lord that Elaine chose to stay at home. She is the love of my life, a great cook, my best friend, a fabulous mother, and my most precious gift from God.

And then there is my pride and joy—Louis Jr. As much as going to church was what Sunday was all about and going to work on Monday was something I looked forward to, Saturday was the day I made sure I reserved for spending quality time with my son. Even as a little five-year-old boy, Louis would eagerly wait for me to take him and his friends to the park to play. We did so many special things together that it's hard to say which activities Louis Jr. enjoyed the most. He loved to play baseball and basketball, go bowling, and spend an afternoon at the movies; and going to McDonald's was always a highlight for him and his friends. We were the best of pals. He was always a great joy to be with.

We were very close, and spending quality time with my son was a high priority in my life. Before bedtime we spent a short time together, and always closed the day with Louis Jr. saying his prayers. What a joy it was to kneel by my son as he gave thanks to God and prayed for the needs of our family and world.

As a lawyer, I have always striven to truly help people and not just make a good income. Taking pride in my work has been a hallmark of my practice, and showing compassion for my clients has been a key factor to building a successful practice. Without compassion, a lawyer is nothing more than a legal technician. But a lawyer who truly loves the people he represents is a special breed. I believe that the truly successful lawyers don't just win cases for their clients but also help them to learn to cope with the difficulties of life—whether they are spiritual, emotional, or legal matters. And I thank the Lord that in my small way, I have been able to help many of my clients beyond the bounds of the legal issues they came to me with.

One such case involved a young man named Earl Munson. Earl was a very decent twenty-two-year-old young man who held down a responsible job and lived with his mom in Brooklyn. One night in the summer of 1987, he decided to go out with a friend and made the mistake of using crack. This was the first time he had used it, and he just plain lost control. That night, he got himself arrested for the robbery of a supermarket and possession of a knife. This was the first time he had ever been arrested, and when I spoke to him about his case he told me he didn't remember what happened.

I was representing Earl on what is called an 18B assignment. Basically, an 18B assignment is where a lawyer at his option decides if he wants to represent a specific assigned case. If he chooses to do so, the court assigns a particular courtroom and case to him, which he is then bound to handle. This was one of the few times in my private practice when I ever volunteered for this type of an assignment.

I met Earl in the bullpen at 120 Schermerhorn Street, the criminal court building, and asked him what had happened. When he told me that he couldn't remember, I was quite skeptical. But after we spoke a little more, I began to believe him. I told him that I would get him out on a parole release on his own recognizance on one condition—that he come down to my office so we could discuss the case in more detail.

As we discussed the case in my office, I felt led to share with him that he needed Jesus Christ in his life to help him to cope with his problems. I told him how Jesus loved him and how He had died on the cross for his sins and the restoration of his fellowship back with God. As I shared this love of God with him, Earl broke down and told me how he was afraid he would wind up in jail and that he was truly sorry for what he had done. Earl, right in the middle of my office, gave his heart to Jesus and turned his problems over to God.

For the next three months, Earl faithfully attended our Bible study and began to truly grow spiritually. He was so excited about his new relationship with God that he shared his story with his family, and soon he was bringing his mother and aunt with him to Bible study.

Earl then decided to assign himself into Daytop to help him deal with his drug situation. During his time at Daytop, as luck (or, I believe, fate) would have it, the DA's office reduced his charge. As a result, the case was dismissed. With the help of the Lord and the caring people at Daytop, Earl finished his time at the center and went back to work. Today, he is active in his church and a very respected member of society.

On a different legal proceeding, I met a very distraught woman who came to my office asking me to handle a divorce she was initiating against her husband because he had repeatedly cheated on her. I sent her husband a letter stating that I was representing his wife, and asked him to come to my office so the three of us could discuss the whole issue.

Shortly thereafter, I found myself right in the middle of a very difficult discussion of marital strife. With the three of us in my office, Tom began to tell both me and his wife how he had met this girl a while back and had fallen in love with her. I could sense from his tone of voice and how he related to his wife that he still cared for her but was now torn between two lovers.

As we continued to discuss all the details and problems in their marriage, I began to share with both Tom and Jane how the Lord loved them very much and that if they both dedicated their lives to serving Jesus and making Him the center of their marriage, He would help them make the marriage work and give Jane the ability to forgive her husband for his unfaithfulness.

The three of us prayed right there in my office, and they promised me they would come to church that next Sunday. They were true to their word, and on the following Sunday both of them came to the International Christian Center.

✞ ✞ ✞ ✞ ✞ ✞ ✞ ✞ **✞** ✞ ✞ ✞ ✞ ✞ ✞ ✞ ✞

When the altar call was given, both Tom and Jane came to the front and gave their hearts to the Lord. Within a short time after this very touching moment, the two of them were happily reconciled to each other and both of them felt as if the Lord had performed a miracle in their lives—which He, indeed, had.

Over the years, I have been blessed to see several marriages, which I was asked to help legally separate, wonderfully restored through prayer and the words of wisdom the Lord has allowed me to share with those contemplating divorce. While most lawyers who are asked to handle divorces only look at dollars and cents, my main focus has always been restoration, even at the cost of losing a fee.

Throughout my career, my approach has always been to help my clients in whatever way I can. Offering my legal expertise is only one aspect of what I believe God wanted me to offer when He told me that I was to have a "ministry of law." Fifteen of my clients were lead to the lord while consulting with me on their legal cases and were "saved" for the work of the kingdom of God.

On one occasion I was sitting in a diner having lunch and relaxing by myself. When I looked up, I noticed a familiar face heading toward my table. Girard was a pretty rough customer who earned his livelihood, at least when I had known him several years earlier, as a purported hit man for the mob. I had defended Girard five years earlier while working for Legal Aid.

Girard really respected me not only as a lawyer but also as a person who had tremendous integrity. When he saw me sitting alone, he walked right over and said, "Hello, Mr. Gelormino. It's been a long time since we last saw each other. Do you mind if I sit and join you for a while?" After we had exchanged warm greetings, Girard began to tell me how he felt his life was in serious danger. He said that the FBI was after him and he felt very strongly that they were going to have him arrested for the suspected killing of a man several months ago. Girard was also very scared because the mob was also after him on a different matter. He basically told me that he was living a life of total fear and didn't know who he could turn to for help.

When he told me he didn't know where to go for help, I knew that God was opening a door. I knew just the right person he could rely upon, not only for help but also for comfort from all his fears.

"Girard," I said, "the FBI and the mob—we can talk about them later. Right now, I want to share something that I believe is the answer you are searching for. His name is Jesus." I spent the next ten minutes telling him that he needed to bring Jesus Christ into his life and turn the burdens of his heart over to Him. I explained that no matter what evils he might have done in the past, Jesus would forgive him if he truly repented and made Him the Lord of his life. After I shared the wonderful Gospel message with Girard, it was clear that he hadn't expected this type of conversation. He abruptly told me that he had some other business to attend to and left the diner in somewhat of a hurry.

Two days later I walked into my office, and when I looked down at my seat my eyes caught hold of a beautifully gift-wrapped box. The little card fastened to the top of the box read: "Thanks for everything—I really appreciated what you shared with me this past Tuesday—Girard." Inside the box was a beautiful shirt that I wore with great joy each time I took it off its hanger from my closet.

Sadly, two days after this event, Girard was found dead. He was slumped over the driver's wheel of a car by the roadside. Two bullet holes were found in his head. I have often wondered over the years if my message ever penetrated into his heart and if Girard turned his eternal life over to Jesus before those two bullets took his physical life. I pray that he did, and I look forward and hope to see him in heaven when I leave this earth.

One of the greatest blessings that I receive from time to time is when I get to represent an old friend from high school or the Little Gents. On one occasion one of my good friends from the Little Gents, Hornsey, came to my office in need of legal representation. When he first came into my office, he kept commenting that he couldn't believe I was a lawyer. He had known for a while that I was, but I guess not until he came to my office did it really sink in. After all, we had been good friends during my gang days, and he never dreamed I would go so far in life.

Hornsey had been recently served with divorce papers by his wife, and he asked if I would represent him. As with all divorce cases I handle, I tried to encourage reconciliation of the marriage, but in this case it was not to be. Hornsey shared with me how his life had not been very satisfying or happy since the days of the Little Gents, and I had the opportunity to share with him how God had watched over and guided me throughout all of the trials in my life. I also shared my conversion testimony and how Jesus had a wonderful plan for him if he would only invite Him into his heart. We prayed right there and Hornsey, with tears in his eyes, accepted Jesus Christ as Lord and Savior of his life.

A month later, I received a collect call from Florida. It was from Hornsey. To my great shock, he shared with me that he was now in a hospice, dying of AIDS, with very little time to live. He asked about our mutual old friend, Mary Sansone. He had been deeply touched by Mary's love many years earlier in the old storefront facility. When I told him she was doing fine, I could feel the happiness in his heart.

Hornsey told me how much he appreciated my prayers and sharing Jesus with him. We ended our conversation with a few words of love and Hornsey said, "When I leave this world, I hope to see you in heaven." One week later, Hornsey died and took up his new residence in heaven.

✝ ✝ ✝ ✝ ✝ ✝ ✝ ✝ ✝ ✝ ✝ ✝ ✝ ✝ ✝ ✝ ✝

As my practice continued to prosper, I noticed an amazing thing unfold. It seemed that the most desperate and needy people always came into my office around 6 p.m., which was the last case of the day for me. I was able to spend more time with them and not have to rush as I would have earlier in the day. God always made sure the timing was perfect.

Reflecting back on the many cases I have been involved with over the years, I am grateful for the opportunity to help many hurting people. And while spending extra time sharing things that went beyond the rule and spirit of the law may have cost me some financial rewards, I know that I am storing up "treasures in heaven." Helping my clients win their legal battles has been important to me, but I know that my talks with them about the Lord, in many cases, have had eternal consequences. I praise the Lord for the opportunity to serve Him through my vocation!

✝ ✝ ✝ ✝ ✝ ✝ ✝ ✝ ✝ ✝ ✝ ✝ ✝ ✝ ✝ ✝ ✝

18 The Bowery Mission

Whenever I feel a little down, I look around this whole wide world at all of the people who have so few material blessings and so much pain and suffering, and I begin to thank God for the many blessings He has bestowed upon me: my wife and precious son, my career, so many wonderful friends, and, yes, even the roof over my head.

Often in America, we take so many things for granted that we become spoiled and out of touch with a world that is very deeply hurting. In a land where the American dream is to own our own home, we forget that many thousands have long ago forgotten this dream ever existed. I am so grateful that we own our own home and that one day seven years ago I met a man who opened my eyes to the plight of the homeless in such a way that it literally transformed my heart into one of pure compassion toward this growing segment of hurting people, who literally are our neighbors.

While my family was attending the International Christian Center in Staten Island, we became friendly with an elder by the name of Mike Vecchio. One of the ministries he really enjoyed participating in was visiting the Bowery Mission in lower Manhattan and sharing the Gospel with the many homeless men who have been frequenting this lighthouse to the lost for many years. I knew of the Bowery Mission; it was well known for helping alcoholics and drug addicts piece back together their broken lives. One night, Neal Emmino and I went with Mike to see what this ministry was all about, and I saw firsthand the pitiful plight of this vast sea of seemingly hopeless men. And little did I imagine that this night would change my outlook on many major areas in my life forever.

Mike asked me to sit up at the altar with him while he was preaching to the men. After he spoke for about fifteen minutes, he asked me to come to the microphone and give my testimony of how I had come to Jesus and how He had turned my life around. As I spoke to the hundred or so men there, it turned into more of a sermon than a testimony. After twenty minutes of preaching, I sat down and watched the reaction of the men I had just ministered to.

While the homeless men were visibly moved by my words, so was the pastor of the mission, John Willoch, who happened to be present that evening. In fact, he was so impressed with my testimony and words of encouragement that he asked if I would like to come back on a regular basis. I, too, was very moved as I looked into the hopeless faces of these men. Little did I know that several years later I would still be sharing the Word of God on the second Tuesday of every month with literally thousands of down-and-out guys who managed to find their way to 227 Bowery.

The Bowery Mission is a Christ-centered mission that offers help to the homeless and hope for those trapped by alcohol and drugs. It has a wonderfully successful six-month program where men are literally transformed by the power of God. After the men clean up their substance addictions, they are given daily Bible study and work chores around the mission. They live at the mission, and when they complete the program they are placed in jobs both inside and outside the mission. I have often stated that as much as I love bringing words of hope and encouragement to the men, these guys really minister to me with their smiles and willingness to share their lives and hurts with me after my message. I tell people that I walk into the Bowery Mission, but I float out of it! The Bible says, "Blessed are those who bring good news" (Nahum 1:15).

Working with the men in the mission for approximately seven years has helped me to mature as a person a great deal. My compassion for the homeless is no longer expressed through passive neglect, but through actively helping them whenever and however I can. It has become my habit for the past several years that whenever I see a homeless person on the street, I go over and give them two things. First, I always reach into my pocket and give them two dollars. And second, I tell them that if they want to get help for their problems to go to the Bowery Mission in Manhattan. The two dollars is their subway fare, and I give them my card and a contact person to see at the Bowery Mission. Over the years, one of my greatest joys in life has been seeing these homeless men show up at the mission and have their lives totally turned around through the help of the caring staff at the mission and God.

Through the years, I have seen firsthand that the Bowery Mission's program works, and the staff truly cares for the men who pass through their doors. I have always said that if you know of a good formula for success, continue to use it.

To me, the Bowery Mission has always been a safe harbor for people who are hurting. One such person who credits this lighthouse on Bowery with saving his life is an old friend of mine from the Little Gents, Danny the Phantom. Like many men who ended up at the mission, Danny never intended to make this a stop on his travels through life.

Like so many men who came to the mission, Danny had things fairly well under control until a series of tragedies hit in a very short period of time. One night in deep desperation, I got a call from Danny, who told me why he was going to kill himself. He spoke tearfully about how his dad had just passed away and his mom had been put in a nursing home. Danny loved his mother, and they had lived together in the same apartment. To top this all off, Danny's brother had just committed suicide.

His whole world was crumbling before his eyes. Danny said he couldn't afford the rent now that his mother wasn't living with him, and that all of the pressures he was trying to cope with were just too much for him to handle. He said that life was no longer worth living and he was going to kill himself like his brother had just done.

Danny told me where he was staying, and I wasted no time in traveling to Coney Island to offer him the advice I had given to many desperate people over the past few years. I shared with Danny that the Bowery Mission was one place I was certain he could go to where caring people could show him that life was worth living. I called up the director of the mission and asked if I could bring Danny into their six-month program. Well, six months later turned out to be a very exciting day for my old friend Danny the Phantom. It was graduation day! Danny had successfully completed the program and started working at a good job on the outside as an assistant to an undertaker. He also became the head of the chapel at the Bowery Mission, and his whole attitude about life was changed radically.

Over the years, my excitement for the Bowery Mission has grown so much that I've gotten several people from our law office Bible study to come and share their testimonies and volunteer their time to help out at the mission. On other occasions, I was able to get Mary Sansone and CIAO interested in hooking up with the mission and doing joint projects together on reaching out to the homeless.

Ministering at the mission was like attending a graduate school on the hard facts of life. As I observed and spoke to the men month after month, my stereotype of what I expected the men to be like was totally shattered. Each man had his own unique story about why he was there. Some were professionals who had lost their jobs. Others couldn't cope with the death of a loved one. Many had had their wives leave them, taking their children along with them. Still others began to drink and take drugs because they had tried everything else in life and nothing seemed to bring them any peace or happiness. In every one of these cases, however, the one thing these men had in common was that they had given up all hope for a better life ahead.

I have learned that there is a very fine line between sanity and insanity, and between having a home and being homeless. I know, because if people like Mary Sansone and Father Kenna had not come on the scene at several points in my life, I don't know where I might be right now.

The more I preached at the mission, the more comfortable I became speaking in front of large audiences. As I shared the message of hope through Jesus Christ, many opportunities began to open up for me to speak at other churches and business groups around the city, especially among the black and Hispanic communities. Through these experiences, I began to see that all people are basically alike. Differences in ethnic origin or any other differences among people are merely on the surface. Within the hearts of all people run the same wants, desires, and needs. Under God, all men and women are created equal, all are equally special and deserving of our love and respect, and all are one and equal in Christ.

During my long association with the Bowery Mission, I have realized that one of the most beautiful things in life is not the acquisition of worldly wealth but the opportunity to help a soul in need. It's hard to describe the joy I receive when, after I deliver a message to the men, I mingle with them and shake as many hands as I can. I always wish them God's richest blessings and often spend time praying with them and listening to them pour out their hearts to me and tell of their great sadness and tragedies. A bond often forms that makes me feel very special inside.

I wish I could say that all the men who came through the doors of the Bowery Mission left renewed in body, mind, and spirit. Sadly, many of them left in the same shape they had come, refusing to accept our message of hope or the love of the staff. Sharing hope and offering help can only aid individuals who are willing to accept it.

It broke my heart to see many of these men refuse the love and kindness offered to them. For whatever reason, they chose to return to the streets and continue their hopeless journey to nowhere. My sincere prayer is that somehow the love we offered each one will one day speak to their hearts and draw them back onto the road of hope that always awaits them.

✟ ✟ ✟ ✟ ✟ ✟ ✟ ✟ ✟ ✟ ✟ ✟ ✟ ✟ ✟ ✟ ✟

19 Rose Gelormino

In March 1994, my dear mother Rose Gelormino was at the twilight of her four-year battle with breast cancer, which had now spread throughout her whole body. I was forty-six years old and wondered what my mother's legacy would be when she would pass and go home to the King of kings and Lord of lords, Jesus Christ. As a child, I remembered my mother suffering from acute paranoid schizophrenia and psychotic episodes. I was told by my brother Anthony that she was afflicted with this horrible illness when she was fifteen years old. Mom was then known affectionately as "Skippy" because of her sparkling personality and her obvious innate intelligence. She was a young teenage girl with great promise and potential ability. However, above all of that she was a young lady of great faith. I was told that she prayed in front of the picture of the sacred heart of Jesus every day for two hours. I wasn't born yet, but everyone who knew her all agreed that she loved life and above all she loved Jesus Christ and her family.

As a child and a young man, I do remember mom praying on her knees every day. Her father (my grandfather) bought a four-story brownstone located at 631 Carroll Street where I was raised as a baby. Unfortunately—and tragically for my mother—my grandfather had difficulty paying the mortgage, so he decided to put my mother to work in a sweets factory, where she worked continuously until she had a nervous breakdown. My father was a good man and unofficially a saint. He saw the beauty in my mother, fell in love, and married her. They had five children together—I was number four. Throughout their marriage my mother's condition worsened, and she was quite often taken away in a straitjacket to a mental hospital so she could get the treatment and later on medication that she needed. She had sustained this illness before medications were available. When she was taken away, the authorities would want to put her in a state-owned and -operated mental hospital. My father would take us to the houses of Aunt Rose and Aunt Anna, his loving sisters.

To say that my mother's illness was very sad and emotionally painful is putting it very mildly. The illness lasted for sixty years. My father spent his life savings to put my mother in a private hospital, Kings Park, where she had been hospitalized many years before when they were first married. He wanted to use that money to buy a house for his family in Long Island. However, it was not meant to be. Her illness was a primary reason for my brothers' drug addictions, and for my anger and self-hatred as a child, which motivated me to form the Little Gents when I was fourteen years old.

The amazing thing about my mother was not her illness or its negative effects on each member of our family, but in my mind it was her unwavering faith in Jesus, and her total belief and commitment to constant prayer, day in and day out, regardless of her condition. I remembered her love and strong faith in Jesus, and her constant and increasing prayer to Jesus while on her knees. The Scriptures say, "What the devil meant for evil God turned to good" (Genesis 5:20). The doctors had expected my mother to die of cancer in 1992, but she stubbornly survived. I couldn't understand her persistence since she always wanted to go "home" and be with the Lord Jesus before she had cancer. When I told her in February 1994 that she should and could go home now, her response was a shock and a surprise to me.

She informed me that she did not want to go home now. This baffled and troubled me. I told my brother Anthony that he should return from Italy, where he was working for the Pope, so he could see Mommy before she passed. When Anthony came home in March 1994, all five Gelormino children, together for the first time in approximately three years, went to visit my mother at the Madonna Residence, a Catholic nursing home. When we were together finally at my mom's bedside, I realized why she had not wanted to go home to Jesus. She wanted to see all of her children together one last time and wanted permission from all of us to pass and go home. Although my mother was barely conscious, her body totally wracked with cancer, she was aware of all of us together and smiled for joy. With the picture of the sacred heart of Jesus on the wall beside her bed, my mother smiled, took her last breath, and passed away in peace, knowing that her five children loved her dearly and had given her permission to return to her Lord and Savior and Maker, Jesus Christ.

At my mother's wake, the many visitors, friends, and relatives asked me how I felt. I told them that I felt happy and sad—happy that she was with the Lord and finally free of suffering after approximately sixty years, and sad because she was gone from this earth. The comfort I took was that I would definitely see her and my father again in heaven through faith in Jesus Christ. I am thoroughly convinced that my mother and her prayers for her children were a prelude to my Gent's Prayer that I prayed in the bullpen at the Criminal Court Building that night I was stabbed and received forty-eight stitches in my back. That prayer is, "Dear Lord Jesus, teach me to use my God-given talents and abilities in a constructive way and to maximize my effectiveness as a human being." That was the night when God spoke to me and told me I would become an attorney, and I did in addition to the many blessings that came about as a result of my mother's prayers. In May 2001, the Brooklyn Psychiatric Center honored my mother's name by establishing the Rose Gelormino STAR program, which provides quality counseling to children of District 15 schools in Brooklyn. Many young men and women have received essential and required assistance through this program in order to realize their potential as human beings. Praise the Lord!

✝ ✝ ✝ ✝ ✝ ✝ ✝ ✝ ✝ ✝ ✝ ✝ ✝ ✝ ✝ ✝ ✝ ✝

20 Appointment by Mayor Rudolph Giuliani and 9/11

When I recited my Gent's Prayer, I never ever imagined how powerful and awesome that prayer was and other prayers would be as I went on in life. After I was accepted into college and law school, received a full scholarship, and then became an attorney—a successful and distinguished private practitioner, a prosecutor for Kings County District Attorney's Office, and a Legal Aid attorney—I realized why my mother was a firm believer in prayer to Jesus Christ. When I started to read the Bible at the age of fourteen, and continued reading it throughout my life, it became quite evident to me that all things are possible through God. If our heart and intentions are correct and right, God will continuously do miraculous things in our lives.

I am married to a wonderful woman who is not only my wife but also a great friend. Elaine and I have a beautiful son who is a great blessing and a "dream." Yes, it is evident that God has answered my prayers and that I am living an abundant life. Yes, all of the promises in the Bible are true and are being answered. This was a powerful revelation to me. I needed to continue to be true to God's calling, grace, mercy, and kindness. It says in the Bible (Luke 7:47) that he who is forgiven much loves much! Yes, God had forgiven me much and, like my mother Rose, I love Him much.

After my mother's death in March 1994, I again prayed to the Lord to use me for his will in a mighty way. I was bold in my prayer life, but I knew that my God was awesome and I would continue to bring much good fruit from the sixty years of her suffering. I asked God to show me what he wanted of me after my mother died. I was still in my successful private practice, the ministry of law, when God clearly spoke to me and said, "Louis I want you to do for the New York City probationers what Mary Sansone and Honorable John Lindsay did for you and the Little Gents through the Neighborhood Youth Corps Program, specifically to provide life skills, vocational training, and employment for these probationers so that when they leave probation they will have a positive self-image, positive self-worth, a job or career path, and not have to commit crimes—particularly violent crimes—again."

This was a big mission, one that would call for me to leave my successful practice ministry of law, but my God, as I already knew, was an awesome God. How could this calling and vision be accomplished? The answer was found, as usual, in that wonderful human being and Christian, Mary Sansone. In the 1980s, Mary's son Ralph had formed an independent political organization called the New Era Democrats (NED). The young people in this group were friends and associates of Ralph Sansone as well as Mary and Zack Sansone. They were outstanding individuals and human beings like Dr. Daniel Ricciardi; Honorable Anthony Annucci; Salvatore Aspromonte, Esq.; Mr. Anthony Papa; Mr. Frank Mainiero, Esq.; Mr. Louis Cossentino; Mr. Joseph Erazo, Esq.; myself; and others. These were young activists who were involved in Honorable Mario Cuomo's successful campaign for governor of New York in 1980 and did not want to join or go to the political clubs at that time. That was the main reason why we were independent and nonpartisan. Only the candidates that clearly demonstrated integrity, character, excellence, compassion, intelligence, and consistency and who were best qualified did we support. I could speak volumes about the uniqueness, greatness, and beauty of Ralph, but there is not enough time and there are not enough words to write about this amazing human being. Suffice it to say that Ralph was an outstanding young man who had the best of his mother, "My Love" Mary Sansone, and his wonderful father, Zack. It was easy for me to get involved in NED because of Ralph's graciousness and my strong connection and affection for the whole Sansone family.

In 1989, a brash, young, accomplished, tough, brilliant, and dedicated U.S. attorney named Rudolph Giuliani had already made great achievements and left his mark as the U.S. attorney for the Eastern District. When Rudy decided to run for mayor of New York City in 1990, Mary, Zack, and the NED supported him wholeheartedly. Although Rudy ran a great race, he lost by a very slim margin. He again ran for mayor in 1993 and again Mary, Zack, and the NED supported him wholeheartedly. This time, Giuliani won and became the 107th mayor of the great city of New York.

When Giuliani was officially sworn in in 1994, he asked Mary to recommend some highly qualified individuals to serve with him in his administration. Time and history would prove that his administration was outstanding, including its response to the infamous September 11, 2001, attack by terrorists. I was in lower Manhattan when the attack occurred; I will speak about this experience shortly.

Because of my unique background and extensive experience spanning over twenty years in the criminal justice system as a defense attorney, private practitioner, assistant district attorney, and Legal Aid lawyer, my name was submitted by Mary Sansone in February 1994. After a series of difficult and extensive interviews by various blue-ribbon criminal justice committees, I was highly recommended. In 1994, Mayor Rudolph W. Giuliani bestowed upon me the great honor and privilege of serving in his administration as deputy commissioner of law, employment, and special programs of the New York City Department of Probation. Yes, the answer to my prayers to God after my mother's death were clearly answered. God and our great mayor quickly put

✝ ✝ ✝ ✝ ✝ ✝ ✝ ✝ ✝ ✝ ✝ ✝ ✝ ✝ ✝ ✝ ✝

me to work in my new position.

Approximately nine years later, God had answered my prayers and more than 7,000 NYC probationers were offered life skills, vocational training, and employment through the Nova Ancora Program, which was modeled on the Neighborhood Youth Corps Program. This program helped probationers who tested negative for drugs and placed them in vocational training and full-time jobs and careers without jeopardizing public safety and, above all, by rehabilitating the probationers.

The Nova Ancora initially met with a negative response within the department. However, as the program began to bear much good fruit, it was expanded with the support of four different commissioners and with the vital and essential help of Assistant Commissioner Eden Weiss. The Nova Ancora staff, the Nova Ancora Program, and its companion PEP (Pre-Employment Project, a life-skills class) were written up in various journals and newspapers. I followed the Lord's direction of doing for the drug-free and motivated probationers what Mary Sansone, CIAO, and Mayor John Lindsay had done for the Little Gents back in 1963. I will forever be grateful to Mayor Rudolph W. Giuliani and his administration, particularly Commissioner Honorable Raul Russi and of course Mary Sansone, for giving me the opportunity, honor, and privilege of doing God's will in helping the needy New York City probationers.

✝ ✝ ✝ ✝ ✝ ✝ ✝ ✝ ✝ **✝** ✝ ✝ ✝ ✝ ✝ ✝ ✝ ✝

21 September 11, 2001

Being a part of the Giuliani administration and God's work that I undertook for almost eight years was a definite blessing and satisfying work. However, nothing that I had done then or before in my life could have prepared me for what occurred on September 11, 2001, a day that will never be forgotten by anyone. It began like any other balmy, beautiful early September day. The sky was dark blue, and the clouds were few. I gathered with the rest of the NED brothers and sisters in Mary Sansone's basement to prepare for the primary Election Day work that was normally required by a very big and powerful political action group, as NED has become. John Orlando, our executive vice president of operations, was instructing the workers on what to do.

We had endorsed and actually campaigned for a number of various citywide and local candidates—those who were best qualified for the office they were running for, regardless of party label. I told Mary I was going to vote for our slate of candidates and that I would return. I did not intend to go to work that day. I was going to take an annual leave day.

After I voted, the hand of God once again played itself into my life. Instead of going back to Mary's basement, I inexplicably decided to take my city car and go to work. I went directly to work at approximately 7 a.m. and arrived at my designated parking spot in front of 33 Beaver Street in lower Manhattan, four blocks away from the Twin Towers. I didn't understand why I came to work that day. I had planned to take the day off, but I did not. At approximately 8:45 a.m. that day, however, I clearly understood why I had made a last-minute decision to come to work. I was reading the *Daily News* and drinking coffee in the office when my secretary came rushing into my office on the twenty third floor and told me that a small plane accidentally crashed into the World Trade Center. I went to my window and looked at the tower burning, wondering who was behind this sinister and evil act. Minutes later, as I was looking at Tower 1 burn from my window and listening to the news reports, I saw something that will forever be etched into my memory: a huge commercial passenger jet crashed at great speed into Tower 2. I felt that the worst was yet to come; only God knew what evil and destruction we, the citizens of the City of New York and in particular in the Twin Trade Centers and lower Manhattan, were about to face. It was now approximately 9:15 a.m.

The explosion was tremendous when the plane hit Tower 2. I went to the commissioner's office for instructions and orders. The commissioner instructed everyone to go to the lobby of the building and await further instructions. Tragically for the city leaders and uniformed services, the Office of Emergency Management (OEM) was located in the Twin Towers and was decimated when the terrorists crashed the planes into the towers. In the lobby of 33 Beaver Street, people were given masks and told to exit toward Battery Park near the water. While in the lobby I heard and felt a tremendous explosion. I was told that they blew up Wall Street, which was one block away. Never in my wildest dreams did I think that Tower 1 would collapse. Who could have ever imagined? I went out into the street and saw people covered with soot, dust, and debris. I went back to the lobby and took the elevator to the twenty third floor to inform the commissioner of my assessment.

As I was doing so, I heard and felt a second tremendous explosion, and debris hit the commissioner's window and shook the building. All hell was breaking loose and chaos was starting to rule. The commissioner and I went to the lobby of 33 Beaver Street, where the probation employees and other occupants of the building were wearing masks and awaiting instruction. They stood nervous but firm, strong and confident, as the soot, dust, and chemicals began to seep into the lobby through its closed doors. It became obvious that there was no concrete plan for exiting since OEM was gone and destroyed and only a few people at that time knew that the Twin Towers collapsed. An unforgettable and unimaginable nightmare was taking place. It was obvious that some people in the lobby of 33 Beaver Street were not physically, emotionally, or psychologically healthy, but these brave people remained in the lobby. Some seemed to be suffering reactions from the dust, soot, ash, and so on, manifesting obvious symptoms of bronchitis and asthma, including myself. As I surveyed the lobby, I saw two individuals who were obviously suffering. They both had serious health problems, and one of them was overweight, and because of their disabilities they came to work every day by way of access-a-ride, a bus that transported disabled individuals back and forth to work.

One of these people was Leta. Due to her medical condition, she could not walk far, and she was sitting in a chair in the lobby. After the first tower collapsed, a huge cloud of blackness began to engulf the building. I could barely see anything outside the building. Everyone who ran outside disappeared into the gray ash. I knew then that I must help Leta and the other individual, Anne. They were sitting in the lobby, holding filter masks and bottles of water. I went outside to the street. I saw chaos, fear, and everyone fleeing toward the water and the Brooklyn Bridge and most people covered with ash. It looked like the "first snow of winter," only not white but black ash. When I finally helped Leta and Anne to my ash-covered car, we made footprints on the ground in the soot, ash, and debris of the collapsed Twin Towers

It was obvious that Leta and Anne would not be able to get medical as-sistance, since all roads and bridges were closed, and chaos, panic, and confusion was ruling in the streets. I asked the commissioner if there was a plan; he said

✟ ✟ ✟ ✟ ✟ ✟ ✟ ✟ ✟ ✟ ✟ ✟ ✟ ✟ ✟ ✟ ✟

not at this time. He was bravely and valiantly trying to get a handle on the situation. I told him I had my plan, and it was to take these two sick and disabled individuals to my car that and bring them to safety, somewhere they could get medical attention. He said I would not be able to do so since the bridges and tunnels were closed. I instantly responded that I was from South Brooklyn and that I would find a way. He wished me God speed.

When we got to my car, it was totally covered with dust, ash, soot, and debris. I didn't think it would start. It was a task helping Anne and Leta into the car, but we all managed to get in. At the last minute, my secretary came as well. Miraculously, the car started and I cleared the windshield so I would be able to see where I was going.

I was praying to the Lord that I would manage to get to the Brooklyn Bridge and do so in a manner that I would not hit anyone, since there were thousands of people running in all directions in panic and shock. I proceeded slowly toward the Brooklyn Bridge, which was approximately seven blocks away. When I miraculously made it to the bridge, a police officer told me that I could not possibly pass over since the bridge was closed and thousands of people were crossing on foot from Manhattan to Brooklyn. I was told to go to the Manhattan Bridge. I truthfully didn't think we would make it to the Manhattan Bridge, which was another six or seven blocks away. I prayed and proceeded on. The scene on the street was surreal, with everyone attempting to leave the city by the bridges. Naturally, most were frightened, shocked, and horrified,

I said another prayer and headed slowly to the Manhattan Bridge. Truthfully, I do not remember how I managed to drive the car through the crowded and chaotic streets. I did make it to the Manhattan Bridge, which was closed and again mobbed with people exiting on foot. Another police officer told me that I could not cross. This time we would not be denied. Leta and Anne were in obvious need of medical assistance. I showed my deputy commissioner badge and told the officer that it was an emergency, and probably a matter of life and death. He said that he would make a way for us to get over the bridge. Going over the bridge I was cursing, very angry that those terrorist bastards attacked our city, destroying the Twin Towers and the human beings—some of them my friends—who were working in those buildings. The unimaginable was being processed in my mind.

As we crossed the bridge, I remembered that my son Louis had gone to his school, NYC New York University, that day and was somewhere in the city. I decided that once I got Leta, Anne, and my secretary to safety, I would return somehow and get my son. I got Anne to her house on 15th Avenue in Boro Park Brooklyn. My adrenaline was flowing, but I was becoming fatigued. After dropping Anne off, I realized that I needed to go to the men's room. So,

✝ ✝ ✝ ✝ ✝ ✝ ✝ ✝ ✝ ✝ ✝ ✝ ✝ ✝ ✝ ✝ ✝

naturally, I went to Mary Sansone's famous basement, which was approximately ten blocks away. We pressed on in my pile of dust, ash, and so on, on wheels and made it to Mary's house. I asked Leta and my secretary to wait in the car.

When I went down to Mary's basement, I had forgotten that it was a Democratic and Republican Primary day. As I descended the stairs to Mary's basement, I received a hero's welcome from all my NED brothers and sisters and Mary, who was working on the campaign.

I went to the men's room and told everyone to look at the condition of my car as I was about to continue my adventure and take Leta and my secretary to their homes. A reporter from Hoboken was there and asked where I had come from. I said to her, "What kind of reporter are you?" She had the audacity to ask me to drop her off at Shore Road in Brooklyn. I don't know why, but I told her to get into the car with Leta and my secretary. I took Leta home, and my secretary spent that night at Leta's place since she lived in the Bronx and I had no way of getting her to the Bronx on the morning of 9/11. I took the reporter to Shore Road, and I called my wife. I thanked God when she informed me that our son Louis was okay and was walking home.

I was completely exhausted and angry. I drove my car still covered with dust, ash, and debris to Bay Parkway and Shore Parkway. After parking the car, I took a long walk by the water to the Verrazano Bridge. I will never forget the tremendous smoke and smell coming from the tragic site of the destroyed Twin Towers, and the wind blowing that smoke and smell into the blue sky. As I walked near the Verrazano Bridge, I prayed to the Lord for peace, courage, strength, and faith. Yes, 9/11 is a day I and all New Yorkers and Americans will never forget.

✝ ✝ ✝ ✝ ✝ ✝ ✝ ✝ ✝ **✝** ✝ ✝ ✝ ✝ ✝ ✝ ✝ ✝

22 The Promises and Challenges of 2002

The rest of 2001 was hectic and busy. Not only did I, my family, Mary Sansone, and the NED have to continue to work hard for the election of our endorsed candidates of choice (particularly Honorable Michael Bloomberg, the compassionate and very successful philanthropist, businessman, and great leader, as well as other candidates for various political office), but we also had to contend with the fallout and traumatic effects of 9/11 in our daily personal and professional lives. It seemed that these circumstances called for constant and continuous prayer for strength, courage, wisdom, faith, and compassion for our political elected leaders more than ever. The churches naturally took the lead in this essential and vital area. Most people were looking for answers through God and their religion. I sought and found many answers, as usual, in the Bible.

The end of 2001 had a bright and positive ending. It was a happy and sad time—politically happy because our candidate for mayor had pulled off an amazing and stunning upset. Michael Bloomberg had become the 108th mayor of New York City. It was also a sad time because our great mayor and a person I had come to love and respect while serving him for eight year, Honorable Rudolph W. Giuliani, was leaving office. I would miss Rudy but looked forward to meeting new challenges under our new mayor, who I knew would prove to be a great mayor as well.

Elaine and I, along with our dear friends Commissioner Matt Daus and his lovely wife Charisse, spent New Year's Eve laughing, dancing, and celebrating at Mayor Giuliani's New Year's Eve party in Times Square. We watched the ball drop like most New Yorkers, and we were grateful and thankful for our many God-given blessings. Elaine and I had been married for twenty-two years, and that was one of my greatest blessings. I thanked the Lord for my existence and faith, and for being used by Him throughout my life. The ball finally dropped while we were in the streets of Times Square and the year of 2001 had officially come to an end.

I decided to start the new year by taking a long-overdue vacation with my son, Louis, who was going into his last semester at The Stern Business School at NYU. Louis was ready to graduate with honors and enter the wonderful, challenging, and interesting world of work in business and finance. We went to the Bahamas for one week and our vacation was enjoyable, fun, special, and—as my son would say—"seamless." It was overdue and physically necessary. The year was off to a great start and much excitement with a new city administration and many new, young public officials. The face of city politics was changing, as it should. The sun was certainly shining, and God's favor was definitely on me and my family. However, little did I know that the dark clouds of trouble would soon begin to present themselves to our family.

In February 2002, my beloved wife and best friend was diagnosed with breast cancer. Her mother and her sister had been victims of this disease, and it now was Elaine's turn, with me beside her, to confront this potentially deadly disease. The diagnosis by two top surgeons was that Elaine had two separate and distinct types of cancers, one of which was traveling rapidly. After seeking various opinions, it was obvious that she would have to undergo a mastectomy—the removal of one breast. I couldn't help but wonder how my wife would deal with this daunting, difficult emotional challenge, both spiritually and attitude-wise. I would certainly pray and request that the pastor as well as the brothers and sisters at the New Hope Church and others pray for her. But the true courage, faith, and strength would have to come from within my wife.

Elaine was scheduled for surgery in March 2003 on a Wednesday. We went to our usual Sunday service at New Hope Church to receive God's grace, kindness, mercy, and faith, and the strength that we sought for the coming surgery and recovery thereafter. After the service our pastor, Roger McPhail, asked the congregation to come up to the altar for prayer. Elaine and I went in response to the invitation. What happened next was divine, supernatural, and beautiful. The pastor placed his hands on her head for prayer, and my wife became unconscious and slowly fell to the floor. She laid there for approximately twenty minutes while the pastor, myself, and others prayed over her. Elaine had been what we called "slain in the spirit" by the Holy Spirit. After Elaine awoke, we went for lunch and I asked her what had occurred. She told me while the pastor was praying for her, she saw Jesus standing in front of her, and then her body went into his body. She asked me what it meant. I told her either that she was healed or that the Lord was offering Himself to her and that He would bring her through the surgery stronger than she had ever been.

Elaine told me that the message she received was that this was not about her body or the cancer but about the "gift of Jesus and faith." That was her message going into the surgery on that Wednesday in March, and that definitely was her loud-and-clear message coming out of the surgery and going forward. God had answered my prayers again big time, as He had always done in the past. Elaine became a spiritual giant and was healthy physically and mentally—used by God to encourage and bless others, including me and our son. "What the devil meant evil God turns to good," and, according to Romans 8:28, "God causes all things to work together for good for those who love God and are called according to his purpose." As it states in Romans 8:32, we are more than conquerors through Christ. Elaine is certainly more than a conqueror through

✝ ✝ ✝ ✝ ✝ ✝ ✝ ✝ ✝ ✝ ✝ ✝ ✝ ✝ ✝ ✝ ✝

Christ. I was once again humbled by the love, mercy, grace, and kindness of my Lord and Savior Jesus Christ.

After Elaine's surgery, the year 2002 saw many beautiful and wonderful events for my family. The most special was for Elaine, I, and other loved ones to witness the momentous occasion of our son's graduation with distinction from the NYU Stern Business School in May. Louis immediately received a good position in a distinguished company in the financial services area. He is and will always be a success and blessed.

Elaine and I finished the year on a cruise with some dear friends. We certainly finished the year that started with promise and potential with more promise and potential. Praise the Lord in spite of the cancer.

✝ ✝ ✝ ✝ ✝ ✝ ✝ ✝ ✝ **✝** ✝ ✝ ✝ ✝ ✝ ✝ ✝ ✝

23 The Aunts

As I look back on my life, the years from age one through twelve are very blurry. Mom's recurring violent sickness caused a great deal of emotional, psychological, spiritual, and physical upheaval for the five Gelormino children, and I am sure for my wonderful and loving father as well. When Mom had her lucid periods when the sickness was not severely altering her personality and being, I could see and feel the innate kindness, caring, love, and beauty in her and understand why my father had married and loved her. However, those lucid periods seem to be few and far between. When my mother's sickness became severe, as it often did in the cycle of her illness, we would have to take her away, usually by force of the authorities, to the state mental hospital.

During those periods when Mom was not at home, we would experience the great blessing and comfort of the love and kindness of my Aunts Anna and Rose. They were my father's sisters and lived in Brooklyn. I would usually go with my Aunt Anna, who lived on Tenth Street and Sixth Street in Brooklyn. My younger brother Jamsie was taken along with me sometimes to my Aunt Rose's home. Both my aunts were married with their own families. Both had their own homes and always had a room available for Jamsie and me. We were always treated as one of their own children. We were sincerely welcomed, loved, and cared for. It usually was a fun time because my cousins had happy and "normal" childhoods. They would play ball, go fishing or scuba diving, and enjoy themselves. We always easily got along with our cousins and their friends and girlfriends as well. This was good for our sense of self-worth and self-image. My aunts and my cousins were a joy and blessing because deep down inside, we knew that they loved my father and mother and us. Unfortunately, these stays with my aunts were short and temporary. My mother would be treated at the state hospital, and then she would return home and the cycle would continue. As a child, I never felt that 631 Carroll Street was my true home because the emotional and psychological trauma and continual haunting shadow of my mother's sickness resided with us twenty-four hours a day, seven days a week. I loved my mother, but I hated her sickness. My Aunt Rose, Aunt Anna, and cousins made our childhood tolerable and sometimes lovely and wonderful because they provided the love that Jamsie and I needed.

The necessary love of a mother was unfortunately was often missing on the fourth floor at 631 Carroll Street. After I was thirteen years old, Mary Sansone as well as my aunts began to give me the love that I desperately needed and craved. The many girlfriends of my youth were not qualified to give me the love I required and needed. However, as I look back, the true love of God—which is always present—was manifested through my aunts, my mother, Mary Sansone, my wife Elaine, Father Kenna, and others throughout my life.

It states in 1 Corinthians (Chapter 13) that love never fails and love conquers. Yes, the love of God as manifested through my aunts, my mother, Mary Sansone, Father Kenna, my wife, and others truly never failed, and certainly conquered all. Praise the Lord. God is good until the end.

✝ ✝ ✝ ✝ ✝ ✝ ✝ ✝ ✝ ✝ ✝ ✝ ✝ ✝ ✝ ✝ ✝

24 My DA Days

Even though things were going fairly well with my law practice, I had developed a sense of restlessness with the day-to-day affairs my office was handling. As I reviewed my career to date, I felt that there were new challenges I wanted to take on in the legal profession.

I was considered by my peers to be a very successful defense attorney. However, for the past several years I had begun to think seriously about trying my hand at the other side of the fence. I had always wondered what it would be like to be a prosecuting attorney. With this thought in mind, I came home one day and discussed with Elaine my desire to temporarily leave my own practice and go to work for the Brooklyn district attorney's office. When I told Elaine why I wanted to become an assistant DA, and that it would also prove a great place to sharpen my trial skills, she said that she would support my decision if this was what I really wanted to do.

While I knew that this decision would be a good career move, I felt a little uneasy since it meant I would have to, at least for a while, sever my ties with the many clients I had come to work and care for over the years. I had developed a real love for and rapport with many of them. As much as I was saddened to have to leave them, many told me that they would miss me also. Despite the emotional separation pains I knew I would experience, I felt that my career would benefit from this change in legal venue. And so it was that by the end of 1989, I made up my mind that my new office would no longer be in Bensonhurst but at the Brooklyn DA's office. I promptly turned my office over to a friend of mine, and while he moved into my cozy little office on 73rd Street I moved into the hectic and very different world of the Brooklyn district attorney's downtown office, located at 210 Joralemon Street. This office has a great reputation and the highest prestige.

My transition was not as easy as I thought it would be, but it was very exciting. The reason why I was so excited about my new job was because of the special new unit I was thrust into called the Trial Cadre. My supervisor knew of my excellent trial skills and felt that he could best utilize my talents by placing me into this special new unit that was just formed three months prior to my arrival at the DA's office.

Basically, the Trial Cadre consisted of from eight to ten elite prosecutors whose job was to help the state prosecute persistent and violent felony offenders. The Trial Cadre was the most prestigious bureau in the DA's office, and I felt honored that they would pick me to be a part of this special team. It was so exciting to be part of this team, and the cases would certainly be challenging and interesting.

While I only served in the DA's office for a little more than a year, I am grateful for the cases I handled and the skills I was able to fine-tune. By the time I left, I had handled five cases. Each case involved a homicide, and every one was a successful prosecution. In two of these cases I tried it to a verdict, while in the three others we reached a successful plea before they went to trial.

The reason the Trial Cadre was formed was to establish a special unit that could investigate and prosecute the high-profile cases that the DA's office often handled. Normally, DAs have to handle several cases at a time. As a result of this, they can't be as effective as they would be if they were able to channel time and energies into a single case at a time. The Trial Cadre was established to remedy this situation. In order to get a solid team behind a case, the DA's office would assign two assistant DAs, two experienced trial attorneys, and an appellate attorney from the Trial Cadre team to handle specific major cases.

During my tenure at the DA's office, I was establishing a solid reputation for myself. Unfortunately, our new elite unit was coming under some pressure because we were not always getting the homicide convictions that everyone was unreasonably expecting. However, one case in particular was about to come the way of the Trial Cadre that was destined to give our group the credibility and respect that we knew we merited and deserved, as well as give me new confidence in my legal abilities.

As a member of the Trial Cadre, the most difficult cases often came my way. It always seems that the more difficult the case, the greater the challenge and the more I put into it. And so I accepted this new challenge: *The People vs. Benjamin (Bobo) Johnson*. It was not even mine to start with. Another assistant DA decided to abandon the case and, as fate would have it, it fell onto me. With no witnesses to be found and only a little more than two months to trial, I had my work cut out for me. There was one thing in my favor, however, and that was a burning desire for justice to be served. It was just nine weeks before Bobo Johnson was to stand trial for murder, and little did I imagine that Jesus Christ was going to be the key to solving a case that nobody wanted to handle. I was assigned a young, talented, and wonderful trial lawyer and soon-to-be good friend, Mr. Neal Doherty, Esq., to second seat with me on this difficult case.

Bobo was no stranger to crime, as thirteen-year-old Jason Gordon had found out. It was just another day for the crowd that always gathered at Herkimer Park in Bedford Stuyvesant. Young Jason's only mistake was being in the wrong place at the wrong time. While riding his bike in the park, little did he know that his gold chain was going to make him just another statistic in a seemingly endless wave of violence in America.

As the record would later show, twenty-four-year-old Johnson approached Jason and demanded he turn over his gold chain. When Jason refused, Bobo left, only to return ten minutes later with a gun. He shot young Jason in the heart, took the chain, and fled.

In a crowded basketball court on a quiet, ordinary weekday afternoon, the all-too-familiar sound of gunshots and sometimes death shattered the silence. Once again, the justice system was asked to come to the aid of a situation that at best could bring about justice but sadly often offer little hope in prevention.

As I read through all the case information, it became apparent that this was going to be a murder mystery with a good news/bad news twist. First, the good news! Ten months previously, Bobo was indicted by a grand jury based on the testimony of Benny Styles, the one and only eyewitness who saw the whole thing from start to finish. The bad news, however, was that Benny became so scared of Bobo's reputation that shortly after his grand jury testimony he vanished from the scene, fleeing New York State—whereabouts unknown!

If being in a gang had taught me one thing, it would have to be street smarts. I learned early in life that the streets are rich with information if you only know where and how to look for it. With the clock against me, I had to find a witness or else watch a dangerous murderer find his way back onto the streets.

I immediately began to conduct my own investigation by returning to the scene of the crime (why not—all good detective shows always seem to do it). I had reasoned that there had to be other witnesses to the murder since it happened in broad daylight right in the middle of a crowded park.

One name was listed on the police report that struck my attention. It was that of Junior Thomas. As I was to soon find out—not from the police record, but from my own detective work—this eight-year-old boy had, like Benny, been an eyewitness to the whole crime. Unfortunately, young Junior was only listed as a name on the report, with no story behind it.

But the story of Junior Thomas is one of great courage and conviction. As I was looking for witnesses in Herkimer Park, Junior Thomas came up to me, somehow knowing I was either a detective or from the DA's office, and began to relate to me that he was a friend of the deceased Jason Gordon, and had witnessed the entire vicious murder. He further told me that one year earlier he had related the same story to the police, but that his grandmother absolutely refused to let him cooperate with the police, fearing for his life.

That name, Bobo, seemed to evoke fear in the hearts of so many. As I recalled from my younger days in the gangs, a person's reputation was quite a valuable asset, especially when it could generate instant fear just by mentioning it.

What stuck me about this little boy was that on both occasions he had volunteered to tell what he had seen to various members of the law, knowing quite well that by doing so he ran the risk of placing his own life in jeopardy.

✝ ✝ ✝ ✝ ✝ ✝ ✝ **✝** ✝ ✝ ✝ ✝ ✝ ✝ ✝

Immediately I made arrangements to have Junior brought down to my office. And what got me excited was that he wanted to go and share the whole story with me, which he did. But now came the hard part: to call up his grandmother and brace myself for what I knew wouldn't be the most pleasant conversation in the world.

When I finally summoned the courage to place the call, I was greeted with the expected fury of one outraged grandma. I had to use all my charm to calm her down, and somehow got her to agree to let me and another young and brash assistant DA, Neal Doherty, come to her apartment to discuss the case.

Convincing Junior's grandma, grandfather, and mother, who were all present at this meeting, to let their precious little boy testify at a murder trial needed a lot more than my usual smooth talking. Whether it was the idea that a white DA took the time to come all the way out to see her, or that I mentioned to her that we should, in the name of Jesus Christ, proceed with the case, she took a real liking to me and soon agreed to let Junior testify.

As a gang leader I had brought fear into the hearts of many, and I am so grateful that God turned my life around so completely that I can now be used to help defend the innocent instead of inflicting pain and fear on them as I so often did in the past. And now I have learned to use my past to help me understand the hurts of others and become a part of the solution instead of the cause of the problem.

With young Junior onboard, I still felt I needed to find Benny, since the testimony of an eight year old might not be enough to convince twelve adults to convict Bobo of murder, especially since it was hard to know in advance how a little boy would hold up under the pressure of a high-powered barrage of tricky questions from a polished defense attorney.

The key to finding Benny once again rested with a grandmother. I started this next hunt by going to the last address Benny had used as his residence. I found Benny's grandma, who happened to be an alcoholic. She told me that Benny had fled a while back, fearing for his life if he testified again against Bobo. The best she could tell me was that she thought he went to live with his aunt in Georgia. Thanks to this lead, I was able to contact the aunt and find out that Benny had indeed lived with her, but had been accused of stealing $10 on his job and been fired. He was now living in a men's homeless shelter in Georgia.

My persistence led to pay dirt as my phone call to the shelter found me introducing myself to the grand jury star witness, Benny Styles. I had only one week earlier been able to convince one very scared and skeptical grandmother to let her grandson testify, but now I had another great challenge—how to get one equally scared and runaway homeless man to change his mind and travel what seemed to be 1,000 miles back to a place he probably had made up his mind never to come back to again.

I took a chance and appealed to Benny, in the name of Jesus Christ, to come back and testify. There was no reason for him to come back and really nothing I had to offer him to make the journey back, but when I said the name of Jesus a small miracle took place. To my surprise Benny told me, "If you had said anything else I wouldn't have come up, but because you said to do it in the name of Jesus Christ I will come back, for I am a Christian."

Within the next day or two, I had secured a plane ticket and with the DA's blessing had Benny flown up to New York. The DA would only put Benny up in a hotel for a week, and then he would have to find another place to live. Fortunately I had been preaching and doing work with the homeless at the Bowery Mission, and the pastor agreed to let Benny stay at the mission until it was time for the trial to begin.

Thinking back now as I write these words, I wonder how I could accomplish so much in such a short time when my predecessor became so frustrated with the case that he abandoned it to another lawyer. Could another lawyer have accomplished as much as I did? Was it the fact that most DAs are so busy that they don't have the time or desire to go that extra mile that separates the good from the great lawyers? Was I just a cut above the rest? Or could it be that there is the inevitable reality that an overworked DA just can't put in the hours and resources that a private firm can devote to a case? Is money what decides who gets justice? Perhaps it's a combination of all of the above. Sometimes justice can get a little complicated, although I saw and felt that all my fellow assistant district attorneys in Kings County were dedicated, hardworking, and good.

It was one day before trial, and I was psyched up to unveil my two star witnesses in court. Unfortunately, while my mind was razor sharp to try the case, my body wasn't. An untimely accident had caused me to hurt my back and herniate a disk. The pain that traveled up and down my back was intense, but my will to see justice prevail helped to send a counteracting signal to my brain to go and handle the trial despite my doctor's warning to rest.

Picking a jury has always been a part of trial law that I enjoy. Having the right jurors can often make or break a case. There is a certain art to the selection process, and asking the right questions can give a lawyer valuable clues about how a juror may react during the trial. One of my favorite questions of prospective jurors is what they like to do in their spare time. In this particular case, three said they enjoy reading their Bibles. Within two days all twelve jurors were picked, and the three Bible readers all made it into the juror's box.

Picture for a moment the courtroom scene—the judge at the bench, two well-dressed and eloquent attorneys in fierce battle, twelve jurors in a section all by themselves, intently staring at everything and listening to every word being said, and a host of other people in various attire and locations all focused on a man accused of murder. Now, picture this intense real-life drama through the eyes of a small eight-year-old boy, two feet shorter and many years younger then everyone else in that room.

Junior Thomas was the first witness to take the stand. While being sworn in, the pressure took its toll and tears began to roll down his face. For five minutes the tears fell, but somehow they served as the key force in stabilizing my very young witness. After this good cry, it seemed as if a new little boy came to life. When I asked him why he was crying, he said, "I am scared." When I asked why, he said one word: "Bobo."

Junior then proceeded to tell the whole story of the cold-blooded murder of his friend he had witnessed a year ago. His tears were so real, but so was his remarkable calmness as he related in detail the scene that had been permanently etched into his memory that fateful day one year ago.

I have rarely seen such courage from a young boy under such pressure. He said to the judge and jury that the reason he wanted to tell his story was because he felt he wanted to do what was right. I am convinced that the combination of Junior's tears and morality, not to mention the almost two days of prepping I spent with him, had a powerful influence on the jury.

It was now time for Benny to tell his story. While I did have two eyewitnesses, they were by no means the picture of what one would consider reliable. One eight-year-old boy and a homeless man who had been fired from a job for stealing hardly seemed to be the type of people a skilled defense attorney would have any trouble discrediting. While Junior had done quite well, everyone now turned their attention to another scared individual.

As Benny related the sordid details of the cold-blooded murder, defense attorney Morgan was preparing for his melodramatic counterattack. His cross-examination was skillfully thought out, and I vividly remember the three questions he put to Benny and the members of the jury.

Feeling he would have little trouble discrediting a runaway homeless thief, he began by saying, "Why are you testifying? Are you testifying because the DA offered you money?" Benny answered, "No." "Or did the DA offer to help you with your case in Georgia?" shouted Morgan. Again Benny said softly, "No." Then the third accusation came: "Did you do it because you are a good citizen?" For the third time Benny responded, "No."

There is one basic rule in trial law that states you never ask a question unless you already know what the answer will be. Morgan readied his final assault on Benny, but he forgot all about the above rule. As if he was closing in for the kill, he turned to the judge, the jury, and the courtroom, and then point blank at Benny and blasted out, saying, "If the DA didn't offer you money, if the DA didn't

✝ ✝ ✝ ✝ ✝ ✝ ✝ ✝ ✝ ✝ ✝ ✝ ✝ ✝ ✝ ✝ ✝

offer you a deal, and if you didn't do it because you are a good citizen, then why did you do it?"

Instantly Benny took his gaze away from Morgan, turned to the jury, and without a moment's hesitation said in a loud voice, "I did it as unto the Lord."

Both Judge Kahn and the defense attorney (both of whom are Jewish) looked at each other with blank stares and said, "What does that mean?" As I looked at the jury box, I saw big smiles break forth from the three Bible-reading Christians. In all my years of trial law, I have never seen such bewilderment from a defense attorney as I did that day. As the final words of testimony were given, the time had now come for our summations.

Morgan was brilliant. He told the jury that Junior's testimony could not be taken seriously because he had just now, one year after the crime, appeared on the scene to testify and that I had forced out of him a concocted story as seen from the eyes of a little boy who obviously was mistaken. He went on to appeal to the jury's common sense by claiming that no one could seriously take the word of a homeless thief from Georgia, who was returning all the way up to New York to testify in a murder case with no motive other than some foolish religious reason.

I certainly had my work cut out for me. For over ninety minutes, I demonstrated to the jury not only that my two witnesses were credible but also that their motives for testifying were sincere, which our justice system needed more of. As I played on Junior's courage and Benny's sense of morality and dignity, I began to feel that the jury understood that my two frightened but brave men were indeed honest and true to their convictions.

As I continued to speak, I felt a surge of inspiration pulsating throughout my entire body. To me, this trial was important not only because justice had to be served, but also because I felt strongly that it was time to make a statement that would boldly stand out in the minds of everyone present that day as well as in the recorded record for all of time and eternity. I had wanted to say the name of the Lord loudly and clearly so that it would echo throughout the halls of justice at 360 Adams Street, the Supreme Court Building. I knew that our country was founded on a strong belief in the Bible and Jesus Christ, and I felt that it was time to charge up the courtroom with a heavy dose of a name that is the personification of justice, and that is the Lord Jesus Christ.

It was our thirtieth president, Calvin Coolidge, who summed it up best when he said, "The foundations of our society and our government rest so much on the teachings of the Bible that it would be difficult to support them if faith in these teachings would cease to be practically universal in our country."

I had hoped that the jury would see that good old-fashioned motives such as doing the right thing and saying that God was still an important part in one man's life would bring high credibility to Junior and Benny. I told the jury that if they wanted to know the truth about what really happened in this case, they could find it all in the stenographer's record. There was only one motive that would move the heart of a man to travel over 1,000 miles to testify against a man he feared with all of his heart, and it was in the record—he did it "unto the Lord."

By now my adrenaline was flowing freely and I decided that it was time to let the halls of justice echo with the name of Jesus Christ. Three times I told the jury that Benny Styles had returned to New York because he was doing it "unto the Lord." And each time, my voice turned its volume to high. The sound of my voice was so loud that people came rushing into the courtroom from all over 360 Adams Street to see what all the commotion was about.

Proclaiming the name of the Lord Jesus that day was a moment I will never forget. I felt so blessed to be an American and a Christian. As a youth my goal and mission in life seemed to be to subvert justice, but now I was boldly helping to bring about justice and make our country and community a better and safer place to live.

It was the jury's turn to evaluate all the evidence and render their verdict. In just two short hours, the jury announced that they had found the defendant guilty of murder in the second degree. Justice had been served!

The case was promptly adjourned for sentencing. Right before the date of sentencing, Bobo, while still in jail, stabbed a twenty-year-old white male over two Oreo cookies. It took thirty-eight stitches in the face to close the wound. Naturally I made sure to get a picture of the young man's distorted face to bring with me to the sentencing. I asked the judge to put Bobo away for twenty-five years to life. Judge Kahn decided on eighteen years to life. As a postscript, Benny came up to my office after the trial and told me that his dream had always been to become a Christian rap star. Interestingly enough, Benny set the entire trial to rap music and sang his composition to my associate Neal and me.

To show that the DA didn't offer Benny any deals, he returned to Georgia and spent time in jail for the stealing he had previously done. When he got out, he gave me a call and said he wanted to come back to New York. I don't know what Benny is doing now, but I will never forget the day a young homeless man said he came back to Brooklyn, to 360 Adams Street, because God was calling him to do so.

After the sentencing, Bobo made it a point to look me straight in the eye as they were taking him away and tell me that he was going to kill me when he got out. I told him, "When you get out, I will be retired and living in Florida." And in my concluding remarks I added, "Why don't you do yourself a favor and read the Bible and get to know Jesus Christ like Junior and Benny did?"

✝ ✝ ✝ ✝ ✝ ✝ ✝ ✝ ✝ **✝** ✝ ✝ ✝ ✝ ✝ ✝ ✝ ✝

I am quite proud of this conviction for two reasons. First, a dangerous human being was placed behind bars. And second, it represented an important case tried to conviction for the Trial Cadre.

While the case was going on, my adrenaline was flowing and somehow I was able to live with the pain of my herniated disk. However, once the case was finally concluded, I guess my body started to feel the full force of the pain. What had happened was that while I was rushing down the stairs to the subway station on my way to the trial, I missed a step and my back went out. I literally crawled back to my home and the next day went to my doctor. They ran an MRI on me and the diagnosis was clear—I had herniated a disk in my back. While the pain was intense, I was right in the middle of the Bobo Johnson case and decided that pain or no pain, I was going to finish this trial.

With the conviction in hand, I decided to stay out of work for a month to try to recuperate from the accident. As soon as I returned to work, my supervisor told me that the DA's office was so impressed with my work that they were transferring me to the Major Offense Bureau (MOB). The atmosphere was similar to what I had gotten used to while working with the Trial Cadre in one way but quite different in another. In both units we were given very high-profile cases, but the MOB had a much larger volume of cases than the Trial Cadre.

As soon as I stepped foot into the MOB, I knew that something was not right. Now, I don't mean that there was a problem with this new bureau. I actually felt that this even broader exposure to the high-profile cases would give me the real challenges I wanted. Unfortunately, while my mind was eager to tackle this new assignment, my back said no. I never knew how important a good healthy back could be until I no longer had one.

As the workload began to pile up at the MOB, the combination of the heavy stress these cases brought with them and the tremendous physical pain I was experiencing every day was just too much for me to handle. I looked down the road a little bit and could see that if I stayed in this new position, I probably wouldn't be able to cope and do a good job, and if I wasn't careful I might slip back into a depressive state of mind.

I quickly decided that my health was too important to allow my career to jeopardize it and that in my present state of health it would be unfair for me to practice law at the Major Offense Bureau since I knew that I couldn't perform physically as a senior trial attorney needed to. In order to be a top performer, you really have to be quite mobile, healthy, and strong on these big cases. There are lots of heavy files to carry around with you as well as the need for a lot of bending. Neither of these tasks was possible for me now. So, after talking it over with Elaine, I tendered my resignation to the Brooklyn DA's office to heal and recuperate physically, mentally, and emotionally. I did not know how long it would take.

✝ ✝ ✝ ✝ ✝ ✝ ✝ ✝ ✝ ✝ ✝ ✝ ✝ ✝ ✝ ✝

While it was a difficult decision, I knew I had made the right one. I felt sad in a way to leave the DA's office because I had made some good friends, but I also was looking forward to regaining my health and maybe then getting back to my old practice and resuming the relationships I had established there.

One of the nicest things that happened to me at the DA's office occurred right at the time I decided to leave. I was deeply moved when I received a call from Joe Hynes, the Brooklyn DA. He asked me to stay on because the entire office was very proud of the excellent work record I had compiled during my short stay there. Even though I was offered a very generous twelve-week paid leave of absence, I declined the offer.

Moving back into my old office and resuming my former legal practice were two things I had little problem readjusting to. It was one of my greatest honors to serve under a great district attorney, Honorable Charles Joseph Hynes, and in one of the most prestigious and respected prosecutor's offices in the world, the Kings County District Attorney's Office.

✟ ✟ ✟ ✟ ✟ ✟ ✟ ✟ ✟ ✟ ✟ ✟ ✟ ✟ ✟ ✟ ✟

25 Looking Back

Looking back! Often when people look back on their lives, true joy, peace, and meaning seem to have eluded them. Instead, when they reflect back on their lives, they find only memories of what could have been. And, sadly, when they look forward, they see only a future fast approaching its terminal point. But as I meditate on where my life has traveled since my mom brought me into this world back in November 1948, I can honestly say that I am grateful for every experience and person I have met along the way.

Would I have changed things if I could do it all over again? I really believe that I wouldn't change much at all, for you see, I have learned over the years that even though it was no fun getting beaten up or having someone take a razor to my back, it was also these very same experiences that served to make and mold me into what I am today. To take only the good and blot out the bad would have served to make Louis Gelormino a very dull, sheltered, and probably unproductive member of society.

Now, don't get me wrong: there are a few things in my life I probably could have done without. Take, for example, the time I got my nose broken for the second time. The first time my nose was broken proved more than anything else to be a great source of embarrassment for me due to the manner in which it happened. On this first occasion, while I was still a member of the Little Gents, I met up with an untimely accident while walking one day up Sackett Street and Fourth Avenue on my way to the old railway, where we had our headquarters. It was always the custom of the Little Gents to kick out the lights around the railway so that nobody could see what we were up to. As I was walking by, Lenny the Mud thought I was a member of the Soviet Lords gang and decided to throw a rock at me to chase me away. While his vision was obviously not very good, his aim proved to be great. He hit me square on the nose. I was a bit aggravated at Lenny, but such are the effects of being a member of a gang—and especially being a member of a gang like the Little Gents, where most of the guys were not too smart. Even though my nose was broken and I was in a lot of pain, I would have felt a lot better if I could have told my friends that I broke my nose in a big street fight instead of at the hands of Lenny the Mud's rock.

The second time my nose was broken occurred just one day after I came out of the hospital, where I had spent three days getting my nose fixed from the first time it was broken. Two years had gone by, and my mom had finally agreed to let me get my nose operated on. This wasn't because she didn't want it fixed, but because we had no medical insurance and it took her that long to save up enough money for the operation. The cost was $600, and that was a lot of money back then. I needed the operation not just for cosmetic reasons but

because my breathing had been affected a lot from Lenny's rock. My mother saved the money by knitting hats for a factory by day and sometimes by night.

Just before I was scheduled to go into the hospital for the operation, we had this fight in Prospect Park with another gang. I was with two of my friends, and we met up with several guys from a rival gang. As we exchanged some unfriendly words, one thing led to another and I beat up one of the guys in the gang pretty badly. I didn't give this incident much thought until the day after I came out of the hospital with my new nose.

I was feeling great. I was once again walking in Prospect Park, but this time I was with my brother Jamsie and two very beautiful young ladies. I was on top of the world—who had it better than me? I was seventeen years of age and had a new nose and a new look. As we were walking through the park, we saw two teams playing football. I didn't think anything of it and just kept walking with Jamsie and our two lady friends. As we walked by the two teams, one of the guys approached me with his full football uniform on. I was quite surprised to see that it was the same guy I had beat up just prior to going into the hospital.

He looked me right in the face and asked, wasn't I the guy who had fought him a week ago? I told him, "I never saw you before in my life—you must be mistaken." I then told him to take a good look at me because "You're making a big mistake." Before I could say another word, he told me, "You're a dead man because I'm gonna kill you."

Within a matter of seconds, the entire football team surrounded us. I told Jamsie to take the two girls out of the park because I knew that this would probably be the end of me. As I stared at these twenty-four or so guys dressed in their full football outfits, I knew that I was kind of in a jam. My only concern was that I didn't want to have my nose busted again so soon after getting out of the hospital, since my mom had just spent $600 on the operation.

As soon as the team had surrounded me, they threw me down and for the next twenty minutes kicked and stomped on me. One guy even put a gun to my head and said he was going to blow my head off but decided not to do it. After this tremendous beating was over, I got up on my knees and looked around. Everything seemed to be going around in circles. One thing I could see was that I was bleeding profusely from various parts of my body.

As I looked up, I heard one guy tell the others, "This guy still hasn't had enough." With that, he kicked me in the nose. Immediately blood started gushing from my nose all over my face, and I knew that my nose job had just gone down the drain. I was so aggravated that I attacked this guy and began to beat him up. This caused the whole football team to jump on me again. I guess they decided after a few more punches and kicks to let me go. After they left me, I literally crawled home. I was a wounded person in many ways that day, but the

✝ ✝ ✝ ✝ ✝ ✝ ✝ ✝ ✝ ✝ ✝ ✝ ✝ ✝ ✝ ✝ ✝

thing that upset me the most was that my nose was again broken.

When I returned home, my mother saw that my nose was busted. She was very upset at having $600 go down the drain. She hit me over the head with a broom. This obviously was not one of my better days, but it was the story of how I broke my nose for the second time, and one of the experiences from my past that I probably wouldn't have minded if it had never happened.

If an objective observer could travel back in time thirty years and view the state of affairs in the Gelormino household, he most certainly would have concluded that survival was the best the Gelorminos could have hope for. My dad had just passed away; my mom continued to go through severe emotional problems; Anthony was heavily into drugs; Jamsie was also involved with drugs and had a very self-destructive personality; and I was a gang leader, rebellious, and going nowhere fast. It looked hopeless for the entire lot of us.

But today all of my brothers and my sister are doing great. It's really a miracle how far all of us have come, considering the circumstances of our upbringing. Sometimes I have to pinch myself to see if it is really possible that I have come so far. While I have always told the good Lord how thankful I am to Him for watching over me throughout my life, as well as for the wonderful people He sent my way at critical times, I sometimes forget that there is also one other special person who in her own way was responsible for our entire family making it out of the pits of despair and poverty—my mom.

Even though this special woman suffered for so many years with serious emotional illness and instability, she always tried her best to show us love and raise us the best that she knew how. And every day, as bad as her condition was, she would get on her knees before a picture of Jesus and pray for an hour on a hard surface floor. There is little doubt in my mind that she spent a great deal of this time bringing before God the names of her children. I am grateful for her prayers and believe that because of her persistence on her knees, we were able to stand tall on our feet. I have learned that we should never underestimate the power of a mother or grandmother praying for her children.

It seems that it took the death of my dad for us to rally together and begin the transformation process for the entire Gelormino family. Perhaps by necessity or maybe out of desperation, we began to pull together as a family from that point forward, and slowly our lives began to transform. There is a remarkable verse of Scripture that seems to convey a very powerful message similar to the experience my family went through when my dad died. John (12: 24) says, "Truly, truly, I say to you, unless a grain of wheat falls into the earth and dies, it remains by itself alone; but if it dies, it bears much fruit." When my dad died, we somehow began to gain strength through the adversity. And some forty years later, our family has indeed borne "much fruit."

✟ ✟ ✟ ✟ ✟ ✟ ✟ ✟ ✟ **✟** ✟ ✟ ✟ ✟ ✟ ✟ ✟ ✟

There is another verse from the Bible (John 12:24) that has served to constantly remind me that our great God works in ways very different from what we might on the surface expect from Him. The Apostle Paul tells us in Romans (8:28): "And we know that God causes all things to work together for good to those who love God, to those who are called according to His purpose."

As I was growing up, it would have been difficult to convince me that God could use the forty-eight stitches I received in my back for any good. How God could use a miserable old German farmer named Fink to be a positive role model for me was something else I could not fully understand. And how in the world could God use the Little Gents to turn me into a real "gent"? These things seemed impossible during my young adult life.

But God was able to use all of these bad experiences for good because He loves me and allowed these incidents to be teaching tools on the road to maturity. He has a plan, purpose, and destiny for my life. I have also learned that how we view things in life makes all the difference in the world. For example, I couldn't understand why my brother Anthony sent me away to Madoosa, New York, to work for slave wages for an entire summer. Looking back, I now see that it was because he really did care for me and knew how much I needed to learn discipline and the value of good, honest work. Farmer Fink, wherever you are, thank you for being one of my best teachers in the world!

I was a rebel without a cause. And I believe that God knew that the only way to bring this rebel in line was through allowing me to go through the trials and tribulations I would encounter along the path of life (although it would take a lot of time and a lot of great people showing me the better way). Fortunately, I have been able to turn all of these negative experiences in my life into positive forces in my character building and vocation.

So much of who I am today rests on who I was in my past. I have successfully channeled the fighting spirit that used to dwell in my hands into one that now flows from my mouth, heart, mind, and spirit. My leadership qualities from my gang days now give me the ability to spearhead many worthy social causes. And my natural ability to relate to people from all walks of life has proven invaluable in all phases of my legal practice.

Looking back on my life to date makes me realize that our God, as great and wonderful as He is, also has a sense of mystery and irony about His ways. Here I was, growing up as a problem to the system of law in America. I tried to outfox the system at every turn. I tried to subvert justice. I even tried to make up my own rules along the way. As a youth, I also greatly feared the district attorney's office. But today I am part of the solution to the problems in our country. I work with our legal system, uphold justice, obey the laws of the land, and have even devoted a part of my life to working for the DA's office. My life is clearly a case study in transformations. As with the prodigal son, I was once dead but now am alive; I was once lost, but now I have been found.

I have served in the criminal justice system in almost every capacity and aspect as an attorney with distinction and excellence and, most of all, to the best of my talents and abilities. The good Lord Jesus has, as usual, given me the grace, strength, courage, knowledge, intelligence, understanding, and wisdom to do so. It's a miracle! Praise the Lord!

Good friends and good times also come to mind as I reminisce about my past. Thinking about Nicky Egghead telling the groundskeeper over the loud-speaker at Ebbets Field to leave the field because he was interfering with our stickball game still brings joy to my heart. Watching Lumpy stick his huge tooth in people's faces during our haunted house ride, though bizarre, is still a fond memory. As is Vinny Mophead hanging himself from the roof of a four-story brownstone and telling the whole neighborhood he was going to jump if his mother didn't stop making him look like a sissy. People like Bobby BeBop, Big Wax, Blackie, Mike the ice cream man, and the unforgettable BaBa are colorful faces from my past. And I'll never forget, thanks to the aerospace program at John Jay High School that was initiated and partially organized by my friends George McGauglin and Hank Boerner, the plane ride around New York City with the then-mayor, Honorable John Lindsay, some of the gang members, and other youths.

While these faces helped to bring color and laughter (not to mention a few broken noses and black-and-blue marks) into my life, others brought compassion, help, and healing. Mary Sansone must have been dispatched to me right from the very throne of God. Her love and compassion were so overwhelming; they proved to be the very elements my wounded self-image desperately needed when I was an angry young man headed down the wrong path in life. Mary came on the scene to begin the slow process of redirecting my path onto the road to usefulness and meaning. I will always be forever grateful to her for looking beyond who I was then to who she believed in her heart I could be, if only I were treated with the special extra care I needed.

Father Kenna not only served as the person who joined Elaine and I together at our wedding, but he was also responsible for teaching me that God really loves me and for counseling me through the darkest period of my entire life. He was not only a priest but also a man who was willing to go beyond what his duties called for. I believe that if Donald Kenna had put his ambitions elsewhere, he could have probably been either an ambassador to other countries or maybe even the secretary of state of the United States of America. His ability to put into practice the love of Christ set him apart from the rest of the crowd.

It seems that during every period in my past, God sent just the right person to guide me on the right path of life. Vinny Riccio was the key in helping me get into college. Friends like Mary were instrumental in helping me make it to law school. And people like Ronald Harvey and his family, and Pete Liacoris, were responsible for seeing that I made it through law school.

Once I gave my heart to the Lord, God continued to send special people my way. One person in particular who has been a very precious brother in the Lord, and who has been there in both the good times and the difficult ones, is my good friend Neal Emmino. On numerous occasions, we have become kind of like a team for God. We have conducted Bible studies, gone on speaking engagements, helped feed the poor, and been there to bear one another's burdens. Of all of my blessings to date, one of the greatest has been my association with Neal Emmino. In addition my pastor, Roger McPhail, and his wife Theresa have been a great spiritual blessing to me and my family.

For some people, strolling down memory lane can be a very painful experience. "If only this had never happened" or "If I could only have done this differently" are what many spend their time meditating upon. Perhaps the greatest lesson I have learned in life, besides the realization that God loves me, is that God indeed works both the good and the bad experiences we go through for ultimate good—if we allow Him to work through our lives.

I choose to look at the negatives in my past as stepping stones toward building positives in my future. And as I enter the next phase of my life, I am quite excited because I have so much to look forward to. I am especially thankful to God for allowing me to continue my journey alongside the four most precious people in my life: my wonderful wife Elaine, my son and great joy, Louis Jr., and of course Mary and Zack Sansone.

✝ ✝ ✝ ✝ ✝ ✝ ✝ ✝ ✝ ✝ ✝ ✝ ✝ ✝ ✝ ✝ ✝

26 Looking Forward

Every time I look back on my life, I get excited at how far I have come through the grace of God. But sometimes we can reflect too much on the past and forget that the future is where we are going to spend the rest of our lives, and it is in the present that we must live each moment one day at a time in faith, hope, and love. It has been said that we are but a speck on a speck. With over 6 billion people alive today, each one of us in one sense represents only a mere speck in this vast sea we call humanity. And since our planet earth is only one planet amidst countless trillions, we clearly are a "speck on a speck."

But since we have a wonderful God who has created us and is constantly watching over us, we know that we are very special to Him. In fact, the thing that gets me really excited about my future is that God says He has something special planned for me. As we read in Jeremiah (29:11), "For I know the plans that I have for you, declares the Lord, plans for welfare and not for calamity to give you a future and a hope."

If I had to characterize my vision for the future, I think I would like to be remembered by society when I leave this world as a person who loved God by helping humankind and loved his family. I believe that God created us to love one another and to bear one another's burdens. Unfortunately, somewhere in the scheme of things we have lost touch with this noble desire and have seen our world become one of strife, not love, and one of war, not peace.

In order to help bring our world back to this original game plan, I have become involved in an organization called CIAO's Council for Understanding Racial Equality (CURE). Cofounded by Mary Sansone, CURE is a very special organization designed to establish and promote understanding between ethnic groups and racial equality for all.

It is Mary's dream that in the not-too-distant future we will be able to purchase a building in Brooklyn for CURE's headquarters and truly expand the organization's vision of promoting love, understanding, and equality both within New York City and to the ends of the earth. CURE is planning a big symposium in the near future. The title and topic is "Education + Organization = Emancipation." We have met continuously with the leaders and representatives of thirty-two various religious and ethnic groups and cultures. They are all committed to participating in the symposium to continue to make New York City the best city in the world. We are praying and expect that our great mayor, Michael Bloomberg, will open the symposium. Our mayor has expressed and demonstrated his desire, effort, and commitment to make the quality of life for all New Yorkers better. CURE's desire is to help diverse groups of people to focus on what we all have in common, and to not use our differences to divide us. I am praying that this dream will soon become a reality and that I, in my own small way, can help achieve this most wonderful goal through God's power and Holy Spirit working through me.

In addition to this important young organization, I hope to continue my active involvement in other community social organizations and causes that do God's work on Earth. An area that has become very dear to my heart is helping the homeless of New York City as well as ex-offenders. One of my greatest joys is my monthly visit to the Bowery Mission. As long as the good Lord gives me strength, I hope to continue to share the Good News with the precious souls who enter the doors of the Bowery Mission: that God loves even the homeless and ex-offenders of the law as well, of course, as everyone on this earth.

One thing I know for sure is that as long as I live in New York City, there will always be tremendous opportunities to help people with real needs. In addition to using my talents on the social front, I also have a desire to make whatever contributions I can in the field of politics. Helping get candidates elected who share our visions for the future of our city and country is one important way I can work to make our nation a better place for Louis Jr. and future generations. All of our endorsed candidates have clearly shown integrity, character, excellence, consistency, stability, compassion, and intelligence and clearly have been and are the best candidates for their public offices. The quality of life for all New Yorkers has been clearly improved because of these selected individuals.

One of the greatest attacks on the very fabric of our society today has come about within the family structure. With the divorce rate reaching epidemic proportions, with child abuse becoming a national disgrace, and with broken homes engulfing our society, we need to do everything we can to bring unity and love back into the families of America. I know, looking back on my own family as a child, that we almost reached the disintegration point on several occasions; but by the grace of God we held together. For each family that breaks up, a chain reaction of negative results occurs. If we can work through our faith in God in the social and political avenues to form programs and pass laws that help build up families and ensure their stability and unity, we stand a good chance of America continuing to be a great nation in the twenty-first century.

I guess it is no secret that I am so high on family. Besides my strong faith in Jesus Christ, my family is the most precious thing I have in life, and I look forward to spending the rest of my life helping our small little unit stay close-knit and productive members of society.

It's hard to put into words the joy and excitement I feel when I spend time with my son. All the trials and stresses I went through as a child are to a large extent totally foreign to Louis Jr. He has only known love, comfort, and security in our home. I am grateful for my past in the sense that I feel I have learned

✝ ✝ ✝ ✝ ✝ ✝ ✝ ✝ **✝** ✝ ✝ ✝ ✝ ✝ ✝ ✝

great lessons on how to raise Louis Jr. by the full spectrum of experiences, both positive and negative, I had as a youngster.

Continuing to watch my son grow and mature into a productive human being is something I am looking forward to with great joy. Both Elaine and I work very hard to be positive role models for Louis Jr. Elaine has the wonderful heart of a mother, which has been one of the most important factors in the development of our son. Showing love and acceptance is perhaps the most important blessing we can ever give our children.

I have lately begun to ponder what my son will be as he grows older. I know that whatever he puts his mind to, he will succeed in and do well. I pray that he will make a positive contribution to society. So far, Louis Jr. has inherited many of Elaine's good qualities and, thank God, none of my not-so-wonderful ones. And, of course, I'm hoping that Elaine and I will be able to spend time with our grandchildren if the Lord so chooses to bless us this way.

Elaine and I have become very close over the years. We have worked hard through our mutual faith in Jesus to overcome our difficulties, and we look forward to spending the rest of our lives together as not just husband and wife but as best of friends and partners for making our society a better place to live. We have a wonderful way of complementing one another. Her support and love and ability to put things in proper perspective have been blessings that are hard to put into words. Elaine, when we first married, was not much of a cook. But I can now say with complete honesty that she has not only won my heart but my stomach. After a hard day at the office, I can't wait to get home to her gourmet homemade cooking. Sitting at the family table with a great-tasting home-cooked meal, surrounded by my wife and son and relaxing around good conversation, is to me a dream come true and a great blessing.

Going on family outings, going to a ball game with my son, and doing the hundred and one other things a family does together are very important to me because these are things that I never really got to experience much while growing up in South Brooklyn. Seeing how my brothers and sister have succeeded in life is also something I take great enjoyment in. I really expect even greater things from Anthony and the Gelormino family, and who knows whether he may even earn a place someday in history! But, more importantly, they may earn a place in the kingdom of God on Earth.

There is also a sad part in looking forward as I have to face the inevitable reality of seeing loved ones pass away. I knew that my mom and father would not outlive me. Having to see the good Lord take them home was difficult. But this sad part of life only serves to point out the shortness of life here upon earth. We never really know when our number is up. When I realize that over 300,000 people die each day on our planet, I stand in awe of how fragile life

✟ ✟ ✟ ✟ ✟ ✟ ✟ ✟ ✟ **✟** ✟ ✟ ✟ ✟ ✟ ✟ ✟ ✟

really is. My philosophy is that we must live every day here as if it were our last day on earth and have an eternal perspective to life. I believe wholeheartedly through faith in Jesus Christ that we will all be judged for our lives lived and be reunited with our loved ones who had faith in the Lord while on this earth.

I know that in order to continue to accomplish the things I want to do in life, I must constantly look away from self and toward God and pray for his continued anointing, wisdom, understanding, and grace. With each passing day my love for God continues to grow, and I pray that my faith in Him will constantly grow stronger as I journey through the final years (which I hope are still many!) of my life. Over the past sixteen years, I have been privileged to be invited to many churches in New York City to share my testimony of how God saved me from a life of gloom and despair and gave me purpose, self-control, peace, joy, freedom, prosperity, and a real zest for living. I hope that the future brings more opportunities to share the message of hope that God has placed upon my heart.

Recently I had the great honor of being a guest speaker at an international conference at Allentown College in Pennsylvania. I was able to minister to a group of over 1,000 Asians, most of whom were young and highly intellectual. Sharing my life and testimony with these young Asians was one of the great blessings of my entire life. Seeing how many of them came up to me after I spoke to share their personal lives is something I will never forget.

If the Lord continues to open up future speaking engagements, I will continue to share my story of how great God really is with whoever comes to hear. And hopefully brother Neal will continue to be my traveling companion as we travel the highways and byways of our great city.

And speaking of New York City—even though we still seem to have some problems, I plan to tarry and live here in my home city no matter how tough things may become. I really believe that the Lord didn't allow me to learn street smarts just to use them to survive my environment. I know He wants me to use them to help others not to have to experience all the hardships I had to go through. Those who truly understand the people and ways of New York, I believe, have the best chance of reaching these people with help and hope. I learned my greatest lessons in life on the streets of New York, and I plan to do everything in my power to use this knowledge to help our current mayor and other public officials to make New York City and its people continue to prosper and become an even safer and more caring place to raise our children.

On a professional side, I will continue to use my God-given talents and abilities to meet not only the legal needs of all folks but also the emotional and spiritual ones. I am looking forward to even greater challenges in the field of government and law, and hope that my life, training, and faith in God will serve as the base for all of my social, spiritual, and political involvements. In the spirit of volunteerism, I want to dedicate my future years to helping my city to continue to thrive. Mary Sansone, CIAO and CURE, and the local churches have always been about the business of helping and blessing people and continue to move in faith horizontally into the marketplace and be a blessing.

On a more personal note, I am also looking forward to seeing more of my old friends from my youth surface through my travels. Over the years, in my professional life such things as house closings, marital problems, and a host of other legal matters have brought several of my old friends and former gang members into my office. Reminiscing about old and new times and sharing our experiences and our faith have always been something I have enjoyed. And seeing what these guys are now doing in life in many cases has proven quite interesting as well as surprising.

I now know only one way to live, and that entails living every single day with commitment, purpose, appreciation, and most of all joy to the best of my abilities, using all of my talents to help my fellow man. If the Lord allows me another thirty more years to live, I hope to follow in the footsteps of my mentor and dear friend Mary Sansone. She, perhaps more than anyone else I know, personifies what a true heart of compassion is all about: sharing with and caring for people in need.

My pastor once told me, "One short life will soon pass, and only what's done for God and our fellow man will last." The Bible also gives us insight on why we were created. We read in Ephesians (2:10), "For we are His workmanship, created in Christ Jesus for good works, which God prepared beforehand, that we should walk in them."

My investment strategy for the future is simple. I am looking forward to storing up a lot of treasures—not here on earth but in heaven! I pray that my story has inspired, encouraged, and blessed those of you who might be going through rough trials and tribulations. If I could leave you with one message, it would be this: Trust in God, and always remember that when you sincerely wish and desire through faith in God to use your talents and abilities in a constructive way and maximize your effectiveness as a human being in God's eyes, we are blessed and will always be blessed even when you may not realize it. I pray that this book instills and develops faith, hope, and love for every reader, particularly love, because it never fails and conquers all (1 Corinthians 13).

Smile—God loves you!

Afterword

The 1960s will be remembered as a time of radical changes, changes that took an unprepared, lethargic society by surprise. In a struggle where freedom was confused with permissiveness, enormous damage was caused.

Youth, the most vulnerable sector of our society, became an easy target. A benign, neglectful attitude, the absence of responsible guidance, left young teenage boys and girls with very little choice. Hate—hate for everything that represented authority—created a general chaos. Gangs were born in every neighborhood. Fights, stabbing, and shooting became everyday occurrences. A bad situation was getting worse.

It was with this background that John Lindsay, then mayor of New York City, sent for me. A conflict between Italian and Puerto Rican gangs was getting out of hand and needed special and immediate attention. I don't know why, but I accepted the task. Maybe it was the challenge. Against the advice of some of the experts, I called Father Anthony of Our Lady of Peace Church on Carroll Street between Third and Fourth Avenue in Brooklyn, New York, to set up a meeting with the leadership of the "Little Gents," an Italian gang that was making itself a reputation in South Brooklyn.

Here I was in the lion's den, facing half a dozen teenagers who were anxious to show their displeasure with my interference in their lives. Hornsey, the toughest kid, was chosen to do the heavy hitting for the gang. Some of their complaints were legitimate. Their welfare was not on any of the city agencies' priority lists. As I listened, I realized that the majority of these teenagers were reachable. My somber appearance, and my secure and determined language, had won their trust. Their faith in me had won my commitment.

Out of the group, a young boy attracted my attention. No special reason; he was always close to me. Was he trying to protect me? Or was he looking for protection for himself? Maybe both. A silent allegiance was formed between us. Our lives became interdependent.

Lou Gelormino, the scrawny little kid from Carroll Street, was not looking for a city program. He was looking for a person to love. He selected me; I adopted him. We never left each other.

Of course, the program was successful. Most of the kids turned out well. At a function years later, I had the opportunity to see some of them. Proud to flaunt their success and show their respect, they came over. They wanted me to know that they had not forgotten what I did for them.

Nothing is 100 percent. Hornsey, the gang speaker at that first meeting, when he was dying of AIDS, put it best when he said, "They listened, and I didn't."

Louis Gelormino, one of the Little Gents who listened, is the best evidence of how much a little love can accomplish.

Mary C. Sansone
Founder and executive director of Congress of Italian American Organizations (CIAO)
Founder of Council for Understanding and Racial Equality (CURE)

✟ ✟ ✟ ✟ ✟ ✟ ✟ ✟ ✟ ✟ ✟ ✟ ✟ ✟ ✟ ✟

About the Author

Born in South Brooklyn, author Louis Gelormino overcame a difficult family environment: the death of his father at age fifteen, his mother's long suffering from a debilitating disease, and his brother's victory in a courageous battle with drug addiction. Louis was delivered from a street gang, "the Little Gents," through the energies and unselfish love of dedicated individuals such as Mary Sansone and the Congress of Italian American Organizations (CIAO). In addition, Louis attributes his success and achievements to his faith in God, which he received from his mother, Rose Gelormino.

As a young adult, Louis committed himself to defeating the adversities of his early childhood. During his high school years, he took on diverse responsibilities as a family worker, youth counselor, and ironworker. He was the first Italian American to be awarded a full scholarship from the College Discovery Program at the Borough of Manhattan Community College of New York (BMCC) and the City College of New York (CCNY).

Upon earning his bachelor's of arts degree, Louis was beginning to taste victory. Next, he was the first Italian American to receive a full scholarship from the Council on Legal Education Opportunity (CLEO) to Temple University School of Law, where he received his jurisprudence (J.D.) degree.

From a humble beginning, through many personal hardships and difficulties, scholastic challenges, and the hurdle of professional obstacles, Louis has achieved the position of deputy commissioner of law, employment, and special projects for the New York City Department of Probation from May 2002 under Mayor Rudolph Giuliani and his present position as deputy commissioner and counsel to the Local Conditional Release Board under present Mayor Michael R. Bloomberg.